D0140736

Rhetorical Public Speaking

NATHAN CRICK

Louisiana State University

Allyn & Bacon

Boston   Columbus   Indianapolis   New York   San Francisco   Upper Saddle River
Amsterdam   Cape Town   Dubai   London   Madrid   Milan   Munich   Paris   Montreal   Toronto
Delhi   Mexico City   Sao Paulo   Sydney   Hong Kong   Seoul   Singapore   Taipei   Tokyo

Editorial Director: Daryl Fox
Editor-in-Chief, Communication: Karon Bowers
Marketing Manager: Blair Tuckman
Editorial Assistant: Stephanie Chaisson
Managing Editor: Linda Mihatov Behrens
Associate Managing Editor: Bayani Mendoza de Leon
Project Manager: Clara Bartunek
Senior Operations Specialist: Nick Sklitsis
Design Director: Jayne Conte
Cover Designer: Suzanne Duda
Composition: Aptara®, Inc.
Cover Image: © Dave Booker/Star Ledger/Corbis

Copyright © 2011 by Pearson Education, Inc.
All rights reserved. No part of this publication may be reproduced, stored in a retrieval system, or transmitted, in any form or by any means, electronic, mechanical, photocopying, recording, or otherwise, without the prior written permission of the publisher. Printed in the United States.

Library of Congress Cataloging-in-Publication Data
Crick, Nathan.
   Rhetorical public speaking / Nathan Crick.
      p. cm.
   Includes bibliographical references and index.
   ISBN-13: 978-0-205-66558-7 (alk. paper)
   ISBN-10: 0-205-66558-6 (alk. paper)
   1. Business communication—Handbooks, manuals, etc.   2. Business writing—Handbooks, manuals, etc.   3. Public speaking—Handbooks, manuals, etc.   I. Title.
   HF5718.C75 2010
   808.5'1—dc22

                                                                     2010017297

2 3 4 5 6 7 8 9 10—CRS—13 12 11 10

Allyn & Bacon
is an imprint of

www.pearsonhighered.com

ISBN 13: 978-0-205-66558-7
ISBN 10:   0-205-66558-6

SPEECH SOURCES

In order to encourage further research on the speeches used as examples in this textbook, whenever possible, excerpts have been taken from speeches whose full text is available on the Internet. The best resource for speeches is www.americanrhetoric.com. Whenever this was not possible, speeches were taken from popular compilations of speeches readily available at any university library. These texts include the following:

Reid, Ronald and James Klumpp. *American Rhetorical Discourse*. (Long Grove, IL: Waveland Press, 2005).

Ritchie, Joy and Kate Ronald. *Available Means: An Anthology of Women's Rhetoric(s)*. (Pittsburgh: University of Pittsburgh Press, 2001).

Safire, William. *Lend Me Your Ears: Great Speeches in History* (New York: Norton, 2004).

Suriano, Greagory R. *Great American Speeches* (New York: Gramercy Books, 1993).

Zinn, Howard and Anthony Arnove. *Voices of a People's History of the United States* (New York: Seven Stories Press, 2004).

CONTENTS

PREFACE

I distinctly remember the first time I taught public speaking. On asking a more experienced peer for advice on how to design the course, I received the following recommendation: "The first thing to do is throw the book out the window." It was, in general, advice worth following. With that experience in mind, I designed this book specifically so that it would not be thrown out a window—or, if such a fate were to befall it, such defenestration would not occur because it exerted so much energy glorifying the obvious.

I have tried, in this book, to reconnect public speaking with the rhetorical and wholly democratic tradition of eloquence—of the act of appearing before others to express one's truth with beauty and excellence. Toward this end, I have emphasized that aspect of public speaking which is often quickly passed over by textbooks in haste to present the latest in flow charts and moral catechisms—the act of appearing before others. Throughout this book, I have presented public speaking as an action that occurs in the company of others who share experience on matters of common concern. This is why rhetoric, as a form of public speaking, remains vital to democratic life even in a global, technological age. Although rhetorical public speaking is arguably about the act of persuasion, it is more importantly an action of gathering together people to appear before one another in a shared space of their common world.

It is in that collaborative spirit that I would like to recognize several people who have helped inspire this textbook and/or played a role helping it "appear" in print: John Lyne, who first brought me into the rhetorical fold; John Poulakos, who taught me to love the logos; Peter Simonson, who made me to take tradition seriously; Andy King, who welcomed me to the South; Loretta Pecchioni, who suggested the idea to me in the first place; Zachary Gershberg, who valiantly taught this text when it was just a Word document; the graduate students and instructors at LSU, who endured years of teaching works in progress; and Jennifer Gremillion, Kensie Hingle, Karon Bowers, and all the supportive people at Pearson/Allyn & Bacon who assisted me in bringing this book to fruition. Let us hope this book has a long and happy life.

INTRODUCTION

On December 5, 1955, Dr. Martin Luther King, Jr., made what was to become the speech that formally inaugurated the Civil Rights Movement in America. Days earlier, Rosa Parks had performed one of the most celebrated acts of civil disobedience in American history: she refused to give up her seat on a bus to a white passenger, thereby willingly violating the segregated-seating ordinance of Montgomery, Alabama. Hardly a "tired" woman performing a spontaneous act, Parks was then secretary of the Montgomery chapter of the National Association for the Advancement of Colored People (NAACP) and was, rather, "tired of giving in." Her courageous and committed action inspired the formation of the Montgomery Improvement Association (MIA), under the leadership of Dr. King and fellow minister Ralph Abernathy. The MIA urged African-Americans to boycott the segregated city buses. The first mass meeting of the MIA was attended by several thousand people in the spacious Holt Street Baptist Church. Because both the sanctuary and the basement auditorium were filled, an audience outside listened via loudspeakers. After introductory hymns and sermons, Reverend King gave the address that would propel him into the leadership of one the most powerful social movements in the United States. Although the successes of the movement was hardly the result of a single individual or a single speech (indeed, King was himself largely propelled by the force of a social movement that had been growing in strength for decades), this event nonetheless demonstrates how rhetorical public speaking plays a vital role in the political history of a nation.

The purpose of this book is to give students a practical understanding of how public speaking can function as a rhetorical intervention—as an act of persuasion intended to alter how other people think about and respond to public affairs that affect their lives. The audience for this book is the **engaged citizen**—that individual who is an active participant in the democratic process of debate, deliberation, and persuasion as it relates to issues of public concern. The guiding rationale for this book is that the success or failure of democratic social life depends on the cultivation of engaged citizens, each of whom has the capacity to act rhetorically in the public sphere. In other words, democracy suffers when we base our educational system on the naïve faith that individuals instinctively possess the skills of public advocacy. The reality is that citizens are made, not born. Part of that educational process involves instilling in people the belief that free speech is their right and individual expression is their duty. The other part of the process is to give them the knowledge, skill, and confidence to perform that duty and to judge the performances of others when the situation demands it. One unique function of a class in public speaking is to provide a structured and supportive environment in which to develop these skills in preparation for an active life. This textbook is designed to facilitate that process by providing the tools—understood as methods—that promote the creative expression of engaged citizens.

It is from this methodological and pedagogical perspective that one should interpret the examples used in the book, many of which exhibit "radical" sentiments that seek emancipation for certain marginalized groups or support for controversial positions. Their inclusion is not determined by their political views. They are included because they demonstrate, in the most vivid terms, the challenges faced by public speakers who wish to confront dominant conventions, norms, and attitudes. Moreover, these examples are chosen because they represent strategies for generating social change within certain historical moments of crisis. Methodologically, a historian of public speaking finds the most interesting examples of rhetoric on the margins of culture. Understandably, this does *not* mean that these strategies were particularly *effective* or *virtuous;* it means only that the strategy was explicitly and creatively employed in such a way that makes it useful for the purpose of elaboration. Instructors and students who do not find their own views expressed in the examples of the book should bring them to the table during the span of the course to generate productive discussion through engagement.

The controversial nature of these speeches also provides an opportunity to discuss the ethics of rhetoric. By "ethics," I do not refer to whether a speaker's beliefs match up to some formal catechism or obey some polite convention. The **ethics of rhetoric** are determined by how well the speaker has fully considered the broader consequences of his or her actions beyond the immediate moment and has acted conscientiously with respect to that evaluation. Part of the responsibility of rhetorical theory is to make speakers aware of just how much impact a single speech might have in a complex and interconnected world in which "good intentions" are not enough to produce desired consequences. The ethical study of public speech helps people to avoid getting trapped into such a situation by providing the tools to survey a broader social environment before acting. Based on this "holistic" ethical ideal, a large part of what distinguishes this book from other texts on public speaking is its continual emphasis on the speaker as a part of a larger social whole.

Finally, the book emphasizes that public speaking is an art. As an art, it is learned through practice. Nothing replaces the pure experience of simply talking in front of others. This experience cannot be quantified or measured. The value of any conceptual material, therefore, must be judged with respect to how it enriches and broadens the experience of the student in the act of speaking. The Roman rhetorician Quintilian wrote, "An art consists of perceptions consenting and cooperating to some end useful to life" and involves "a power working its effects by a course, that is by method;" consequently, "no man will doubt that there is a certain course and method in oratory."[1] A successful course in public speaking will seek to educate students in a method of channeling the power of the spoken word toward ends that are useful in life.

---

[1] Quintilian, quoted in *The Philosophy of Rhetoric,* in *The Rhetorical Tradition: Readings from Classical Times to the Present,* ed. Patricia Bizzell and Bruce Herzberg (Boston: Bedford Books of St. Martin's Press, 1990), 329.

A DEFINITION OF RHETORIC

This book is thus oriented toward the cultivation of public speaking as a rhetorical art. The modifier "rhetorical" is meant to distinguish the subject from the broader category of public speaking, which involves any situation in which one speaks in a public setting. **Rhetorical public speech** *is the art of addressing pressing public concerns by employing deliberate persuasive strategies before a public audience at a specific occasion in order to transform some aspect of a problematic situation by encouraging new forms of thought and action.* This definition can be broken down into the following parts:

(1) *the art:* Referring to rhetoric as an art distinguishes it from a mere instinctual or unreflective talent. *Art* thus does not mean an intuitive creativity or genius lacking in method. Quite the opposite, art requires the application of rational concepts and methods in the creative process of guiding situated judgment.

(2) *of addressing pressing public concerns:* Except for matters of idle curiosity, the only reason we voluntarily expose ourselves to rhetorical discourse is because it speaks to a shared concern that is in the forefront of our consciousness. We listen to rhetoric with the hope that the person speaking might be able to suggest a path out of our current predicament or a solution to our current problem.

(3) *by employing deliberate persuasive strategies:* Persuasion is often accidental or a product of sheer luck. This does not alter its *function* as a persuasive message, but it does change how we evaluate it in terms of *art*. In contradistinction to rhetorical criticism, which can evaluate anything that strikes us as persuasive, the productive art of rhetoric concerns itself with improving how something is produced, and one cannot improve accident or luck.

(4) *before a public audience:* The *public* character of the audience means that it addresses an audience of relative strangers who come together to address areas of common concern. Persuading an audience of friends may still employ rhetoric, but that rhetoric generally appeals to the unique bonds of those friends rather than their shared characteristics as part of a larger public.

(5) *at a specific occasion:* This aspect addresses the situated character of rhetoric *as a form of public speaking* and not simply a genre of persuasion. One can, of course, create rhetorical discourse in the form of a written or visual medium. The use of the Internet has certainly led to an explosion of attempts at long-distance persuasion. But rhetorical *public speech* more narrowly refers to rhetoric delivered in the physical presence of others.

(6) *in order to transform some aspect of a problematic situation:* Rhetoric seeks to change some aspect of the natural or social environment that is *felt* to be problematic by members of a public. This shared experience of uncertainty, anxiety, and urgency focuses people's attention on a speech that gives it a unique power. Absent such a situation, the same speech might be experienced not as rhetoric, but as a form of poetry, news, or entertainment. It is not the speech itself that determines its character, but the total context in which it is spoken.

(7) *by encouraging new forms of thought and action:* The means by which rhetoric transforms that environment is by encouraging other people to change

their attitudes toward objective things in the world. Rhetoric is thus an indirect form of action. It makes changes by changing what people think and do with hope that their behaviors might resolve some shared problem.

Because rhetoric becomes rhetoric only within urgent contexts of judgment, rhetorical public speech is a fundamentally *ethical* activity insofar as it forces one to take a stand about what "good" we should pursue and how we should pursue it. Paradoxically, however, the very problematic aspect of the rhetorical situation often throws into question the conventional ethical standards that had guided previous action. Thus, rhetorical public speakers must do more than seek mere tactical "success;" they must also determine what success would look like in such a situation and then justify that vision on the basis of a reflective ethical judgment.

To understand the significance of the modifier *rhetorical* for "public speaking," one must look to the history of the two terms. Rhetoric has a more recent origin than public speaking. The latter originated the day that language was used to address a crowd. One can imagine early human beings announcing the birth of a child, organizing a hunting party, celebrating a ritual feast, or giving orders to a group of people. Rhetoric, however, means something more specific than the sheer act of speaking in front of others. It is one thing to say words in public; it is another to deliberately construct an argument using the tools of reason (*logos*), credibility (*ethos*), emotion (*pathos*), and style (*lexis*) to challenge and transform some aspect of public sentiment in the face of opposition.

THE GREEK ORIGINS OF RHETORIC

In the Western world, rhetoric didn't appear as a discrete art until a rudimentary democracy came to the Greek colony of Sicily around 466 B.C.E. At that time, the tyrants had been overthrown and the citizens had to find a way to properly and justly redistribute the property that the former leaders had unlawfully confiscated. Their novel solution was to have citizens argue their cases in courts of law. Because these courts required ordinary citizens to speak in their own behalf, techniques for argumentation became a marketable commodity. As a result, the first "handbook" for rhetoric was produced around that time, providing instruction in the basics of speech composition and delivery for a fee.[2]

As democracy spread through the Greek world, particularly in Athens, and expanded from the law courts into political and social forums, instruction in the art of rhetoric flourished and became progressively formalized, first by the development of a class of itinerant teachers called the Sophists and later by the more institutional education provided by the schools of Plato and Aristotle. This is not to say that rhetorical practice in Greece was an egalitarian enterprise. Access to education was restricted to those with financial resources, and the ability to even participate in politics was restricted to a relative minority of male citizens—women and slaves being two major groups excluded from public life. The birth of rhetoric thus did

---

[2]George A. Kennedy, *Aristotle, On Rhetoric: A Theory of Civic Discourse*, 2nd Ed. (Oxford: Oxford University Press, 2007).

not lead to a "Golden Age" for everyone. Many of the powerless remained power-less, in part because they were denied both access to the political forum and the artful tools necessary to influence others.

Nonetheless, rhetoric and democracy contributed to the others' development because both were concerned with facilitating the process of collective judgment, even if for a relatively small—if expanding—group of free citizens. The more the burdens of advocacy and judgment were placed upon the shoulders of individual citizens, the more urgent that training in rhetoric became; and the more citizens became skilled in rhetoric, the more they craved and demanded participation in the decision-making processes of governance. It was thus in Greece that rhetoric established its position as an *art*—not in the sense of being a form of creative self-expression, but in the sense of being a practical skill based on a body of knowledge, much as we think of engineering or architecture.

In Greek culture, there were three distinct perspectives on rhetoric that are still useful in understanding the broader relationship between rhetoric and democracy: the Sophistical, the Platonic, and the Aristotelian. The most controversial perspective was held by the Sophists, who were teachers of rhetoric who professed to be able to have the ability of making the weaker argument the stronger. The Greek **Sophists** arose in the 5th century B.C.E. in Classical Greece when political conditions brought about the need and opportunity for citizens to acquire the skills to participate in the new democratic empire. In providing education in *logos* (meaning reason, argument, and critical thinking) for a fee, the Sophists acted as traveling universities. The Sophistical attitude was thus one of supreme confidence in the creative power of the word in the hands of the citizens. In this way, the Sophists were the first *humanists*. Rhetoric, for them, was a way of trying to bring about better experiences in the world in whatever way they could. Consequently, they tended to emphasize creativity and experimentation in language in the hope that the best ideas would win out in the end by producing happiness.

The Sophists' boast that they could turn the weaker argument into the stronger was often interpreted to mean that they intended to undermine traditional ethics through false reasoning. However, as John Poulakos points out, the literal translation of the Greek leads to a far more conventional interpretation. It simply takes "weaker" (*to hetton*) to refer "to that argument or position which commands less power because the majority shuns it or is not persuaded by it," and "stronger" (*to kreitton*) to refer "to that argument or position which is dominant because the majority has found it more persuasive than other alternatives." From such a perspective, the function of sophistical rhetoric is to "reverse in some measure the established hierarchy of things" by employing "the resources of language and its surrounding circumstances to move what is regarded as weaker to a position of strength."[3] In this sense, to argue that slavery is a violation of human rights would have been a relatively "weak" argument in eighteenth-century America, one that was then made stronger in part through the efforts of rhetorical public speakers such as Sarah and Angelina Grimke, William Lloyd Garrison, and Frederick Douglass.

---

[3]John Poulakos, *Sophistical Rhetoric in Classical Greece* (Columbia: University of South Carolina Press, 1995), 65.

However, those who employed rhetoric often did so for personal gain in neglect of the larger public good. **Plato,** in particular, accused rhetoric of being the use of "empty words" to distract us from "reality" and deceive us about the truth in the pursuit of narrow pleasures. Plato, in other words, was an *Idealist,* but not in the sense we use it today to mean a sort of youthful and naïve optimism about the future. Plato was an Idealist because he believed that only "Ideals" were real and that our everyday existence in the world was but a shadow of that reality. Consequently, he emphasized our duty to search for, comprehend, and then convey the nature of the Ideal to those in a fallen world in order to bring it closer to the true reality that exists in the word of a rational God. For Plato, rhetoric was a kind of "pastry baking" that makes sweet-sounding speeches without any nutritional value. Consequently, he saw the Sophists—who were paid teachers in public speaking, much as are modern-day professors of communication—as a breed of social parasites. Plato's ultimate solution was thus two-pronged. On the one hand, he wished to ban all rhetoric that was not based on prior philosophical inquiry into the nature of the fixed ideals of the Good, the Beautiful, and the True. On the other hand, he encouraged a form of rhetoric that could inspire people to pursue genuine virtue and thereby liberate themselves from bodily pleasures. In his *Gorgias,* Plato asked,

> What of the rhetoric addressed to the Athenian people and other free peoples in various cities—what does that mean to us? Do the orators seem to you always to speak with an eye to what is best, their sole aim being to render the citizens as perfect as possible by their speeches, or is their impulse also to gratify the citizens, and do they neglect the common good for their personal interest and treat the people like children, attempting only to please them, with no concern whatever whether such conduct makes them better or worse?[4]

If the Sophists were rhetorical optimists and Plato a rhetorical pessimist, Plato's student **Aristotle** was a rhetorical Realist. Aristotle was educated at a time when the heights of the Classical Era of Sophistical optimism was long past and when the devastating Peloponnesian war that had produced Plato's skepticism of political rhetoric had finally come to an end. Aristotle's Athens was a democracy, but no longer an empire; it was a city filled with intellectuals trying to make sense of a long, complex, and tragic history. Aristotle thus understood rhetoric through a historical lens, seeing it as an experimental tool for figuring out empirical truth by trial and error. Thus, he wrote,

> "We must be able to employ persuasion, just as strict reasoning can be employed, on opposite sides of a question not in order that we may in practice employ it in both ways (for we must not make people believe what is wrong), but in order that we may see clearly what the facts are, and that, if another man argues unfairly, we on our part may be able to confute him."[5]

The goal for Aristotle was not to praise or condemn rhetoric, but to identify the situations in which it was useful and to develop methods of invention and de-

[4]Plato, *Gorgias,* 502e.
[5]Aristotle *The Rhetoric and the Poetics of Aristotle,* trans. Roberts, W. Rhys, ed. Edward P.J. Corbett (New York: The Modern Library, 1984), 1355a30.

livery most appropriate for those situations. Aristotle was therefore a *Realist* in the scientific sense of the word. He advocated for a more "scientific" rhetoric that drew its conclusions on the basis of systematic inquiry into lived reality.

These three attitudes toward rhetoric—the Sophistical, the Platonic, and the Aristotelian—still thrive within contemporary culture. The Sophistical attitude emphasizes the importance of *kairos,* or "timeliness," which means that a speaker has to grasp the right moment in the present to make a rhetorical intervention. The Sophists reveled in such energetic moments, both by creating them and by responding to them, much in the way that participants in the blogosphere highlight all the sensational moments of the present and revel in the diversity and flux. Plato, however, would be annoyed by the cacophony of noise emitted by the contemporary news media. For Plato, the genuine orator did not concern himself with the passing issues of the day. His mind was concerned with, "tracking down by every path the entire nature of each whole among the things that are, and never condescending to what lies near at hand."[6] In other words, if the Sophists were entertainers and courtroom lawyers, Plato was a religious poet and constitutional law professor. Lastly, Aristotle reminds both of his predecessors that people exist in historical time, in which stretches of calm and certainty are punctuated periodically by moments of crisis that require us to make the best judgments we can with limited resources. His model is the prudent politician who is capable, of course, of quietly crafting policy, but also of making a rousing speech when the situation demands it.

The lesson the Greeks teach us is that a genuine art of public deliberation will combine all three of these attitudes in the appropriate balance order to create a coherent rhetorical whole.[7] One therefore need not choose absolutely among them: there is a way of combining each of their insights in the goal of producing a discourse that simultaneously acts in the moment and directly attends to the experiences of the audience while still keeping the broader scope of one's actions in mind. Assisting in this difficult task of invention and performance is the goal of this book.

[6]Plato, *Theaetetus,* 174a.

[7]On the comparison between the three perspectives on rhetoric, see Everett Lee Hunt, "Plato and Aristotle on Rhetoric and Rhetoricians," *Reading on Rhetoric,* 100–159.

Introduction to Public Speaking

The two chapters in this section provide a coherent overview of the basic elements necessary for successful public speaking. It is designed to provide a broad but general outline of the elements of public speaking, much like an aerial view of a landscape. Clearly, such a perspective may seem too expansive if one approaches it with the expectation of mastery. However, to borrow a sports analogy, one does not learn to play baseball first by learning to run, then by learning to hit, then by learning to catch, and then only afterwards, finally putting it together into a game. One learns baseball by being taught the rules of the game, and then only afterwards, focusing on specific parts of the game that contribute to a mastery of the whole.

Similarly, one does not learn public speaking by piecemeal. A public speaker learns by writing a whole speech, and then only afterwards, concentrating on developing those aspects that are in need of improvement. Consequently, much of the material that often gets isolated in separate chapters has been concentrated into a single chapter in order to provide students of public speaking with all the basic rules of the game in one place. To be used effectively, these "rules" should be taken more as goals and rules than as artful methods. They identify the parts that are needed to fit together into a whole speech. However, the other chapters in the book will provide the richer form and substance necessary for creating artful rhetoric.

The Canons of Rhetoric

This chapter introduces the basic techniques of public speaking that provide the general framework and methods for putting together any public speech. These include the Five Canons of Rhetoric: Invention, Arrangement, Style, Memory, and Delivery, which comprise specific guidelines for delivery, appearance, writing your thesis, introductions, conclusions, structuring your points, finding sources, doing searches, citation style, visual aids, outlines, note cards, and methods of dealing with speaking anxiety. Mastering all of these techniques will clearly require extensive practice. However, this chapter will provide the basic methods that should then be applied in giving form to the conceptual strategies and persuasive substance explained in subsequent chapters.

Ever since its origin in Classical Greece, rhetoric has been associated with the tradition of "handbooks" that outline the basic techniques of public speaking. Although we take such handbooks for granted in the age of immediate information, these handbooks were revolutionary at the time. Only the aristocratic class had ever had possession of such skills, as demonstrated by the long speeches of Achilles and Odysseus in Homer's *The Iliad*. Never had ordinary people been trained in the art of rhetoric and disputation. The invention of democracy changed all of that. It turned such people into "citizens" who now had the chance and obligation to participate in political life. These handbooks played a vital role in teaching the rudiments of speech organization, logical proof, and narrative structure to those citizens, skills that gave them, as a class, a great deal more political power than they had ever possessed in Western history.

These handbooks were not without their critics, of course. "New" aristocrats like Plato (who sought an aristocracy based not on land or blood, but on knowledge) often ridiculed these handbooks as being akin to "recipe books": add so much of this type of proof, put it in this type of container, stir well, and deliver. For instance, we find this discussion in Plato's *Phaedrus* between Socrates and a young admirer of rhetoric:

PHAEDRUS: There is a great deal surely to be found in books of rhetoric?

SOCRATES: Yes; thank you for reminding me:—There is the *exordium*, showing how the speech should begin, if I remember rightly; that is what you mean—the niceties of the art? . . . Then follows the *statement of facts*, and upon that *witnesses*; thirdly, *proofs*; fourthly, *probabilities* are to come; the great Byzantian word-maker also speaks, if I am not mistaken, of *confirmation* and further confirmation . . . [And] all of them agree in asserting that a speech should end in a *recapitulation*, though they do not all agree to use the same word.

PHAEDRUS: You mean that there should be a summing up of the arguments in order to remind the hearers of them.

SOCRATES: I have now said all that I have to say of the art of rhetoric: have you
            anything to add?
PHAEDRUS: Not much; nothing very important.[1]

Phaedrus's response, "nothing very important," is, of course, meant to be ironic. For Plato, the handbooks were all "style" and no "substance," for they left out all that was really significant to public speaking, which was knowledge of the good, the beautiful, and the true. He believed that the way rhetoric was taught in Greece tended to neglect long-term wisdom and knowledge in favor of short-term power and victory. Thus, the handbooks were like cookbooks for pastry baking: compilations of easily understood tricks in producing sweet words that hungry audiences readily consumed without concern for their long-term health. After all, what use are techniques for arranging a speech if one has nothing worthwhile to say? The devastating Peloponnesian War that had destroyed the Athenian Empire and caused the execution of his mentor, Socrates, led Plato to conclude that rhetoric required the guidance of reason if it was not to destroy civilization.

The Platonic entreaty not to sacrifice long-term good for short-term success remains as important as ever, yet misjudges the nature of handbooks. Not only does Plato attribute too much ethical significance to their existence, but he also credits rhetorical techniques with far too much power. Learning the rules of an art makes one a master of that art no more than learning the rules of baseball; it simply gets one familiar with the game. It is a precondition for participation, not a guarantee of success. Or, to use a structural analogy, rhetorical handbooks provide a "skeleton" for a public speech insofar as it provides a skeletal structure onto which substance must be formed, much as a wooden stick figure provides a stable base onto which a sculptor creates a clay model. The total quality and worth of the object created is determined not only by the skeleton one uses, but also the type of material used and the total form it becomes. The technique that tells one to "be humorous" has no substance; it is just a placeholder. The hard work comes in finding out what, exactly, is funny in a particular circumstance. But this requires a great deal of wit, situational understanding, and insight into human nature. Handbooks can tell us where we might find these things, but it does not tell us what we will find or what to make of them.

The handbook tradition reached its culmination in the Roman work, *Rhetorica ad Herennium*, written anonymously in the first century B.C. but generally credited to be the work of the orator and senator Cicero. This work formalized what were to become the Five Canons of Rhetoric, which are the five methods necessary to employ in creating a successful speech. Subsequent teaching of rhetoric, up to the present day, largely follows this organization. The author writes:

> The speaker, then, should possess the faculties of Invention, Arrangement, Style,
> Memory, and Delivery. Invention is the devising of matter, true or plausible, that
> would make the case convincing. Arrangement is the ordering and distribution
> of the matter, making clear the place to which each thing is to be assigned. Style
> is the adaptation of suitable words and sentences to the matter devised. Memory

---

[1]Plato, *Phaedrus*, 267.

is the firm retention in the mind of the matter, words, and arrangement. Delivery is the graceful regulation of voice, countenance, and gesture.[2]

These canons effectively summarize the basic rules of the game, and any student of rhetoric—no matter how naturally talented—must follow them to achieve success beyond accident or luck. This chapter will thus define the nature of each canon and show what specific techniques are commonly included within each. The goal is to lay out the basic rules and methods of public speaking in order to provide a common ground on which more genuine mastery of the art of rhetoric can be built.

THE FIRST CANON: INVENTION

When Aristotle defined rhetoric as the capacity for discovering the available means of persuasion in each case, he defined rhetoric as an inventional art. Derived from the Latin word *invenire*, "to find," **invention** refers to the act of finding something to say. It is not surprising that the scientific-minded Aristotle would place such emphasis on invention; for it is precisely invention that provides a public speaker with the resources and knowledge that gives a speech its substance and value. Consequently, the author of *Rhetorica ad Herennium* says that "Of the five tasks of the speaker Invention is the most important and the most difficult."[3] The reason is because invention, of all the canons, tends to place the greatest emphasis on discovering what to say concerning the problematic situation at hand, including what to observe about the character of the speaker and the audience. Invention guides the speaker on *what* should be said rather than *how* it should be said, thus committing a public speaker to the scholarly labor of research that is often required for ethical speech in a complex situation. In sum, invention calls on a speaker to determine the following:

1. The nature of the rhetorical situation (Chapter 3)
2. The relationship between speaker and audience (Chapter 5)
3. The motivations of the audience (Chapter 4)
4. What logical and emotional proofs best appeal to the audience (Chapters 6 and 7)

The majority of this book will focus on providing resources for invention, drawing not only from reasoning and logic, but also from an understanding of the broader historical, political, and sociological context of a situation. To begin, however, one must start with the basic techniques of research and argument.

Sources

The power of invention often derives from the integrity and breadth of one's **sources**. Finding sources that are respected by your audience is paramount to

---

[2]*Rhetorica ad Herennium*, (Loeb Classical Library, 1954). Available from the University of Chicago <http://penelope.uchicago.edu/Thayer/E/Roman/Texts/Rhetorica_ad_Herennium/1*.html> (accessed 16 April 2010).

[3]Ibid.

persuading them that you are both informed of the situation and sympathetic to their attitudes and concerns. Except in special circumstances, most people generally tend to respect the same sources—usually those coming from representatives of some established public or private institution such as a university, a news organization, a research bureau, or a "think tank." Generally, specific strategies for finding sources can be found on at any university library, and there are dozens of websites that maintain updated links to helpful databases, including the following:

> *University of California–Berkeley:*
>
> http://www.lib.berkeley.edu/instruct/guides/primarysources.html
>
> *Indiana University:*
>
> http://www.indiana.edu/~tltl2/www_history/01_welcome.htm
>
> *Duke University:*
>
> http://library.duke.edu/research/finding/primarysource.html

Here are some general considerations about how to go about finding sources:

1. *Websites:* In the Internet age, it is tempting to believe that you can simply go to a web browser and do a search on your topic idea and get all you need. As a first step, this is usually appropriate. Sites like Wikipedia offer a good overview of a topic and provide a basic framework of understanding that allows you to narrow your focus on more particular aspects of the subject. For general knowledge that does not need citation, these kinds of sources are valuable. However, due to the lack of guaranteed accuracy and the presence of explicit bias, Internet websites that are not associated with a reputable organization are unacceptable as interpretive or background resources. They are simply personal tools to get you started. The only time websites are acceptable is when they provide the primary material for analysis.

2. *Newspapers, magazines, or other journalistic sources:* These are helpful to provide quotes and basic facts about your case studies. Historically they also provide an insight concerning how facts were "framed" by the journalistic standards of the day. Newspapers are especially helpful in finding examples to use in introductions and conclusions, as newspaper articles are written with a similar incentive to "get attention and interest."

3. *Books written about your subject by respected authors:* These generally provide a wealth of primary material as well as interpretative resources to help back up your claims. Books by university presses are generally more respected than books by popular presses. Of course, books also have a lot of material you will not use in a speech, thus making searching difficult. A good strategy is to first go to the index to see whether your particular interest is represented by a category entry. Often, a quick index search in a biography or history will give you a wealth of details that gives a speech character.

4. *Academic journal articles:* These usually present a very specific argument about an aspect of your case studies from either a scientific or a theoretical perspective. Even if they may not be directly relevant to your argument, they often provide good models for how to critically analyze objects for the purposes of drawing meaningful conclusions. The best electronic database for essays from

communication and rhetorical scholars is "Communication and Mass Media Complete," accessed via the EBSCO search engine. The database includes all the essays from journals like *Quarterly Journal of Speech* and *Philosophy and Rhetoric.*

5. *Government documents:* Documents prepared and distributed by government agencies are often very useful when looking for data or analysis on general social conditions that can be measured by some objective standard. In general, the value of government documents is found in statistics.

Doing Proper Searches

When using electronic database searches, particularly newspaper and magazine databases, you need to try many different strategies. First, you should always avoid relying on general terms alone, such as "global warming" or "civil rights." You should always try to pair general terms with specific terms to narrow the search. Try adding specific names, places, dates, or "catchwords" that will call up more relevant searches—for instance, "Global warming Gore documentary controversy," or "intelligent design Dover 2006 debate," or "Malcolm X violence social change." Second, once you find one source, you should also scan it for more keywords that might be unique and helpful. Lastly, always check the bibliographies of articles and books to find new sources. Even if they are not immediately helpful, these new sources might, in turn, cite other articles and books in their own bibliographies that are helpful. This is a useful source for search tips:

Finding It Online: Web Search Strategies:

http://www.learnwebskills.com/search/

Topics of Invention

During the research process, it is helpful to distinguish different categories of proof that may be useful in constructing an argument. These are called "topics of invention" (in Greek, "*topoi*", which means "places to find things"). **Topics of invention** represent the kinds of proof available for a public speaker.

1. *Definition:* Often, a speaker persuades simply by providing a more correct and precise definition of a situation, object, person, or action. For instance, the Founding Fathers often distinguished between a "democracy" (which was direct majority rule by the people) and a "republic" (which was indirect representative government by elected leaders). Making definitions clarifies not only the speaker's position but also the situation in which one is acting.

2. *Division:* This is a subset of definition, in effect breaking whole terms into their constituent parts ("A republic requires fair elections, a parliamentary body, separation of powers, and the rule of law") or combining parts into a whole ("I may be a New Yorker, and you might be a Virginian, but we are all Americans."). Division allows one to make more careful distinctions and avoid the fallacies and problems that arrive from overgeneralizations and category confusions.

3. *Comparison:* After defining and dividing terms, a speaker can then make comparisons based on similarity and difference. These comparisons provide a

more detailed map of the environment in order to aid in judgment. ("Those who died in the Boston Massacre are akin to the Greeks who died at Thermopylae, sacrificing themselves for the sake of freedom.").

4. *Relationship:* A relationship is more than a comparison; it puts two or more things in causal relationship to one another, either in terms of direct cause and effect ("Oppressive taxation of the colonies has led to revolt.") or in terms of historical lineage ("The colonists are the children of the English king.").

5. *Circumstance:* The most situational of the topics, circumstance argues whether or not some future situation is possible or impossible, based usually on an empirical diagnosis of the situation combined with references to past situations that show something to have happened or not ("Achieving freedom without war has never happened in history. The only possible revolution occurs through the sword.").

6. *Value:* Arguments from value include those dealing with comparisons of the just and unjust ("To refuse an unjust law is more just than to obey it."), the advantageous and disadvantageous ("We gain more from freedom than we lose from separation."), the virtuous and the base ("It is as shameful to allow oneself to be oppressed as it is to oppress others.").

Evidence for Invention

If the topics for invention provide a place on which to find things, evidence represents the specific things found. There are three general types of evidence, including testimony, **examples**, and statistical facts.

1. **Testimony:** Inspiration for a speaker can also come through the testimony of others whom the audience respects. Testimony can prove that something exists or has happened by drawing on the personal experience of others ("I have seen warships in Boston Harbor."), it can give a "human touch" to a story by using colorful quotes to exemplify some point ("I saw the young man bleeding to death in my arms."), or appeal to the words of experts of authorities as your evidence ("John Locke has proven that government only rules by contractual consent of the governed, meaning that if one party breaks that contract, as the king has done, we may rightfully liberate ourselves from its constraints.").

2. **Examples:** These include descriptions of actual or hypothetical events, people, objects, or processes that can embody an idea or argument in a concrete form so that audiences can "see" what it means ("If one wants to know the nature of tyranny, go to Boston. There, the streets are filled with armed men, the courts have been abolished, and young men are killed in the streets.") and/or act as evidence to prove the existence or define the nature of something ("War is upon us, as evidenced by the battle of Concord and the presence of British troops marching through our countryside."). Examples can be drawn from newspapers, history, biographies, science, or personal experience. Examples function as evidence to support the styles of reasoning.

3. **Statistics:** Direct use of numeric facts and statistics are generally helpful to either show the magnitude of something ("Over 90% of the colonists now support a revolution.") or the probability of something ("Given the number of warships in Boston Harbor, it is impossible that war shall not come to us."). A carefully

placed statistic can lend great credibility to an argument if done properly. However, too many statistics can ruin the flow of a speech and make it sound too "technical." Also, one should be very careful about the sources of the statistics. It is very easy to twist statistics to imply very different things depending on the way they are calculated. Quote only those statistics from sources that are both reliable and also that you know will be trusted by your audience.

Writing Your Thesis

The culmination of the process of invention is the development of a concrete goal—its specific purpose—as well as something to say to achieve that goal—a thesis. A specific purpose is the answer to the question, "What is this speech trying to do?" while a thesis is the answer to the question, "What is this speech trying to say?" Especially for beginning speakers, the quality of a speech stands or falls with how well the thesis helps to achieve the specific purpose. The thesis is the center around which every aspect of a speech revolves. Conveying a thesis to the audience gives a speaker a concrete focus necessary to create a logical and coherent message and provides an audience reference point to understand the speech.

1. **Specific Purpose:** A specific purpose is an expression of an interest in a particular goal that the speaker finds interesting and that may have value for an audience. It involves four characteristics as follows:
   a. the kind of speech one is giving (Chapter 2)
   b. the audience to which this speech is delivered (Chapter 5)
   c. the occasion for the speech (Chapter 3)
   d. the effect on the audience that the speech is supposed to have (Chapter 4)
   Examples of specific purposes might include "to persuade my parents over dinner to buy me a car" or "to commemorate the Battle of Normandy during Memorial Day in front of a public audience to make them remember the sacrifices of veterans" or "to persuade the school board to support school uniforms during the monthly school board meeting." For a speech delivered in a public-speaking class, the audience can be the actual class or some imagined situation, depending on the decision of the instructor. In general, however, speeches given to actual audiences (the class) generally have more value because one can gauge an actual rather than a hypothetical response.
2. **Thesis:** A thesis is the specific argument that seeks to achieve the specific purpose. It is usually a single sentence that sums up what the entire speech is arguing, including a claim and reasons in support of that claim. Whereas a specific purpose is written for the speaker in order to help to *develop* a concrete idea during the writing process, a thesis is the *product* of that process. Thus, for the specific purpose "to persuade my parents over dinner to buy me a car," a thesis would be "You should purchase me a car because I have proved myself responsible, I require transportation to and from my job, and I need a car if I am to ever to get a date." A thesis should:
   a. *Be specific.* A thesis should be specific. Vague and generic thesis statements always lead to speeches that are vague, confused, and lack impact. The more specific you can make a thesis, the more focused your speech

will become and the greater impact it will have on an audience. Instead of "Our country should fight for peace," one could write "The U.S. should negotiate a settlement with country X by sacrificing interest Z."

b. *Focus on a single topic.* Avoid including too many topics in a speech. An audience can only follow a few lines of reasoning in a sitting, and a speech that attempts to go too many places will lose them. Too many topics also generally lead to superficial arguments that do not get to the "heart" of an issue.

c. *Be audience centered.* Consistent with the definition of rhetoric, any topic should be developed only with respect to the situated interests of an audience.

d. *Make a clear claim.* A thesis should always have a single, clear argumentative claim being made (e.g., "We should build this bridge."; "This person is noble."; "This policy works."; "The universe is infinite."). The claim is usually a restatement of the overarching goal of the specific purpose.

e. *Present reasons/details.* Following the claim should either be *reasons* in support of the claim or *details* about how it will be elaborated. The claim "We should build this bridge . . ." is generally followed by reasons like "because it will ease traffic, create a scenic walkway, and stop litter." But the claim "The universe is infinite . . ." should be followed by details like "and I will show how it expands in all directions, has no center, and possesses infinite possibility." A thesis might also have some combination of both reasons and details.

Documenting Sources

Through the invention process, make sure you keep a careful document of your sources. A simple model is the Modern Language Association (MLA) citation style. Use this in recording your sources in an outline, making sure also to retain the page numbers:

1. *Journal or magazine article:* Paroske, Marcus. "Deliberating International Science Policy Controversies: Uncertainty and AIDS in South Africa." Quarterly Journal of Speech 95.2 (2009): 148–170.

2. *Newspaper article:* Mitchell, Gordon. "Scarecrow Missile Defense." Pittsburgh Post-Gazette 8 July 2001: E-1.

3. *Book:* Danisch, Robert. Pragmatism, Democracy and the Necessity of Rhetoric. Columbia: University of South Carolina Press, 2007.

4. *Book article or chapter:* Keränen, Lisa Belicka. "Girls Who Come to Pieces: Shifting Ideologies of Beauty and Cosmetics Consumption in the *Ladies' Home Journal*, 1900–1920." Turning the Century: Essays in Media and Cultural Studies. Ed. Carol A. Stabile. Boulder, CO: Westview Press, 2000. 142–165.

5. *Website:* Furness, Zack. "My Dad Kicked Ass for a Living." Bad Subjects. Oct. 2001.

A useful guide is found at Purdue University:

http://owl.english.purdue.edu/owl/resource/557/01/

Discussion: Often, the term *invention* is used as a synonym for *magic*, or to create something from nothing. But as all magicians know, there is a lot of labor behind the illusion. Based on your own experience with other arts (music, dance, painting, poetry, etc.), how does "invention" work in these arts as a kind of method for "finding," like it does in rhetoric? What did you find, and how did you learn what to look for?

THE SECOND CANON: ARRANGEMENT

After going through the process of invention, a speaker now must organize the various proofs into a coherent form that has a beginning, middle, and end. **Arrangement** is thus the capacity to put things in order. In the Classical Roman oration, the arrangement was quite rigid and included the following parts:

a. Introduction (*exordium*): State purpose and establish credibility.
b. Statement of Facts (*narratio*): Provide an overview of the situation.
c. Division (*partitio*): Outline what is to follow and specify main point.
d. Proof (*confirmatio*): Present arguments and supporting facts.
e. Refutation (*refutatio*): Refute counterarguments.
f. Conclusion (*peroratio*): Sum up claims and reinforce with emotional appeal.

Contemporary speeches need not follow such a strict pattern. However, this does not mean that anything goes. A good speech follows *some* arrangement. This is because a speech is different from a website, which allows and even encourages a fragmentary presentation. A speech, being an oral performance, must have a logical, temporal sequence if an audience is to maintain interest and to acquire understanding. Thus, the following guidelines are helpful in arranging a speech:

Introductions

1. *Function:* An **introduction** lets an audience know what a speech is about and tries to convince them that it is also worth hearing. An introduction should thus be clear and interesting, combining elements of argument and narrative, reason and emotion, or fact and value. Specifically, the functions are as follows:

   a. *Capture audience's attention.* Making an audience interested in listening to what you have to say is *the* most important function of an introduction. Why? If they are not interested, then nothing else you say will matter because they won't hear it.

   b. *State topic of the speech and purpose.* Once you capture attention, you must retain it. You do so by making clear what your speech will be about so they will be prepared to sit through a more formal argument that may not be as "flashy" as your introduction. State your thesis as succinctly as you can.

   c. *Relate the topic to your audience.* No topic is intrinsically interesting. Maintaining an audience's attention usually requires that they feel invested in what you have to say. Relating a topic to the interests and experiences of an audience creates this feeling of investment because what you say has value for *them*.

   d. *Set a tone.* Letting an audience know whether you intend to be serious, ironic, funny, critical, or deferential, is what it means to "set a tone." Doing so puts your audience in a frame of mind so that they know what to expect, just as audiences prepare themselves for a different "tone" at a comedy club than at a graduation ceremony or a funeral.

e. *Preview main points.* Although not always necessary, laying out the basic sequence of arguments can be helpful, especially when making a fairly complex or lengthy speech. However, previews are generally inappropriate for commemorative or introductory speeches because they are too formal.

f. *Provide a transition to the body of the speech.* Always let your audiences know when the introduction is over and the actual body of the speech has begun. This encourages them to listen with a different set of expectations. Since they have committed themselves to listening to the speech, they no longer need speakers to "get their attention." They now want to hear the details. A transition lets them know when this shift has occurred.

2. *Strategies:* The following are some helpful techniques to "get attention and interest" before stating your thesis and moving to the body.

a. *Use a quote.* Everyone enjoys hearing interesting quotes from famous people. Quotes should be relatively short and easy to understand and drawn from a person readily recognizable to and respected by the audience. These quotes should then be relevant to your own topic and preferably your argumentative claim as well.

b. *Startling fact.* Stating some dramatic fact either reveals some problem in graphic form (like the fact that thousands of people die from some disease every day) or it demonstrates the relevance of your topic (like the fact that amount of candy eaten in a year, when stacked on a pile, would reach the moon). Speakers then proceed from this startling fact to argue the less exciting details that are necessary to understand and give meaning to that fact.

c. *Begin with a question.* To ask a question is to put your audience in the position of judgment. What would they do if such a thing occurred? What would they think about this or that idea? The intention of this strategy is to generate perplexity that your speech presumably would resolve. A poor question has an obvious answer, such as "If you had a choice, would you abolish cancer?" A good question actually raises some moral issue, such as "If your family was hungry, would you steal bread?"

d. *Refer to a current event.* Usually drawn from news stories, current events demonstrate why your topic is relevant to everyday contemporary life. These events may be *tragic* (like a child imitating violent video games in real life), *inspiring* (like a person who struggled to overcome cancer), or simply *odd* (like a man who thinks he is the king of Canada). In either case, they are used to show how violent video games, cancer cures, or psychological disorders are relevant issues to talk about.

e. *Tell a story.* A story in an introduction functions a lot like a fable. For instance, the "Boy Who Cried Wolf" conveys a lesson about trust. A story is a way of embodying some message by using plot and character as symbolic of a larger theme. Stories can come from personal experience, news, or history, or can be completely made up. However, completely fictional stories of the hypothetical variety are generally ineffective because the audience does not take them seriously. A good story relates some actual event, even if that event is your grandfather telling you a fictional story as a child.

f. *Perform a demonstration.* A technique with only very narrow applications, performing a demonstration involves actually doing some physical action to make a point. Anyone who has taken physics knows the typical kind of science demonstration meant to demonstrate how Newton's laws function. A demonstration can also be *entertaining* (like doing a magic trick), or *controversial* (like showing how a condom works). In either case, it catches attention through actions rather than just words.

g. *Refer to literary material.* This strategy combines the strategy of quoting and telling a story. This is the one case in which fictional stories are effective because they derive from literature rather than just your imagination. The best source, of course, should be familiar to and appreciated by your audience, especially when it has acknowledged cultural significance for a larger community.

h. *Use humor.* As anybody who has ever attended a religious service knows, humor is not always reserved for "light" topics. Humor can be effectively used in any situation. It takes a very sensitive touch to use humor when the "tone" of the speech is not a humorous one, but when done well it can be an effective way to "break the ice" with an audience.

i. *Create suspense.* Also, a variation on telling a story to create suspense you must set up conditions that may lead to some potential climax, thereby keeping your audience on the edge of its seat. This suspense can be created through narrative or through demonstration. The risk of this strategy is that if the climax is not very interesting, then audiences feel let down. Also, suspense implies that you are not telling the full story, leading to the possibility that audiences may not know what you are actually speaking about until it is too late.

Conclusions

1. *Function:* Whereas the purpose of the introduction is to get attention and interest, the purpose of the **conclusion** is to leave a lasting impression. Performances of entertainment can be judged purely on the quality of the experience as it occurs, but the effectiveness of rhetorical public speech requires an audience to subsequently *act* upon that performance. A conclusion helps to ensure that this purpose is achieved. Specifically, the functions are as follows:

   a. *Summarize main points.* Although not usually effective as a rhetorical style of presentation, if done explicitly (as in, "To summarize, I have argued X, Y, and Z"), a conclusion should usually reaffirm the basic claims and arguments of a speech. The important thing is to embody these claims and arguments in a new way that makes them more interesting and poetic.

   b. *Help the audience remember the speech.* Sometimes this can be achieved by calling attention to the physical environment so that your speech is linked to some memorable object or event that is present. Other times you recall something important or imaginative in the earlier part of the speech and emphasize it again so as to leave them with a lasting "impression." Remember that complex memories are almost always recalled by simple associations.

c. *Leave with a call to action.* Often times, persuasion requires a lengthy detour through factual accounts, narratives, reasons, and explanations. A conclusion should show how all of these things lead to a specific action that is within reach of the audience. The phrase "think globally, act locally" in many ways summarizes the form of a rhetorical speech. One spends the large part of it thinking big only to end on a simple action, like recycling, giving to charity, or boycotting a business.

d. *Clearly end your speech.* Let people know when you are nearing the end of your speech. A conclusion should help an audience "wind down." It allows them time to think about what the speech meant to them. Letting an audience know that you are about to end gives them a sense of "closure" that makes a big difference in the quality of the lasting impression.

e. *End on a positive note.* Even with speeches that articulate the most graphic and devastating conditions, audiences want to know that there is some hope in making the world a better place. It is important to give audiences this hope at the end of a speech so that they leave believing they can make some small difference. This does not mean being naively idealistic. It simply means not giving in to apathy or pessimism.

2. *Strategies:* Here are the basic strategies for leaving a good impression.

a. *Startle your audience.* After a long speech, sometimes audiences get too relaxed or even bored. A conclusion that makes some startling claim or demonstration can "wake them up" and make them pay closer attention to your concluding arguments.

b. *Challenge your audience.* Similar to startling them, a speaker can also take the risky move to challenge them. This usually involves a combination of critique and imagination. To challenge an audience means they are not living up to their potential, but to imagine means they have a better future ahead of them.

c. *Come full circle.* A very effective way of concluding a speech is to refer back to the introduction and pick up where it left off. If it asked a question, then answer it. If it told a story, carry on the plot. If it quoted a famous philosopher, quote that philosopher again. This does not mean simply repeating what is already said, but continuing a line of thought and bringing it to a proper conclusion.

d. *Visualize a positive future.* One way of ending on a positive note is to dramatize the great future that will come about through the committed actions of the audience. This is the basic strategy of much advertising that features before and after sequences. Thus, you not only want to tell people that their future is going to be better; you want to visualize that future for them in order to develop an emotional attachment.

e. *Visualize a negative future.* The opposite strategy is to visualize the negative future that would come about from inaction or choosing a different action. By analogy, this would be the future of choosing the "competitor's product." Instead of a popular person wearing a colorful line of new clothes, one would show a sad and lonely person wearing his or her old wardrobe.

f. *Ask a question.* Unlike the introduction, which poses a question which will then be answered, this question should leave the audience with something to ponder.

g. *Use a humorous anecdote.* An anecdote should sum up a major point already made in a funny way that encourages the audience to talk about it after the speech is over.

h. *Employ quotations.* This strategy is similar to using an anecdote, except that it relies on the words of someone famous who has the weight of authority.

i. *Tell a story.* Often used effectively to give "moral lessons," a story at the conclusion of a speech sums up in narrative what was already explained using logic.

Structuring Main Points

Any speech, no matter how ceremonial, should always contain one or more clear **main points**. The structure of a main point is similar to a thesis in that it presents a concrete claim that will subsequently be elaborated or proved. The difference is that a thesis summarizes the whole speech whereas a main point summarizes a part of that speech. Thus, the main point is closely aligned with the idea of a topic sentence in composition, which is the sentence that establishes the tone and purpose of each paragraph. For example, the thesis "We should establish more national parkland because it preserves wildlife, creates more opportunities for outdoor adventure, and connects people to the natural environment" would then be broken down into the following series of main points that expand on the ideas presented:

- First, the survival of many species of large predators, like wolves and mountain lions, depends on having free range to a wide expanse of undeveloped land.
- Second, national parks provide a destination for the many outdoor enthusiasts who desire to use the space for recreation.
- Third, national parks are the best means of creating a sense of stewardship with the environment, an attitude that is necessary for the health of the planet.

Clearly articulating these points helps the speaker to better organize the speech and helps the audience to follow a complex train of reasoning. After defining your main points, using transitions, previews, summaries, and signposts help to create a smooth continuity to the speech as one progresses from point to point.

1. *Transitions:* Once you have sufficiently articulated a main point and concluded a section, it is necessary to provide a "bridge" to move your audience from one idea to another. A transition provides this bridge by showing the connection between the two ideas and the need to proceed from one to the other. For example, a transition between points 1 and 2 in the preceding example could be accomplished by the following transition: "This space can be used not only by animals, however, but by humans who wish to 'get away from it all.'" This passage shifts our attention from one object (wildlife) to another (park visitors) that are nonetheless connected by the idea of how the park can be "used" in a practical sense.

2. *Internal previews:* An internal preview is a sentence within the speech that lets an audience know what they are about to hear—for example, "I shall show through a series of testimonials how experience with natural parks changes the way that individuals see themselves as connected with nature." Previews of this kind are helpful with a long speech that contains complex details. For shorter, less complex speeches, internal previews are often unnecessary.

3. *Internal summaries:* A summary is the opposite of a preview. Instead of telling people what to expect, a summary reminds them what they have heard so as to reaffirm some important point. For example, at the end of the first section you could write, "All of these animal species I have described would find it hard to survive without continuous land preserved for their habitat." A summary should restate the idea of the main point but do so in a way that refers to the specific forms of evidence presented in the section.

4. *Signposts:* A signpost is a way of saying to your audience "You are here." It marks a path along the way and lets them know your location. In the articulation of the main points, these took the form of "First, Second, and Third." Other signposts include "To begin," "In conclusion," "Next," and so forth. These very simple tools make a big difference in the way an audience follows along.

Arranging Main Points

How will your main points be ordered? A poor speech will simply throw information together in a haphazard way. A good speech will present an audience with a clear progression of ideas that they can easily follow and know what is coming. If a speech does not fit into any of these orders, then it is likely that the speech will be too disconnected to be effective. These are the basic ways of structuring main points:

1. *Chronological:* Speeches that involve some process of time are suitable for chronological order that describes something from beginning to end. For example, chronological order is useful when doing biographies (the life of Martin Luther King, Jr.), events (the Pamplona running of the bulls), or processes (how life may have developed on Mars).

2. *Geographical:* Whereas chronological order deals with differences across time, geographical order deals with differences across space. The classic geographical speech is a kind of "world tour" in which the speaker shows the different manifestations of something in different regions, whether the subject-matter is language, culture, science, economics, history, war, or art. But geography can also be used in a more general sense of describing anything spatially, whether it is a microchip, a crime scene, a state capital, or the universe.

3. *Cause–Effect:* The cause-and-effect order almost always deals with speeches concerned with informing an audience about factual knowledge needed to address some problem. Consequently, they almost always deal with issues of process (like the ways AIDS is transmitted or how smoking causes cancer), because a process is by definition something that causes change over time.

4. *Pro–Con:* The pro–con order is the counterpart of the cause–effect order in that it deals with the analysis of solutions which respond to problems. A pro–con order examines a particular solution to some problem and articulates its positive and negative qualities in order to provide an audience with sufficient objective knowledge to make a decision (like the potential environmental benefits of regulating carbon dioxide emissions compared with its economic downsides).

5. *Topical:* The most general organizational structure is "topical," which simply means a series of related qualities or characteristics of your subject-matter. Examples are "The four unique aspects of Louisiana cooking," "The hierarchies

of English feudalism," and "Varieties of world religions." These do not fit into any of the above orders but still are speeches with thematic connections.

6. *Problem–Solution:* Quite simply, this speech lays out the problem and presents a clear solution. It can also incorporate the pro–con format within this structure.
7. *Comparative Advantage:* Also a variation on the pro–con structure, the comparative advantage puts two competing solutions side-by-side, and shows how one has more advantages than the other.

Monroe's Motivated Sequence

One of the most common rhetorical structures is **Monroe's Motivated Sequence,** which adapts the Classical model of arrangement and puts it into a more simplified, persuasive form. Alan Monroe was a Professor of speech at Purdue University who developed a special sequence designed for policy speeches that encourage immediate action. Although largely just an application of basic public speaking strategies, **Monroe's Motivated Sequence** has a simple form and clear labels that make it easy to remember and apply on short notice.

1. *Attention:* Like any good introduction, get the attention and interest of your audience: "Little Margaret was an otherwise happy child. She liked television, she liked ice cream, and she liked to play with dolls. She also was six years old and weighed over one hundred pounds."
2. *Need:* Another word for "problem," *need* establishes the necessity to address some issue by graphically articulating why we "need" to act: "Childhood obesity is becoming a national epidemic. Over 30% of children under the age of eight are now considered obese. This leads to poorer school performance and chronic health problems."
3. *Satisfaction:* Another word for "solution," *satisfaction* lays out what is required to be done in order for an audience to feel that its needs have been satisfied: "We need to implement an aggressive health campaign in this nation that brings healthy lunches and active gym classes to the schools and also delivers a targeted marketing campaign to parents to encourage healthy eating and exercise."
4. *Visualization:* This step relies on heightening emotions by visualizing the wonderful state of affairs that will occur after satisfaction: "With such steps, Little Margaret could achieve a more active and energetic lifestyle in which she and other children leave the couch to play outside in the fresh air and sun."
5. *Action:* Now that an audience has been suitably inspired, this step tells them what they can do to help by laying out specific things to be done: "These changes must come from you. Become an active member in your school board and advocate changes at a local level while writing your congressional representative to support new health initiatives."

Outlining

The outline is one of the primarily tools for helping to arrange all of your ideas into a concrete form. **Outlining** allows you to organize the "highlights" of a speech into sections and put them into a linear progression of beginning, middle, and end. In its final form, an outline represents the last stage of your speech preparations that precede the actual writing or delivery of a speech. It includes your specific purpose and thesis at the top of the page. It is then broken down into the introduction, main points, and conclusion, with supporting arguments and evidence in between. And a final outline should be careful to accurately record all quotations in full, as well as dutifully record all facts as faithfully as possible. Looking at the final outline thus gives a reader a sense of "substance" or content of a speech, even if it lacks a coherent "style" or form. For example, here is an outline based on a traditional model:

Specific Purpose: To persuade my audience that video lottery should remain illegal in Pennsylvania.

Thesis: Because video lottery takes money from those who can least afford it, increases gambling addiction, and destroys the character of small towns, by keeping video lottery illegal in Pennsylvania, we are essentially stopping problems our state could face before they even start.

INTRODUCTION

1. The story of Susan Piercey
   A. Susan had a tremendous addiction to video lottery machines.
   B. Susan was a "Beautiful intelligent girl who always had a smile and a few words for everyone. She was the type of girl who was always concerned about other people's problems." (1)
   C. Over the course of ten years she lost more than $100,000 to state video lottery machines. (1)
   D. Susan drowned into deep depression and committed suicide.
   E. Her mother Cathy Piercey stated, "For governments to condone and support province-wide VLTs is nothing short of legalized theft of those who use them and those who are left to deal with the aftereffects." (1)
2. Video lottery has become a much debated topic as of late.
   A. A changing of governor has led to concerns of change in the video lottery laws.
   B. Governor Rendell favors installing video lottery machines at the state's four racetracks, as well as at future racetracks that have not been constructed yet. (2)
3. Thesis: Because video lottery takes money from those who can least afford it, increases gambling addiction, and destroys the character of small towns, by keeping video lottery illegal in Pennsylvania, we are essentially stopping problems our state could face before they even start.

BODY

I. Video lottery is often played by those who cannot afford to play.
   A. Brad is a 46-year-old man who collects welfare each month.
      1. What he has left after paying the rent, he blows on the video lottery machines, around $240. (3)
      2. Brad states that most people who play the slots are people who can't work and need government help. "[The government] is taking it out of one pocket and putting it into another because the majority of people who play can't work." (3)
      3. Brad has tried to commit suicide before, jumping off of a three-story building only to break his ankle and pelvis. (3)

B. Gambling addiction of the poor leads to starving and homeless children.
   1. Kevin Head, leader of a Salvation Army food bank says "[Video lottery casinos] are like a big funnel. People go in and they just can't leave. I know in my gut there are people going without, there are kids going without food." (3)
   2. Food banks and other programs have seen an increase in people needing support due to gambling addiction over the past ten years. (3)
   3. Those who make less than $20,000 are at a much greater risk to face gambling addiction than someone who makes more than $20,000 a year. (3)
      Transition: Those people who make small amounts of money or live in poverty are not the only people who are harmed by gambling. Addiction can hurt the rest of the population as well.

II. Addiction
   A. Video lottery addiction leads to an increase of crime and theft.
      1. White collar crime to fund gambling addictions has been on an increase. (4)
      2. Bud Snow of the Halifax Police Department states "At one time, most of our large internal thefts were drug related. Now they're more or less gambling related." (4)
   B. Video lottery leads to high levels of addiction in states where it is legalized.
      1. It is estimated that in states where video lottery is legal that 4% of the population has a gambling problem. (4)
      2. People are more likely to gamble when video lottery is available in their own state as opposed to having to drive across state borders. (4)
   C. Many addicts get too deep into debt and do not know where to turn.
      1. Gamblers Anonymous® has a tremendous increase in states where video lottery is legal. (5)
      2. Some gamblers feel it is not their fault and they should sue or turn to the police.
      3. Detective Kelly of the Halifax police department says, "We've had a number of calls, but there's nothing we can do. They need a credit counselor or clergy. It breaks my heart to hear it. Families are being destroyed." (4)
         Transition: Those who gamble are not the only ones that are being hurt. Citizens of the towns and cities that have casinos are also seeing the effects of video lottery in their everyday lives.

III. Video lottery damages small towns and cities
   A. Advertising for video lottery has changed the look of many towns.
      1. In reference to video lottery advertisements, Luella Everitt, a citizen of Quiet Dell, West Virginia, states, "When you come off the interstate, you see it before you see the church. That bothers me. This has gone from a quiet, nice little community to I don't know what." (3)
      2. Advertisements and video lottery casinos themselves have been placed in locations extremely close to churches and schools. (2)
   B. Many restaurants that used to focus on families and food now focus more on video lottery machines. (1)
   C. The personal atmosphere draws people to small towns and cities as opposed to large video lottery casinos.
      1. This leads to an increase in noise and traffic. (3)
      2. Dave, a video lottery player from West Virginia says, "I would never go to a casino. To me, a casino is a place you go to lose your money. These small places, they don't feel that way." (4)

CONCLUSION

I. Video lottery leads to a number of problems for citizens of states that have legal video lotteries.

II. Those who do not directly participate in the video lotteries are also affected by their towns being overrun by video lottery casinos, as well as seeing loved ones suffer through gambling addiction.

III. By not allowing video lottery in Pennsylvania, we can keep some problems that face states with legal video lotteries out of ours.

BIBLIOGRAPHY

1. Lamp, G.P. (1998). *Gambling with our future*. East Lansing: Michigan State University Press.
2. Ruce, P. (1999, October). Rolling the dice. *Atlantic Monthly*, pp. 67–77.
3. Smith, G.W. (1998). The political impact of video gambling. *Communication Monographs, 62*, 154–172.
4. Price, H.B. (1998, May 26). Why do we love video gambling? *New York Times*, p. A23.
5. Gamblers Online. (1999, October 26). The effects of video gambling. [Online]. Available from http://www.gamblersonline.com/News/video_gambling.html (accessed November 2, 1999).

Guidelines for producing a finalized version of the outline can be found on these university websites:

Purdue University:

http://owl.english.purdue.edu/owl/resource/544/02/

University of Washington:

http://depts.washington.edu/psywc/handouts/pdf/outline.pdf

In the classroom, whenever a speech is delivered, a final version of the outline should also be turned in. This allows an instructor to reflect upon its structure and logic after the initial focus on its delivery and performance. However, using this "final" model as a *way of developing the speech itself* may not be the most productive method. If one starts with a final, polished outline as an example, speakers assume that an outline is only worthwhile if it effectively represents a finished product. In actual fact, the opposite is true. Outlines are often more valuable when they are incomplete, because they help identify the gaps that need to be filled. In the *creative stage*, an outline should thus represent a combination of a rough draft and a brainstorming session. The rough draft aspect records the basic arguments, facts, quotes, and strategies that one feels confident are useful. The brainstorming aspect puts them together with ideas and possibilities that may not yet have any clear structure or backing.

The point of developing such an outline before a speech is precisely to put ideas on paper so that you can communicate your thoughts to yourself and a constructive critic (the teacher) for the purposes of putting them into a more coherent order through experimental revision and encouragement. To assume that the only "good" outline is a fully finished one is thus to misunderstand the entire point of outlining. Both students and instructors should thus use outlines *as a tool for collaborative communication* during the process of invention and development, not as an exercise in translating an already finished speech into a different format for its own sake.

Note Cards

When doing an extemporaneous speech, note cards function as a kind of outline. But note cards should be even shorter than an outline, with information acting primarily as reminders rather than a manuscript. Again, only quotes, transitions, thesis, and introductory and concluding remarks should be written out. While it is tempting to add more "just in case," the fact is that the more one writes on a note card, the more a speaker is tempted simply to read out loud, thereby ruining the purpose of extemporaneous speaking. Note cards should also not be too "packed" with information, but should be written in clear, bold letters with a lot of "white space" so that one can easily see what comes next without having to hunt within a clutter of words. Here is an example of how parts of the outline of the speech above might be turned into a note card:

Susan Piercey addicted.

Best friend, Karen Turner, said she was a "Beautiful intelligent girl who always had a smile and a few words for everyone. She was the type of girl who was always concerned about other people's problems."

Lost $100,000 in 10 yrs.

(as reported in Gordon Lamp's book, *Gambling with Our Future*) Susan depressed and committed suicide

Her mother Cathy Piercey has stated, "For governments to condone and support province-wide VLTs is nothing short of legalized theft of those who use them and those who are left to deal with the aftereffects."

Discussion: As exemplified in the kindergarten activity of making a collage, arrangement is clearly the counterpart of invention and is equally creative. One can find a lot of interesting things to piece together on a board, but it takes added skill to arrange those pieces to create a unified image pleasing to the eye. What other nonrhetorical activities can you think of that involve this chronological relationship between invention and arrangement in which one precedes the other? Which step do you think requires the most effort and talent in each example?

THE THIRD CANON: STYLE

Style is the compliment to invention; whereas invention provides the "content," style provides the "form." It deals with how to express ideas rather than where to find them. However, this distinction between form and content should not be taken as an absolute division. Style may be "ornamentation," but the Latin term *ornare* is substantive and means "to equip, fit out, or supply." A soldier was thus "ornamented" with the weapons of war, meaning that a soldier without style was not, in fact, prepared to fight as a soldier. Similarly, rhetorical **style** is not the frivolous decoration of ideas; it is the filling out and forming of ideas in order to allow them to stand on their own and organize themselves as a coherent whole. Just as the military is made up both of individual soldiers and whole platoons, style includes both particular parts of the speech ("figurative style") as well as the tone of the speech in its entirety ("formal style"). It is important to keep this distinction in mind, for often speakers focus too much on the style of the parts at the expense of the whole.

Figurative Style

Figurative style focuses on providing short, refined, effective parts of a speech that give clarity and power to specific ideas or images. It includes not only examples and the use of concrete words, but also what are commonly called "tropes and figures." A **trope**, like a metaphor, is called a "figure of thought" because it recombines ideas and associations in our minds ("This bedroom is a pigsty"). A **figure**, like alliteration, is called a "figure of speech" because it deals more with how a phrase sounds to the ears ("The day dawned to our delight"). The absolute distinction between tropes and figures has largely been abandoned, but a general distinction in tendency still remains valid. However, as each of these forms of figurative style are derived from the ability of words to take on multiple meanings, it is important that we start with meaning.

Meaning: For something to possess **meaning** is for it to stand in a functional and/or referential relationship to other things. For instance, the string of letters "ltbea" does not mean anything, but the string of letters "table" does. In the dictionary, *table* means "an article of furniture supported by one or more vertical legs and having a flat horizontal surface." In the thesaurus it is associated with the words *counter, bench, stand, board, surface,* and *slab.* However, it can also be defined as "a set of facts or figures arranged in rows and columns" and be associated with the words *list, chart, tabulation, record, roll, index, register, digest, diagram, inventory, graph, synopsis,* and *itemization.* Or it can be defined as an act of "suspending discussion of a proposal indefinitely." The word *table* thus possesses many literal meanings because it is a part of a universe of discourse.[4]

Given the plurality of meanings associated with any word, it is clear that a word only gets its meaning in **context**. That context includes both the other words surrounding that word (as in "Please sit at the table" instead of "Please table that proposal") as well as the situation in which those words are spoken ("table!" can thus be interpreted by movers as a command to bring the table to the moving van without having to say anything else). There are four different types of meaning:

1. *Denotative meaning* is the "literal" reference of a word that is most universally associated with its contextual use. Denotative meanings are the building blocks of language because they provide the basic meanings that everyone can agree upon to coordinate common actions. "We need to provide a joint naval force to fight *piracy* in international waters" (spoken to the United Nations).
2. *Connotative meaning* is the emotional judgment of attraction or repulsion that is associated with the denoted object, event, process, concept, action, or person. This meaning is the negative or positive valence that we attach to a word to give it a certain tone. "Increased taxation to pay for irresponsible policies is a veritable act of *piracy* on the citizens of the nation" (spoken at a protest rally).

---

[4]For more on meaning, see C. Ogden and I. A. Richards, *The Meaning of Meaning* (New York: Harcourt Brace Jovanovich, 1923).

3. *Associative meaning* is the spectrum of secondary denotative and connotative meanings that an audience associates with the primary object of reference. In other words, it is all the other things that spring to mind after one thinks about the intended reference. "Who are you, a pirate?" (Uttered to a friend who bought a parrot).

4. *Practical meaning* is the actual effect brought about by one's choice of language. It is what a word "does" rather than what it "refers to." Consequently, practical meaning is explicitly tied to the immediate context in which something is spoken. "Pirates!" (Shouted to the ship's captain on seeing a vessel approaching).

Concrete Words   A **concrete word** has a meaningful reference to specific and readily identifiable qualities or actions in order to give an audience a more vivid experience of some thing or event. Usually when people think of concrete words, they think of nouns. For instance, the word *it* might turn into *the red table*, the word *country* into *Brazil*, or the word *insects* into *fire ants*. However, it is important to point out that a concrete word does not refer only to nouns. Concrete words also apply to verbs and adjectives. In terms of verbs, the weakest way of writing is the use of the "passive voice," which makes the subject a target of an action rather than the initiator of one. Consider, for example, "The book <u>was</u> <u>read</u> today" or "He <u>is being</u> punished." Notice how much more "concrete" it sounds to write, instead, "Janet <u>read</u> the book" or "His father <u>punished</u> him." Also, overuse of the verb *to be* tends to make a speech repetitive. A sentence like "I am mad" can be turned into "My blood boils," and "Rain is good" can be turned into "Rain gives life." Finally, adjectives can also be made more concrete. Rather than sticking to generic adjectives like good, bad, happy, sad, helpful, harmful, and the like, try to pick out the specific aspects of a thing that makes it those things. For example, "That's a pretty car" can be made into "That old Mustang sports shiny chrome fenders."

In other words, the more specific you can describe something, the more vivid the image will be in the mind of the audience and the more they will enjoy your speech. Thus, concrete words appeal especially to feeling and imagination, allowing an audience to picture itself within a different environment. This is especially important when rhetors have to articulate experiences that are unfamiliar to an audience by using language that *is* familiar. They also play a central role in arguments that employ *pathos*, since we usually get emotional only about things we can concretely imagine.

Examples: An example is a brief narrative or description that demonstrates the meaning of an idea through a specific case. Examples are one of the most important ways of doing this because they allow audiences the time to ponder an idea before moving on to the next one. They also provide vivid memories that an audience can later recall even after they may have forgotten the idea it was supposed to demonstrate.[5] However, as long as the example remains, people can usually, with

---

[5]For more on the persuasive use of examples, see Scott Consigny, "The Rhetorical Example," *Southern Speech Communication Journal* 41 (1976), 121–134.

some effort, remember what a speech was really about. There are two main kinds of examples: actual examples and fictional examples as follows.

1. *Actual examples* are descriptions of real things that exist or have existed, that happen or have happened. The main sources of actual examples are history, the news, personal experience, or science. Thus, one could use the Salem witch trials to exemplify intolerance, a feature story about a New Orleans family to exemplify the struggles after Hurricane Katrina, a personal story about one's immigrant grandfather to exemplify personal courage, or a scientific discovery of an Egyptian tomb to exemplify ancient wisdom. Actual examples are important for making speeches appear thoroughly researched and backed by evidence rather than simply being expressions of personal opinion. Actual examples thus function both to *prove* one's point as well as to demonstrate it.

2. *Fictional examples* are descriptions of events that are only imagined to have happened in the past, present, or future. There are two kinds of fictional examples: third-person examples (referring to "he" or "she") and second-person examples (referring to "you"). *Third-person fictional examples* describe the actions of other people as if they actually happened until usually revealing at the end that it is just a story. For example, one might say "Joe was an aspiring actor until he started doing drugs and then had an overdose and died. Joe is not a real person, but there are thousands of people like Joe every day." The most effective third-person examples come from stories taken from literature or other popular forms of art that are commonly known by an audience. The other kind of example is a *second-person fictional example,* which places the audience in a hypothetical situation that asks an audience to envision doing something. For example, one might say "Imagine you were walking down the street and saw a homeless man being beaten. Would you rush to save him or walk away?" Second-person examples usually offer an audience some choice in order to get them thinking about the problem that the speech then proceeds to address. Fictional examples can be helpful in demonstrating the meaning of a speech, but being pure fabrications, they generally lack the authenticity and power of actual examples. As a general rule, a speaker should choose actual examples over fictional examples whenever possible.

Tropes: A trope tends to emphasize the way that words can have more than one meaning. Often, tropes have literal meanings that are different, or even opposite, from their practical, connotative, or associative meanings. For instance, the statement "the man is a lion" does not literally mean that a man is a lion. As I. A. Richards explains, the meaning of this metaphor grows out of the interaction between the *tenor* and the *vehicle*. The **tenor** is the underlying message or principle idea that is intended to be conveyed ("the man is courageous"). The **vehicle** is how the tenor is embodied and expressed in a specific figure ("the man is a lion"). In this sense, the same tenor might be expressed by the vehicle "he roared into the fray" or "he castoff the cloak of fear" or "he spit into the face of death." However, the *meaning* of the metaphor is *not* simply its tenor. *The* meaning *is the interaction between the tenor and the vehicle.* Each of those vehicles *alters* how the tenor is interpreted for an audience, for an audience, and thus changes the meaning of the metaphor. Many of the tropes can be understood in a similar way, with the meaning being some combination of tenor and vehicle.[6]

1. *Metaphor:* A description of one thing directly in terms of something of unlike nature to emphasize a particular quality ("My love is a beautiful rose.").
2. *Synecdoche:* The use of a part of something to stand in for the whole of it ("After the World Trade Center bombings, we were all New Yorkers.").
3. *Metonymy:* A description of something personal and abstract in terms of a concrete object associated with it ("The other baseball team has its two big bats coming up.").
4. *Irony:* The use of a word or phrase in such a way that it conveys the opposite meaning ("Lucky for us, World War I was the war to end all wars.").
5. *Simile:* Explicit comparison between two things of unlike nature (generally using "like" or "as" to make it explicit ["She runs like a deer."]).
6. *Personification:* A description of abstract or nonhuman objects as if they possessed human qualities ("The waves leapt forward and pulled me back into the ocean.").
7. *Hyperbole:* The use of extreme exaggeration to highlight a specific quality or idea ("When my boss started yelling at me, I could feel the whole office building shaking.").
8. *Oxymoron:* The placement of two terms together that seem contradictory ("There is no such thing as a smart bomb. They are all equally mindless.").
9. *Paradox:* The statement of an apparent contradiction that nevertheless contains a measure of truth ("How strange it is that getting cancer saved my life. Only now have I come to value what is important in the world.").

Figures: A figure uses language that departs from its conventional structure and usage, but does not emphasize in the same way the different meanings of words. It tends to emphasize the musical sense of rhythm and sound over the more cognitive structures of reference. Whereas tropes are pleasing to the mind, figures are pleasing to the ear. Following are some different kinds of figures:

1. *Parallelism:* Placing similar rhythmic structures, words, phrases, or clauses into repetitive sequence ("Rich and poor, young and old, they came here to live, and we embraced them with love.").
2. *Antithesis:* The juxtaposition of contrasting ideas, often in parallel structure ("Do not weep for my death, but cheer for my life.").
3. *Alliteration:* The repetition of words that begin with the same consonant sound ("The soft, slow, surge of the silent sea.").
4. *Epistrophe:* The repetition of the same word or group of words at the ends of successive clauses ("When we came, they were here. When we left, they were here.").
5. *Repetition:* The repetition of the same word or groups of words at the beginnings of successive clauses ("We shall fight in the land, we shall fight in the sea, we shall fight in the air.").

---

[6]See I. A. Richards, *The Philosophy of Rhetoric* (Oxford, UK: Oxford University Press, 1936).

Formal Style

The overall tone and feel of a speech represent its formal style. It is the total impression left upon us by a speech after its completion that allows us to reflect upon it as a whole experience. In *Rhetorica Ad Herennium*, formal style is broken down into three general categories:

- **Grand style** uses a smooth and ornate arrangement of impressive words in order to move an audience to contemplative great thoughts. Such a style might be used in a presidential inaugural address, a ceremonial eulogy, or a social movement oration.
- **Middle style** uses more common words but puts them together into a more sophisticated form than everyday speech in order to please an audience with its novelty and wit. Speeches given at graduation ceremonies, in courtrooms, or at church services use this style.
- **Plain style** uses only the most ordinary speech and phrasings of the day in order to present ideas in the simplest and most accessible way possible. As the goal of the plain style is a kind of teaching, it often is used in salesmanship, in political discourse, and in organizational settings.

It is important to keep in mind that these styles are clearly responses to situated contexts. A grand address is usually inappropriate for a press conference, and a plain style is unsuitable for a State of the Union address. This sense of what style is appropriate to a given situation represents **decorum**. Like all rhetorical concepts, decorum must be understood in relationship to its context rather than as a rigid set of commands. Decorum represents a keen insight into what kind of action a situation demands. Thus, as seen in the action of Rosa Parks, there is no contradiction in the fact that sometimes decorum requires one to violate commonly accepted standards of behavior in order to act appropriately in a given context. Formal style is thus accomplished when one's total speech attains eloquence by perfectly channeling the energies of a situation. More about formal style will be addressed in Chapter 9.

Visual Aids: A visual aid is different from visual rhetoric. In visual rhetoric, the image is the form of persuasion itself—as in a billboard, a political cartoon, or an iconic photograph. This textbook, focusing on the act of speaking, will not address the complexities of visual rhetoric. A **visual aid**, by contrast, is a part of figurative style, using an image to more effectively convey a specific idea or emotion. Such aids include the bar graphs and tables of speech of administration, the personal objects often used in introductory speeches, the graphic images and statistics used in speeches of advocacy to dramatize problems, and the photographs or symbols useful in commemorative speeches in stimulating memory and emotion. Visual aids perform two major functions:

1. Simplify complex information that otherwise could not effectively be explained.
2. Graphically visualize an event, object, person, or process whose details are necessary for understanding a speech.

To be effective, visual aids should be large enough to see and colorful and interesting enough to capture an audience's attention. However, more is not necessarily better. We are often so inundated with visual aids that we often assume that we should always try to use as many visual aids as possible. But as a general rule, visual aids should be kept to a minimum and should never be forced into a speech simply to "dress it up" if there is no reason for them to be there. If a good description can describe something with eloquence, then a picture of that event does not "add" to the speech. It replaces or competes with it. Visual aids should never be in competition with the speaker or the speech. Anytime a visual aid takes attention away from the speech itself, it has failed in its purpose as an *aid*. In other words, a visual aid should be used to supplement a speech by performing a task that only a visual aid can perform. For example,

1. A *bar graph* will easily compare the gross national products of twenty nations at a glance.
2. A *line graph* will show the growth and decline of a nation's economy over a decade.
3. A *pie chart* will demonstrate the economic wealth of ten different social classes.
4. A *map* will show where the highest concentrations of population are in a nation.
5. A *representation* will reveal the process of offshore oil drilling.
6. An *object* will best show the amount of butter people were allowed during World War II.
7. A *flowchart* will show the steps that it takes for grain to get to market.
8. A *photograph* will show how far glaciers have retreated in twenty years.
9. A *chalkboard* drawing will spell out what NAFTA stands for.
10. A *handout* will provide an audience with the specific language of a proposed law.
11. A *posterboard* will show different types of fabric manufactured in the 1900s.

The U.S. Occupational Safety and Health Administration website has a useful summary of strategies for visual aids:

http://www.osha.gov/doc/outreachtraining/htmlfiles/traintec.html

Spoken Citation Style   Lastly, style deals with the proper way of relating information. Especially for informative speeches, it is vital not only to acquire but to cite and quote accurate sources to give yourself credibility. Here are some guidelines for how to smoothly incorporate citations into your speech.

1. *Well-known and uncontroversial facts:* There is no citation needed for the obvious. Do not clutter a speech by citing things an audience takes for granted.
   a. GOOD. "Over 2,000,000 people were killed in the Civil War."
   b. BAD. "According to *Encyclopedia Online*. . . ."
2. *Unknown or controversial facts released by people and institutions in press releases:* When your information comes directly from the source and you have access to that source, just cite that original source by name. Do not cite any subsequent news publication that may have repeated this information.
   a. GOOD. "The Economy Institute released a report in June that claimed environmental restrictions hurt economic growth."
   b. BAD. "*The Times* reported in July that a report by the Brookings Institute in June said. . . ."
3. *Unknown or controversial facts published secondhand by news publications:* When a newspaper has cited some startling fact, make sure to

cite *both* the source and the news publication that first reported it. The fact is that sometimes news reports will "spin" facts in certain ways, so it is important to acknowledge that you are getting it second hand.

   a. GOOD. "Hodgedale Industries recently was reported in *The New York Times* as saying that its medical screening technologies have saved over 2,000 women's lives in the year 2001."

   b. BAD. "*The New York Times* claims that Hodgedale Industries has saved. . . ."

   c. BAD. "Hodgedale Industries has saved. . . ."

   d. BAD. "Hodgedale Industries claims to have saved. . . ."

4. *Quoting famous people:* Generally, important quotes by famous people only need a citation by the name of the person, not the time, place, or manner in which the passage was written or spoken.

   a. GOOD. "Socrates once said that "the unexamined life is not worth living.""

   b. BAD. "In 430 B.C., Socrates was once quoted in Plato's *Critias* that. . . ."

5. *Quoting professionals or experts:* For all other quotes, cite the name, status or position, and the forum in which the quote appeared.

   a. GOOD. "In last week's *Boston Globe*, Dr. Singh, an engineering professor at MIT, claimed that 'there is no evidence that missile defense will ever be a feasible system.""

   b. GOOD. "In his book, *Defending America*, engineering professor Dr. Singh claimed. . . ."

   c. BAD. "Dr. Singh said. . . ."

   d. BAD. "*The Boston Globe* reported that 'there is no evidence. . . .'"

6. *Citing bare, uncontroversial facts reported in newspapers:* For isolated facts that do not merit a lot of attention, just cite the publication in which that fact appeared.

   a. GOOD. "*The Washington Post* reported last year that 5% of the population is illiterate."

   b. BAD. "15% of the population is illiterate."

   c. BAD. "In a study done by *The Washington Post* based on a sample of 4000 people in San Diego. . . ."

7. *Using stories or anecdotes found in magazines or websites:* When you use examples, it is important to make them sound like stories. The temptation is to ignore the need for citation. However, it is very important to cite the source and its author to give examples credibility. You simply need to find a discrete way to fit it in without ruining the flow of the narrative.

   a. GOOD. "Anna had just arrived from Russia when she was arrested by police, who accused her of spying. She was put in a cell for two months and was not able to see anyone. Her story, finally told last August in *The New Republic*, raises serious questions about our civil liberties."

   b. BAD. "Anna had just arrived from Russia when she was arrested by police, who accused her of spying. She was put in a cell for two months and was not able to see anyone. Can we let this happen in the United States?"

   c. BAD. "In a recent issue of *The New Republic*, a story appeared about a girl. . . ."

Discussion: We are constantly challenged to judge when a style has "substance" and when it is just "superficial." In terms of our judgments of self, the former is associated with reflections of "character" (like the unique habits of a superstar athlete) and the latter is indicative of mere "fashion" (like that athlete's name-brand merchandise). In what other spheres of our public life is style judged to be superficial? Do you think this distinction between substantial and superficial style is valid?

THE FOURTH CANON: MEMORY

The art of memory naturally followed style because once a speech was written an orator in the Classical Age had to memorize it before delivery. At its most elementary level, then, memory as the fourth canon simply referred to the ability to memorize a text. This skill is still valuable, but in an age of the teleprompter it has become far less vital. More important is memory as a source of invention and as a goal of persuasion.

Memory serves as a source of invention both individually and publicly. **Individual memory** represents the storehouse of beliefs, phrases, principles, reasons, experiences, and examples that any particular speaker can use to construct the body of a speech. Particularly in impromptu occasions, memory provides a speaker familiar places on which to stand while inventing arguments on the spot. Much like a jazz musician who combines a number of familiar riffs in an improvisation, a speaker with a wealth of resources in memory can create a rhythmic speech seemingly from nothing. **Public memory** represents the storehouse of social knowledge, conventions, public opinions, values, and shared experiences that a speaker can appeal to within that speech and be confident that they will resonate meaningfully with that audience. For example, William West says of memory

> The study of memory encompasses not just ideas of memory at a particular historical moment, but entire regimes of memory, ways of privileging certain types of knowledge, certain values, certain ideas, beliefs, symbols—in short, and entire cultural ethnography coalesces around the apparently innocuous ability to remember the past. Memory serves as the locus of personal history and individual identity.[7]

What is also rhetorically important about memory is that it is undergoing constant reinterpretation. Memory is a story whose scenes are selective and whose plot is malleable. At an individual level, we tend to remember only those things that affected us in some way, however small, and over time these memories connect with other memories and alter their meaning. The time your cranky neighbor broke your baseball bat after you hit his house with the ball was a single traumatic memory as a child, but as an adult it becomes one part of a larger story about the frivolity and adventure of youth. And the more times you tell that story, the more it grows and changes. The family member who tries to remember the "good times" engages in this process of reinterpretation by altering the narratives that make up our memories.

Public memory is different, as it exceeds the lifespan of the individuals who make up a public. For instance, by constant memorization and repetition, public memory preserves these famous words spoken by John F. Kennedy even for those who were born after his death: "Ask not what your country can do for you. Ask what you can do for your country." Kennedy and his speechwriters created a

---

[7]William West, "Memory," *Encyclopedia of Rhetoric*, ed. Thomas Sloan (Oxford, UK: Oxford University Press, 2001), 483.

stylistic figure that has become firmly lodged in American public memory and can be readily recalled to our consciousness by any public speaker who makes a passing reference. In a political environment that moves at such a rapid pace as ours, creating such a lasting object in the public memory is a rare and significant accomplishment. In this way, public memories of this type can act as a reservoir of feelings, images, and stories from which a rhetor can draw. Especially, if a rhetor shares common memories with his or her audience, the appeal to collective memory can be very powerful in gaining interest and focusing attention.

Because public memories are always being reinterpreted, a rhetor usually has the freedom to try to change the meaning of that memory after recalling it in the audience's mind. In this way, rhetors provide new narratives with which to reinterpret already existing memories of an audience. To finish the phrase "We all remember seeing the planes strike the World Trade Center" with the thought "and realizing how America no longer could hide behind its borders" is different than finishing it with the thought "and wondering 'How could God let this happen?'" In effect, rhetors often "suggest" how we should remember past events in the hope that their interpretations will resonate with the memories of an audience. When they do, audiences often feel as if a rhetor were "reading their minds" because the new memories they narrate feel like their own. For the rhetor, the expectation is that in future situations they will then act as if they *are* their own.

Discussion: Some of the most interesting rhetorical tensions arise within a clash between individual memory and public memory. It is not infrequent that those people immediately involved in some major event remember it much differently than the form in which it is preserved in public memory—for better or worse. For instance, a war that is remembered by civilians is much different than the one recalled by the soldiers who fought it. Have you ever been involved directly in an event that was later memorialized in public memory? What was similar or different in its representation? Do you think individual memory is usually more accurate than public memory, or vice-versa?

THE FIFTH CANON: DELIVERY

The last canon, **delivery**, predictably addresses the way a speaker physically performs the speech. It differs from style because it deals with the actual speaking rather than the words that are spoken. Although conceptually the simplest of the canons, it perhaps is the most difficult to master and requires a great deal of training and experience. It also is one of the most important. A speaker may say brilliant things, but if delivery is lacking, nobody is going to pay attention to what is said. Not surprisingly, then, the pressure that accompanies delivery leads many people to have intense speaking anxiety that is difficult to overcome. It is thus appropriate that discussion of delivery begins with this challenge.

Speaking Anxiety

Fear of public speaking traditionally ranks among the top three fears that people have. Being nervous, scared, and worried before making a public speech is completely normal. Michael Beatty identified eight factors of a speech situation that tend to increase **speaking anxiety**: the novelty of the experience, the formality of the occasion, the subordinate status of the speaker, the degree of conspicuousness felt by the speaker, unfamiliar environment, the dissimilarity and degree of attention from others, the degree to which one is being evaluated, and prior history.[8] Added to these situational factors is also the degree to which speaking anxiety, for many people, is akin to an inborn, genetic predisposition.[9]

Dealing with speaking anxiety is thus a complex challenge, as each speaker's anxiety will be unique and derived from different sources. The following are some basic strategies for dealing with speaking anxiety that can be employed by any speaker in preparation for a speech[10]:

1. *Nervousness is natural:* Being nervous is a biological manifestation of the "fight or flight" mechanism. It shows that your body is preparing you to deal with a challenging situation. The goal is not to get rid of nervousness but to harness that energy and use it to your advantage.

2. *Everyone experiences it:* Speaking anxiety is universal. Even the greatest speakers get anxious because so much is riding on their words. But the feelings they experience are the same as a beginning student. The difference is that they have more tools to deal with that anxiety.

3. *You appear more relaxed than you feel:* Anxiety rarely manifests itself in overt signs of stress that can be seen by an audience. The most common expressions of stress are shaking hands and flushed faces, but usually they bother the speaker more than the audience.

4. *Have something important to say:* Nothing rattles a speaker more than standing up only to find that one's speech is boring even to oneself. Hastily written speeches made simply to "get it over with" are, more often than not, the causes of speaking anxiety because one starts judging one's own speech as a failure. Taking the time to say something you want to say makes speaking a much more pleasurable experience.

5. *Visualize success:* Like almost any coach in competitive sports will tell you, if you focus on the little things, you will get so caught up in minutiae that you lose sight of the "big picture." As simplistic as it sounds, sometimes success comes from visualizing oneself succeeding.

6. *Release tension before speaking:* Purely on a physical note, clenching muscles or exerting energy in some way loosens you up and often gets rid of nervousness that has been built up in your muscles.

7. *The audience is usually on your side:* With rare political exceptions, people do not attend speeches to watch people fail. They attend speeches to listen to

---

[8]M. J. Beatty, "Situational and Predispositional Correlates of Public Sspeaking Anxiety," *Communication Education,* 37, (1988c), 28–39.

[9]M. J. Beatty et al., "Communication Apprehension as Temperamental Expression: A Communibiological Paradigm," *Communication Monographs,* 65, (1998), 197–219.

[10]For more on speaking anxiety, see Virginia P. Richmond and James C. McCroskey, *Communication: Apprehension, Avoidance, and Effectiveness,* 5th ed. (Boston: Allyn & Bacon, 1998); Peter Desberg, *No More Butterflies: Overcoming Stagefright, Shyness, Interview Anxiety, and Fear of Public Speaking* (Oakland, CA: New Harbinger, 1996).

people they find interesting. Hence, the audience will almost always wish for a speaker to do well. Despite the fact that they are ultimately "judging" your speech, they are a jury that hopes you succeed.

8. *Practice:* Nothing replaces simple practice. Simply knowing the words of a speech is not sufficient for a good performance. You need to feel at "one" with the speech so that your words and actions occur naturally together. Practice until you have memorized the speech and then practice again until you have completely internalized it. Usually, shoot for reading a speech out loud to yourself three times before delivering it to your audience. Reading it "in your head" *is not* the same as reading out loud. Actually verbalizing the words helps your mouth get used to saying the words and your ears get used to hearing them.

9. *Experience makes you more confident:* The more you speak in public, the easier it will become. It really is as simple as that. We learn by habit, and public speaking can become a habit once you break through the initial fear. By the end of a public speaking class, one may even begin to find pleasure in this habit.

This series of "tips" address the basics of putting oneself in the right frame of mind for public speaking. However, not all speaking anxiety can be dealt with by such simple attitude adjustments. From the extensive literature on speech anxiety, Graham Bodie has compiled a more systematic and clinical list of treatments.[11]

1. *Systemic desensitization:* This procedure attempts to change unconscious negative associations with speaking situations. First, it introduces students to methods of relaxation (like meditation), and once relaxed, a trainer has them visualize a series of speech situations, beginning with the least stressful and progressively increasing in perceived anxiety. Through repetition, individuals become more familiar with public speaking situations, thus normalizing them.

2. *Cognitive modification:* This treatment deals with negative and irrational cognitions of public speaking that take the form of beliefs, "I can't do this" or "It's too frightening." With a trained therapist, individuals discuss specific fears about public speaking, including one's self-evaluation, after which the therapist shows its irrationality and provides a coping statement ("I can handle this") that can be used while speaking.

3. *COM therapy:* Another method of treatment is to change an individual's orientation toward the function of public speaking. For those who hold a "performance-oriented" view, public speaking is like a trial by jury in which one is to perform and be judged. COM therapy attempts to change this orientation into a "communication-oriented" view in which public speaking is more like conversation in which each party is simply taking longer turns.

4. *Visualization:* Similar to systemic desensitization, visualization also begins with relaxation techniques, but instead of focusing simply on familiarizing oneself with the public speaking context, it focuses on visualizing success within that context. Visualization is thus a natural extension of cognitive modification.

---

[11]Graham D. Bodie (2010, January), "A Racing Heart, Rattling Knees, and Ruminative Thoughts: Defining, Explaining, and Treating Public Speaking Anxiety." *Communication Education*, 59, (1), 70–105.

5. *Skills training:* Skills training is another way of saying that practice, experience, and mastery will improve the confidence and public speakers.
6. *Performance feedback:* Another term for *constructive criticism*, performance feedback involves using nonverbal, oral, or written responses to a speaker's performance directed toward improving that performance. Notably, research shows that negative comments (when given in a constructive and honest spirit) are more helpful than positive ones, as they give the speaker a sense that they know the problem and have the means to address it.

After years of research, studies have shown that no one method tends to work for all individuals. Each person faces his or her own particular type of anxiety and must develop a method tailored to that person's needs. However, employing a variety of methods at different times, each overlapping the other, tends to have more benefit than adopting only one.

The Components of Delivery

Trying to improve delivery all at once is often as futile as learning to improve one's golf swing simply by trusting one's intuition. Improving delivery often requires focusing on parts of a delivery one at a time, mastering each one before moving on to the next one. Crucial to improving delivery is having an external critic judge your performance. The following is a list of elements that a speaker might ask a critical audience to evaluate before delivering the final speech.

1. *Eye contact:* The most important component of delivery is eye contact. There is something inexplicable about the power of eye contact, but the fact remains that we feel more engaged with a speaker who is looking directly at us. To avoid eye contact with an audience is to convey the message that you do not care about them; and if you don't care about them, why should they listen to you? Even if it is just for a few seconds at a time, eye contact makes an enormous difference to how a speech is received.
2. *Articulation:* To be clear, words should be spoken so as to make them stand out to our ears. In the very word "articulation," one can say it blandly or can say it by punctuating its highs and lows (e.g., Are–TIC–you–LAY–shun). Mumbling your way through a speech can make even the most eloquent language boring.
3. *Pronunciation:* Of course, one should also know how to correctly pronounce your words. Practice difficult names or words so that they flow off the tongue.
4. *Pitch:* In music, to have "perfect pitch" is to know how to sing a C major on command and have it in perfect tune. Pitch refers to the musical tone of your language, how it goes up and down through different "notes." Hearing a speech is more pleasurable when it is not just a monotone. One of the great qualities of Martin Luther King, Jr.'s oratory was the fact that his sermons often had the musical quality of a hymn.
5. *Volume:* Public speaking requires more than one's usual level of volume. For soft-spoken people, the volume required for public speaking often makes them feel like they are shouting and being obnoxious. Almost never is this the case. Indeed, it is virtually impossible to deliver a speech by shouting because one runs out of breath after a few words. The importance of volume is that if

an audience has to strain to hear you, its members will have that much less of their attention on what you are actually saying.

6. *Dialect:* Many people have *dialects*, a term that refers to local phrasings common in a particular group that may be different from those of the audience. Simply be aware that certain ways of saying things may not be universal, even with people who may technically speak the same language.

7. *Rate:* Similar to the issue of volume, public speaking requires a slower rate of delivery than in conversation. For many people, the rate requirements make them worried that they are boring the audience to death. But because public speaking involves more complex chains of reasoning and more sophisticated style, audiences need more time to process a speech in order to follow it through all its twists and turns. Unlike reading, an audience has no opportunity to go back and read something again if they missed it. Keeping a reasonable rate allows them the time to keep up with the logic of the speaker. However, this does not mean that one maintains only a single rate. At certain moments the rate should increase for dramatic effect, such as at the end of the speech or at times when one is telling a story. In any case, varying one's rate gives a speech more energy and makes it more entertaining.

8. *Pauses:* As a function of rate, a pause gives both the audience and speaker a chance to "rest." Especially after coming to some conclusion and before starting a new line of thought, a pause gives the audience a chance to reflect on what has been said and signals to them that they should be prepared to start down a new path. Also, a pause can be used for dramatic effect to build tension, such as before the punch line of a joke.

Appearance

Appearance matters. Make sure that you present yourself in such a way that adapts to the circumstances of the occasion—that has *decorum*. If you step onto a stage with an appearance that already violates the norms of your speech genre, than your speech is effectively finished before it begins.

1. *Clothes:* There are no universal expectations for clothes. The idea that one should always dress formally for a speech is a standard of the 19th century, not the 21st century. Sometimes, after all, it is better for presidents to "roll up their sleeves" when speaking to working Americans rather than come dressed in a suit and tie. Simply choose clothes that reinforce the persona you wish to present to your audience.

2. *Posture:* Generally, stand up straight and avoid leaning on the podium, shifting feet, or crossing legs. This does not mean you must stand still like a tree trunk. However, generally you want to look composed, even if you are moving around.

3. *Gestures:* A speaker should avoid nervous, repetitive gestures and should concentrate on making conscious movements that reinforce the points of the speech. Simple things like lifting a finger, opening one's arms wide, clasping hands, and the like often make a big difference on how the audience engages with the speaker and understands the message.

4. *Facial expressions:* Like gestures, one's facial expressions should mirror the tone of the speech. Looking happy, concerned, amused, frustrated, and the like

make the audience feel that a speaker truly "feels" the speech and is engaged personally with the language. These often do not come spontaneously, however, but as part of conscious practice. There is no substitution for having someone watch you and give advice.

Delivery Form

One of the most basic elements of any speaking genre involves the expectations for how the speech is going to be delivered. The choice of how you will deliver your speech has important consequences for how it will be received by an audience. The choice also opens up and limits certain possibilities for how a speech will be written, how much information it will contain, and how long it will be.

1. *Manuscript:* Reading from a manuscript means writing out every word of a speech and delivering it as written. Except in cases with a teleprompter, the manuscript should be on a podium and the speaker should have practiced the speech to the extent that much of it has been partially memorized. This allows a speaker to look down briefly to keep his or her place but still maintain eye contact with an audience. In this regard, it is helpful to write marks on the speech for when to breathe (~), when to look up (↑), and when to look back down (↓) so that you can memorize particular sections that you think warrant a more significant delivery. Manuscript reading allows for a careful sculpting of stylistic language (in the cases of commemorative speaking) or complex arguments (in deliberative speaking) that would otherwise be difficult to convey. Manuscripts are most proper for formal occasions in which the audience expects and demands this kind of complexity and subtlety. However, manuscript may provide a "crutch" that speakers rely on too much, which causes them to effectively ignore the audience and deliver the speech as if one was simply reading out loud.[12]

2. *Memory:* Delivering from memory is to write a manuscript first and then rehearse it until one knows it by heart. At its best, it has all the advantages of manuscript style without the disadvantages, for it allows a speaker to engage an audience directly and to walk around a "stage" without being tied to a podium. However, speeches from memory also put one at great risk. If one forgets even the smallest part of a speech, there is the danger that one's mind might go blank like an actor in a play, at which point there is nothing to help the speaker find his or her place. In addition, relying on memory makes it almost impossible to adapt to an audience during the speech, such as when external interference occurs or when a speaker simply realizes that something isn't working. Speeches from memory are thus best when they are short and have only a few simple points, such as a wedding toast or an argument in a public meeting. They also are excellent for storytelling exercises, as stories are easier to remember and audiences enjoy hearing stories from people as if they simply sprung naturally from memory.

3. *Impromptu:* Delivering impromptu speeches means to speak without preparation on a subject given to you at the moment. This form is the most natural and

---

[12]See James C. Humes, *Talk Your Way to the Top* (New York: McGraw-Hill, 1980).

spontaneous and thus often the most interesting to hear. However, it also limits one's ability to sculpt a careful argument and also provides no safety net should one run out of ideas. The classic case of impromptu speaking is parliamentary debate, in which a subject is announced and debaters have just a few minutes to come up with opposing arguments. Exercises of this kind, also helpful in public speaking classes, allows you the freedom to be creative and to gain experience speaking before audiences without having anything "at stake." In public, impromptu speaking may be required during deliberative meetings, like in the boardroom, the town hall, or the family kitchen, and also during celebratory occasions in which people are called upon to make a speech about themselves or others. And sometimes impromptu speaking is simply a way to entertain friends.

4. *Extemporaneous:* The essential feature of this speech is the note card, which includes key points, quotes, and transitions drawn from a larger outline but leaves the speaker to fill in the gaps during the actual delivery of the speech. This form provides structure but allows for adaptation in such a way that, ideally, the speaker will be able to connect with the audience on a personal level while still making a formal argument or presentation. A good note card will thus be easy to read, will not be cluttered with information, and will support the speech by providing both information and delivery instructions, like when to look up, when to make a gesture, when to speak loudly, and when to go slow. Extemporaneous speeches are ideal for people making "official" presentations in front an audience that feels free to break in and ask questions at any time. The speaker is able to deal with such interruptions because he or she still has all the important information in front of them, and they can flip backward and forward without completely disrupting the flow of the speech.

Discussion: Although attention to delivery in public speaking often feels forced, we in fact modify our delivery all the time to suit different occasions. The words, pace, volume, and articulation of our language varies depending on whether we are speaking to parents, friends, employers, teachers, or strangers. What is an example of the biggest difference between your delivery when the audiences change? And between which audiences?

KEY WORDS

Appearance   32
Arrangement   9
Conclusions   11
Concrete words   21
Context   20
Decorum   24
Delivery   28
Examples   6
Figurative style   20
Figure   20
Grand style   24
Individual memory   27

Introductions   9
Invention   3
Main points   13
Meaning   20
Middle style   24
Monroe's Motivated
   Sequence   15
Outlining   15
Plain style   24
Public memory   27
Sources   3

Speaking anxiety   29
Specific purpose   7
Statistics   6
Style   19
Tenor   22
Testimony   6
Thesis   7
Topics of invention   5
Trope   20
Vehicle   22
Visual aids   24

SUMMARY

The canons of rhetoric are necessary guides in creating and delivering a rhetorical public speech. Although they are guides only, they nonetheless help isolate distinct characteristics of a speech that allow for concentrated inquiry and improvement. To demonstrate their importance, let us begin to analyze the speech that we will use throughout this textbook to exemplify the concepts of rhetoric—that of Martin Luther King, Jr.'s address to the Montgomery Improvement Association on December 5, 1955, at Holt Street Baptist Church. Striking about the context of the speech was the pressure on King to invent, arrange, and deliver the speech within a short amount of time. King wrote that he composed the entire speech only twenty minutes before delivering it—a speech that he says "was expected to give a sense of direction to a people imbued with a new and still unplumbed passion for justice." He continues:

> With less than fifteen minutes left, I began preparing an outline. In the midst of this, however, I faced a new and sobering dilemma: how could I make a speech that would be militant enough to keep my people aroused to positive action and yet moderate enough to keep this fervor within controllable and Christian bounds? I knew that many of the Negro people were victims of bitterness that could easily rise to flood proportions. What could I say to keep them courageous and prepared for positive action and yet devoid of hate and resentment? Could the militant and the moderate be combined in a single speech?
>
> I decided that I had to face the challenge head on, and attempt to combine two apparent irreconcilables. I would seek to arouse the group to action by insisting that their self-respect was at stake and that if they accepted such injustices without protesting, they would betray their own sense of dignity and the eternal edicts of God Himself. But I would balance this with a strong affirmation of the Christian doctrine of love. By the time I had sketched an outline of the speech in my mind, my time was up.[13]

What King delivered at Holt Street Baptist Church, in other words, was an extemporaneous speech that was delivered on the basis of a rough outline. Even more significantly, all of his arguments were invented on the spot by drawing on the resources of *individual memory* (as in the case of his scriptural quotations: "And we are determined here in Montgomery to work and fight until justice runs down like water and righteousness like a mighty stream") and *public memory* (as in his reference to the principles of American freedom: "And certainly, certainly, this is the glory of America, with all of its faults. This is the glory of our democracy. If we were incarcerated behind the iron curtains of a communistic nation, we could not do this. If we were dropped in the dungeon of a totalitarian regime, we could not do this. But the great glory of American democracy is the right to protest for right"). In twenty minutes, King managed to invent all the arguments he needed by drawing on the topics he knew would rouse his audience.

The arrangement of the speech fits a basic problem–solution model, with the first half reviewing the problem of racism generally and racist bus segregation specifically, and the second half outlining the principles of nonviolent political action and articulating a vision for a hopeful future. Interestingly, King's speech also seems to conform to Monroe's Motivated Sequence. For instance, we have the following passages:

- *Attention:* "We are here this evening for serious business."
- *Need:* "On so many occasions, Negroes have been intimidated and humiliated and oppressed because of the sheer fact that they were Negroes."

---

[13]Martin Luther King, Jr., "Address to the First Montgomery Improvement Association (MIA) Mass Meeting" (Montgomery, AL, December 5, 1955). Available from Stanford University's website, http://www.stanford.edu/group/King/publications/autobiography/chp_7.htm (accessed on April 16, 2010).

- *Satisfaction:* "I want it to be known that we are going to work with grim and bold determination to gain justice on the buses in this city."
- *Visualization:* "We, the disinherited of this land, we who have been oppressed so long, are tired of going through the long night of captivity. And now we are reaching out for the daybreak of freedom and justice and equality."
- *Action:* "As we stand and sit here this evening and as we prepare ourselves for what lies ahead, let us go out with a grim and bold determination that we are going to stick together."

Lastly, King's address achieves its full power primarily from its style and delivery. Most of the speech deals not with specific arguments and assertions, but with a series of overlapping tropes and figures that approach the grand style. This style also matched King's delivery, with his uniquely rhythmic, low, and powerful voice. Recognizing that it was a time of great suffering but also of great hope, King knew that decorum demanded that he confront the enormity of the situation with equally powerful words. Hence, he concluded the speech on a grand note: "Right here in Montgomery, when the history books are written in the future, somebody will have to say, 'There lived a race of people, a *black* people, fleecy locks and black complexion, a people who had the moral courage to stand up for their rights. And thereby they injected a new meaning into the veins of history and of civilization.' And we're gonna do that. God grant that we will do it before it is too late."

Of course, King was not able to produce this speech just because he had read the canons of rhetoric. He was able to produce the speech because he had spent years studying theology, reflecting upon the relationship between religion and civil rights, and giving weekly sermons that addressed these subjects as they related to the lives of the people in his congregation. Yet rhetorical training was nonetheless a necessary condition for him to be able to act when the situated called for him to act—and as such it is a necessary condition for cultivating engaged citizens.

CHAPTER 1 EXERCISES

1. Select a speech on americanrhetoric.com that you will explore throughout the semester. This will be called your "rhetorical artifact." No two students should have the same speech. Now outline the speech according to the basic outlining structure that was previously discussed, such as breaking the speech into its main points, identifying its thesis, and documenting its evidence and sources.

2. Break yourselves into four groups. Each group should concentrate on making a speech that argues the same point. (This argument should not require research and should be simple and creative, i.e., "Everyone should get a dog" or "Chickens should not cross roads."). Each group should select a different strategy of introduction, conclusion, and way of structuring main points. Each group should then present your argument, and the class should judge which was the most persuasive.

3. Have the instructor provide every student the same short editorial or opinion piece. Each student is then responsible for making an impromptu speech of a few short sentences which argues some point (it does not matter what) that explicitly quotes the article for support. The intention here is to develop the skills of verbal citation style.

4. Bring in one of your favorite poems that employ many of the tools of style. Memorize it and deliver it in front of the class.

5. Choose an editorial from a national newspaper. Translate that editorial into two note cards (written by hand). Deliver a speech from note cards that conveys the argument of the editorial as if you were the author (i.e., without actually quoting the article or citing it as an authority).

6. Select a famous passage by an American president that is part of public memory. Have everyone in class memorize it and deliver it differently. Discuss how delivery style altered the meaning of the speech and what it reminded you of.

7. As a class, select a particular topic of controversy. Everyone do a search for sources that tries to find (a) a website, (b) a book, and (c) an academic journal article. Compare these sources as a class, and determine which sources are most appropriate for the topic and which methods were most productive in finding them.

Genres of Public Speaking

This chapter defines the appropriate contexts for public speaking and identifies the genres that are appropriate for distinct occasions. The idea of a "context for public speaking" is contrasted with contexts for written speech and online communication, thus providing a clearer picture of when giving a speech is actually the most appropriate form of communication. The notion of rhetorical "genre" then refers to different arrangements of elements in a composition or discourse that is appropriate to certain occasions. Identifying what kind of genre is appropriate within a situation is perhaps the most important consideration any public speaker can make, for it provides the proper "form" in which claims can be made and ideas structured and expressed. Although the number of speech genres is, literally, countless, they generally can be divided into speeches of introduction, identification, deliberation, solicitation, commemoration, enrichment, administration, and advocacy. The goal of this chapter is to provide a general method of organization and invention that enables a public speaker to achieve a level of decorum.

In Classical Greece, most public affairs were dealt with through the medium of face-to-face public speaking. Speeches in the courts (law), in the assembly (politics), and at ceremonial events (culture) structured and guided the collective life of the city-state. When Aristotle defined the three dominant rhetorical genres, he based his definitions on what he saw in actual life. **Forensic speech** occurred in law courts, dealt with the past, and addressed matters of the just and unjust. **Deliberative speech** occurred in the assembly, dealt with the future, and addressed matters of the expedient and the inexpedient. **Epideictic speech** occurred at ceremonial events, dealt with the present, and addressed matters of praise and blame. As the foremost scholar of Greek civilization, Aristotle could not ignore rhetoric precisely because it was so ingrained in almost every aspect of their world. For a Greek philosopher to ignore rhetoric was to ignore what it meant to be a Greek in the Classical Age.

So it is natural to ask, given the pervasiveness of electronic communication in the Modern Era, whether Aristotle would have bothered to write the same book when faced with the Internet, television, cell phones, photographic images, movie, radio, and all the other technologies from the past hundred years. Would rhetorical public speaking still play a central role in his analysis? Or would it be replaced by the blog entry, the sound bite, the viral video, the podcast, and the text message? Indeed, one might argue that modern technology will soon make the art of persuasion obsolete altogether. Writing in 1954, social critic Jacques Ellul observed with some trepidation how scientists predicted that there "will no longer be any need of reading or learning mountains of useless information; everything will be received and registered according to the needs of the moment. There will be no need of attention or effort. What is needed will pass directly from the machine to the brain without going through consciousness."[1] As the power of electronic communication grows, this prediction—once relegated to the realm of science fiction—seems to grow even more real.

In order to understand the power and significance of the act of public speaking, one must confront this issue directly. All too often, public speaking is taught as if the context and subject matter were taken for granted. One is therefore given a list of different types of public speaking—informative, demonstrative, ceremonial, persuasive, entertaining, motivational, introductory, and the like—and an accompanying list of methods that are appropriate for each speech. But this assumes that there exist public speaking contexts in actual life which demand such speeches. Yet more often than not, the question is not what type of speech to give, but whether or not to give a speech at all! Why, after all, give a speech demonstrating how to bake a cake when one can post a video? Why give an informative speech about the history of the civil rights movement when one can forward a PDF file? Why bother making introductory speeches to every person in a new workplace when one can send a group e-mail? And why prepare a speech at all if it is better simply to have a conversation on the phone? In an age where communication via electronic technology is the first choice for most people, assuming that public speaking remains our dominant medium of communication is not to address the reality of collective life in the twenty-first century.

But does electronic communication dominate every aspect of our lives simply because it is available? That question can only be answered by looking more closely at the unique qualities of each media. If we take the writing of Marshall McLuhan as a guide, the Internet exaggerates all the characteristics of previous electronic media, like the telegraph, radio, movie, and television, which appear to eclipse the function of both written and oral speech. McLuhan writes that "it is the speed of electric involvement that creates the integral whole of both private and public awareness. We live today in the Age of Information and of Communication because electric media instantly and constantly create a total field of interacting events in which all men participate."[2] McLuhan associates the following qualities with the electronic age:

- **Decentralization:** The Internet does away with the "center and margin" organizational structure that concentrates core functions in one place. In oral societies, there always remained a common area where people would gather to do business. In literate societies, these centers became the great cities around which was spread rural and industrial areas connected by road and mail. However, as indicated by the phenomena of telecommuting, with online communication, centers are infinite and everywhere. For many people, the office is replaced by the communication technology one fits in a pocket or a backpack.
- **Implosion:** Whereas the written word led to "explosion," or the capacity for expansion made possible by long-distance communication, the Internet leads to "implosion," or the ability to make close what seems far away. As indicated by the increasing reach of portable communication technologies, the Internet

---

[1]Jacques Ellul, *The Technological Society* (New York: Vintage Books, 1964), 432.
[2]Marshall McLuhan, *Understanding Media: The Extensions of Man* (Boston: MIT Press, 1994), 248.

allows for concentration of global resources back to a point. No longer is it an issue to send a letter across the world. With laptops and now handheld technologies, one has the "world at one's fingertips." The world comes to us.

- **Mosaic form:** First witnessed with the printing press, the mosaic form of communication does not follow a linear progression like a literary novel. Rather, it places many different messages in juxtaposition, allowing a reader to jump around at will and thereby create a message out of an improvising combination of different parts. Internet websites hyperlinked to one another are an example of an online mosaic form which makes the reader into both consumer and producer.
- **Icon:** The icon is a visual symbol that synthesizes many different meanings and presents them to a reader as a unified experience. Many famous photojournalistic photos are iconic in this way, summing up a whole event in a single image.[3] Because the speed of the Internet creates the necessity to gain attention of users quickly, it tends to place emphasis on the production of iconic forms that can be understood and retransmitted quickly.
- **Immersion:** The culmination of electronic media is the feeling of being involved in everything that is happening here and now. Unlike literacy, which produces isolation and distance, and oral speech, which produces a sense of shared participation in a particular situation, electronic media produce a feeling of being involved in everything that happens everywhere. It thus translates distance into breadth and participation into absorption. The result is the "human interest" story that makes readers feel as if they are emotionally involved in the event as it is unfolding in real time.

Discussion: Think of the website that you most frequently visit throughout your day. Where do you access it? (*Decentralization*) What do you feel is being brought to you from a distance? (*Implosion*) How many different layers of text and graphics are present at one time? (*Mosaic*) What particular images can you recall which were particularly striking to you? (*Icon*) And when have you felt the need to check the website so as not to miss anything that is currently happening? (*Immersion*)

However, whatever the utopian hopes and terrifying fears generated by the appearance of the Internet, little indicates that online communication has made the book and the speech obsolete. The Internet has certainly created that sense of being a "global village" that McLuhan prophesized, breaking down the stark divisions among peoples by creating a sense of being connected as a whole. However, although the rise of electronic communication has permanently affected almost every aspect of our personal, cultural, and political lives, it has not obliterated (except with a few exceptions, like papyrus and the telegraph) older forms of communication. Not only has the novel stubbornly refused to die, but public speaking also remains as vibrant as ever.

For instance, despite the ability to reach the whole nation online, political candidates still spend ever-increasing time and money speaking at rallies, community

---

[3]For more on the photojournalistic icon, see Robert Hariman and John Louis Lucaites, *No Caption Needed: Iconic Photographs, Public Culture, and Liberal Democracy* (Chicago: University of Chicago Press, 2007).

centers, and special events where supporters eagerly gather to listen. Families are now flung across the nation, yet the death of a loved one brings them all to the same place to hear words of remembrance. Televangelists have been around for decades, yet millions of Americans still travel to places of worship every week to gather together in shared praise. Commemorative events like the Fourth of July or the Presidential Inaugural are now streamed online at any time, and yet people will even endure harsh natural elements to be able to say that they were there. And while telecommuting and teleconferencing have increased the scope and efficiency of business, the rituals of the board meeting, the national convention, the interview, and the sales pitch remain staples of corporate culture.

To understand how written, oral, and electronic forms of communication can coexist, we must compare the different features that make each the appropriate medium for specific contexts. For democratic theorist John Dewey in the 1920s, when the Internet was not even yet a fantasy in the mind of an inventor, the important difference was between written and oral communication. Refusing to privilege one over the other, he felt that cultivating balanced communicative habits with both media was vital to sustaining the cooperative institutions of political life. Written speech has a linear pattern and logical coherence that makes it suitable for effectively arranging and disseminating complex ideas, whereas oral speech tends to emphasize on the total quality of shared experience that makes it more suitable to sustain relationships and to creat connections among diverse groups of people. He wrote:

> Signs and symbols, language, are the means of communication by which a fraternally shared experience is ushered in and sustained. But the winged words of conversation in immediate intercourse have a vital import lacking in the fixed and frozen words of written speech. Systematic and continuous inquiry into all the conditions which affect association and their dissemination in print is a precondition of the creation of a true public. But it and its results are but tools after all. Their final actuality is accomplished in face-to-face relationships by means of direct give and take. . . . The connections of the ear with vital and out-going thought and emotion are immensely closer and more varied than those of the eye. Vision is a spectator; hearing is a participator. Publication is partial and the public which results is partially informed and formed until the meanings it purveys pass from mouth to mouth.[4]

For Dewey, written speech highlights the power of language to create a network of causal relationships, to weave together a web of meanings, and to project possibilities into the future based on knowledge of the present and past. In effect, written speech gives order to a complex world, as exemplified in the scope and power we grant to the discourses of science, religion, economics, and history. He thus relates writing to "vision" not only because one has to literally look at the words, but also because it creates the experience of being an observer from a distance. By contrast, by connecting via the ear, oral speech tends to create the experience of being surrounded by and immersed within an environment. Oral speech made in the presence of others brings ideas and possibilities to life within the objects, people, and events of one's surroundings. When successful, oral speech draws people together to share what is created in that moment, an effect which is often associated with ritual ceremonies and celebrations.

---

[4]John Dewey, *The Public and Its Problems* (Athens: Ohio University Press, 1954).

McLuhan's analysis supports Dewey's reading. For him, the dominant aspect of the spoken word is the creation of "audience participation," not just in the understanding of the words but in the comprehension of the total speech situation that "involves all of the senses dramatically." In oral speech, "we tend to react to each situation that occurs, reacting in tone and gesture even to our own act of speaking." When we speak, we are not just conveying information; we are forming relationships between ourselves and the audience, the audience members with each other and everyone with the total environmental context. At each word spoken, one must manage a delicate process of adjusting to constant **feedback**, or the return messages that are constantly being sent by the other people involved in the communicative process. Oral communication is thus a means of inviting people to participate in a shared, **tactile** experience that involves what McLuhan calls the profound and unified "interplay of the senses."[5]

In contradistinction, written speech is marked by isolation, reflection, distance, specialization, and fragmentation. In writing, one does not participate together in a shared moment; one composes or reads in private, taking each word and each sentence at a time, and threading together a total sequential narrative that often has a sense of past, present, and future. McLuhan observes that "writing tends to be a kind of separate or specialist action in which there is little opportunity or call for reaction. The literate man or society develops the tremendous power of acting in any matter with considerable detachment from the feelings or emotional involvement that an illiterate man or society would experience."[6] By "acting without reacting," McLuhan means the ability to reflect on ideas or situations—not with just an overt, physical response—but by quietly writing down one's thoughts in logical or poetic form. Writing, that is to say, makes possible the monk, the poet, the scientist, and the philosopher. Whereas oral speech tends to place emphasis on participation in the whole, written speech makes possible detached inquiry into a part.

In Dewey's ideal, the balanced relationship between written and oral speech brings about the best of both spectator and participant experiences, allowing people to stand outside a situation and contemplate it from a distance while also, periodically, immersing themselves into the shared life of a community. The introduction of electronic forms of communication has not refuted this ideal as much as supplemented it. With the Internet and other electronic media, we have now added the utopian possibility of immersing ourselves in the total life of the planet in a single moment. This creates opportunities for expanding the horizon of one's experience to distances unheard of a century ago. Social networking sites and global communication systems now create the possibility of reaching thousands if not millions of people instantaneously. Yet despite all of this, we still demand the detached solitude of the literate life and the tactile experience of partaking in the spoken word. Each medium serves its own function and must be appraised by that function.

In order to guide judgments about what medium of communication is appropriate for what types of situations, this chapter will define three different speech contexts: the context for written speech, the context for online communication, and the context for public speaking. After these distinctions, the contexts for the spoken word will be

---

[5]McLuhan, *Understanding Media*, 77–79, 314.

[6]McLuhan, *Understanding Media*, 79.

broken down into different genres of speech, including those of introduction, identification, deliberation, solicitation, commemoration, enrichment, administration, and advocacy. The aim of this chapter is not only to provide methods for specific speech situations, but more importantly, to help determine when it is best to speak at all.

THE CONTEXT FOR WRITTEN SPEECH

The term *written speech* means more than just the writing of words. In the Internet age, much that is "written," like an e-mail, a text message, or a blog entry, is actually better understood as an electronic form of communication. **Written speech**, as it is used here, refers to the primary media of a literate culture that privileges sequential ordering of parts, a specific point of view, an explicit logical progression, a complex arrangement of information, and a spirit of objective detachment. Written speech refers to those objects that we wish to study in private, to dwell over and reflect upon, to use as a reliable guide for judgment. Objects of written speech include annual business reports, scientific journal articles, the Bible, handwritten letters, diaries, legal judgments, novels, the United States Constitution, technical manuals, poetry anthologies, new procedural guidelines, to-do lists, biographies, economic projections, and philosophies. Because of the nature of the medium, the context for written speech tends to be of a much broader scope than that of oral or electronic communication. A written document takes time to compose and to publish in the promise that the message it contains will retain relevance for some time to come. Indeed, documents like the Bible or the Constitution are intended to speak to us for eternity.

Most written speech, of course, has a much more limited scope of relevance, but that scope nonetheless includes more than the present moment. Situations that require immediate attention, judgment, and action simply operate too quickly for written speech to address (unless those situations have already been accounted for by previous writing that has been understood or is readily available). Therefore, perhaps the paradigmatic case of written speech as a rhetorical response to a complex and enduring problem is the publication of "reports" produced by research committees and commissioned by government or industry to provide frameworks for action based on a careful research into the current situation. Ideally, these reports are then studied by relevant authorities, after which time they present their judgments on how to act. It is in this way that the conclusions of otherwise nonpartisan groups such as scientists, judges, economists, theologians, and historians actually function rhetorically in the broader political environment. Even though their intention may not have been specifically to "persuade," the publication of their research acts to guide judgments about public affairs in a powerful and convincing way.

From a rhetorical perspective, situations that call for a persuasive response through written speech tend to possess the following qualities:

- A pervasive problem that endures across durations of time and breadth of space
- Sufficient time to deliberate upon a proper response without the need for immediate action
- Significant resources to draw upon in analyzing the problem
- An audience with the willingness and capacity to deliberate over a period of time upon a single issue

Given this type of situation, rhetoric that takes the form of written speech generally attempts to accomplish the following goals:

- Provide a distinct perspective on a situation that offers a useful point of view
- Give order and coherence to a disordered and chaotic condition
- Replace short-sighted fears and desires with far-sighted judgment
- Replace over-heated involvement with cooler forms of detachment
- Encourage delayed individual reflection over immediate group response

None of these characterizations means that written speech automatically responds to these situations or accomplishes these goals. Numerous examples can be brought forth to prove the opposite. This list is rather intended to highlight how the written word is uniquely suited, above other media, to function in these contexts. For instance, sometimes it is better to write a letter of apology than to give one in person, to provide a written manual rather than to explain a procedure, to print out an article rather than send it by e-mail, or to document the reasons for a judgment rather than argue them in a public setting. To put it succinctly, written speech is the best response when we wish to give an audience material to "take home and study."

Discussion: The best way to understand the unique character or written speech as a print form is to compare the same text presented in two different media. What is the difference, for instance, between checking out a book from the library and reading it as a PDF file online? What is the difference between writing and receiving a handwritten letter and just sending an e-mail? And when do you feel you need to "send a card" with writing inside of it versus simply sending an e-card?

THE CONTEXT FOR ONLINE COMMUNICATION

Although electronic forms of communication include many technologies of the mass media, most of us will primarily make use of online forms of electronic communication, like e-mail, teleconferences, website postings, and text messaging. **Online communication** is thus meant to refer to text, image, audio, and video messages sent and received by individuals on computer-aided technologies but capable of being received simultaneously by an infinite number of users and also being recalled by those users at any time. As indicated by McLuhan's analysis, online communication tends to foster mobility and decentralization and at the same time create a sense of constant feeling of being "in touch" with other people. In addition, it tends to favor messages that have an iconic or mosaic form over those which feature more primarily linear narratives or arguments more fitting to written speech.

There are several specific features of online communication that make it unique. First, it allows for multiple messages to be sent and received simultaneously and at rapid speed. This creates an enormous competition for time, as it creates an almost permanent backlog of messages awaiting consideration. In this environment, messages are naturally developed to capture one's immediate attention and be received and understood in a short amount of time. Second, the capability of multimedia messaging further heightens the competition for attention, such as a simple e-mail might be supplemented with embedded images, attached files, and background graphics or sound. Third, it creates a situation of receiving a message in private at the same time that it is capable of being broadcast to a group. This reduces the sense of "privacy" that written speech tends to produce while at the same time allowing a message to be freed from its situational context. Fourth, the capability of saving and resending messages allows them to spread widely and rapidly, thereby allowing both successes and mistakes to be immediately broadcast to all members of a group, from a group of friends to a global audience. Fifth, it creates the possibility of anonymity if the message is sent with a blind or disguised sender, thereby liberating the message not only from context but from authorship.

The majority of our online communication tends to be informal in quality—despite the intended content. Even in organizational settings, official e-mails are often laced with personal observations, jokes, compliments, or complaints that have a conversational tone. E-mail, in particular, fuses composition and production in one function, thereby fostering a type of discourse which is loose and impromptu rather than formal and reflective. In addition, online communication makes ease and entertainment permanent features of its use. Even governmental websites are designed to be appealing to the eye. On the positive side, this makes online communication ideal for situations that require readily accessible information or the rapid dissemination of striking ideas, events, or images. Whereas websites are there to present information or perform a function for anyone who needs it at any time, e-mails and text messages allow individuals to send specific messages to anyone in an instant. On the negative side, online communication tends to lack durability. As quickly as messages are produced, they are destroyed or replaced. Also, online communication tends to lack a sense of shared or situated context. Whereas even a book needs to be read somewhere, online communication has the sense of being received everywhere and nowhere.

Rhetorical situations that call for a persuasive response through online communication thus possess the following qualities:

- Dealing with an event that is of short duration and requires immediate response
- Widespread interest in that event which produces heightened emotional tensions seeking expression
- A rapidly changing situation that makes people desire the latest information
- Little time to dwell upon the complexities of the situation or reflect upon its past or future
- A communication environment where many messages are competing for attention

Rhetoric that takes the form of online communication generally attempts to accomplish the following goals:

- To communicate with individuals in a diverse population across a wide area
- To signal, or call attention to, a specific event, object, person, or quality
- To direct action in the immediate present, often in the form of a command
- To stimulate the senses and satisfy emotional cravings
- To generate a common interest in a particular subject matter

Once again, nothing denies that online communication may also transmit complex information that functions similarly to written speech in certain contexts. It only indicates that the medium is more suitable to respond to more immediate situations. Rhetorically, online communication plays a particular significant role within social movements, both in terms of its organizational capacity during rallies and protests as well as in terms of maintaining an actively interested support based on mass e-mails, videos, text messages, and other media that keep relevant "current events" in the consciousness of the audience. Online communication has made organized movements possible that are of global scale and that can act almost immediately anywhere in the world.

Discussion: When have you been without access to online forms of communication for an extended length of time? What did you feel you were missing? What functions did you feel unable to perform? Did that give you a sense of peace or were you actually more anxious? What does this experience tell you about your relationship to online communication?

THE CONTEXT FOR PUBLIC SPEAKING

If written speech tends to invite individual cognitive reflection in solitude while online communication heightens the feeling of collective immersion in an immediate event, public speaking generates an atmosphere of shared experience within a dramatic situation. For **public speaking** is not so much about the words spoken as the fact that they are spoken *publicly*—which is to say, spoken within a shared space that includes both the words and the total environment in which they are uttered. Public speaking is different from mass communication. **Mass communication** disseminates a message, but it is received in a different environment than that in which it was produced. It reaches a "public," as an organized body of acting citizens, but it is not a *public* speech. A **public speech** is an oral communication delivered by an individual to a public audience gathered in a shared physical environment to listen collectively and respond to that message in the present.

Even a speech videotaped and rebroadcast is not the same as the speech heard by those physically present. A public speech is a shared event that often has a past and a future. The speech includes all the events that led up to it (including the travel required for people to reach the same place, the time it takes to gather together and to wait, and any preceding events that introduced it) and the actions that follow it (including conversation with others about the speech, any proceeding events, and the final departure of the guests). The public speech is not separate from its history. It *requires* its history to be meaningful. Those who watch a speech on television may remember certain words or phrases used, and perhaps an image of the audience flashed before the screen, but their memory of watching the speech is tied up with the physical context of where it is watched—a living room, a bar, a classroom, and the like. For the people actually present, the speech is an event that is a part of a larger drama, even if it includes merely the conversation with co-workers before and after the boardroom meeting.

What makes it so difficult for those versed in the language of written or online communication to appreciate the uniqueness of public speaking is the habit of isolating the message from its context and judging it as if it were just a pamphlet or an e-mail. But the unique thing about public speaking is not the content or even the style of the words; it is the fact that they are spoken in the company of others in a common, shared space. This almost intangible quality is more easily experienced than explained. It is the difference between being part of a graduation ceremony and receiving the diploma in the mail, between going to a place of worship to hear a sermon and reading a religious text at home, between making a toast at a wedding and sending a card of congratulations, between hearing an inspirational speech before a big game and receiving an e-mail of that speech, or between announcing the birth of a child before one's family at Thanksgiving and distributing a video of that speech online.

The fact is that public speaking is a unique and complex experience that cannot be reduced to the simple content of the message. For instance, despite the fact that written communication allows for more complicated factual and logical argumentation and online communication makes possible more sophisticated multimedia presentation. McLuhan observes that oral communication tends to be far more complex in terms of its ability to comprehend and bring together a diverse number of environmental elements into a coherent whole. He notes that individuals who live in dominantly oral communities "are made up of people differentiated, not by their specialist skills or visible marks, but by their unique emotional mixes."[7] Therefore, although oral communication is certainly less capable of precise diagnosis than written speech and is more restricted in scope than online communication, it is far more powerful in situated settings to bring about a feeling of meaningful group participation in a dramatic moment. These kinds of settings often are more capable in producing distinctly memorable events with the possibility of generating lasting relationships and commitments. Although less frequent than occasions for written or online communication, public speaking is far more capable of producing monuments of shared experience that acts among as a firm ground on which further written or online communication is built.

So what is the context for rhetorical public speaking? They include the following characteristics:

- An issue that is forefront in the consciousness of a public or publics
- A speech situation that occurs within a larger dramatic context with a past and a future
- The necessity or desire to make a judgment in a timely fashion
- The lack of time to wait until further inquiry which mandates drawing on the best available information
- The ability for members of an audience to gather in a shared space
- The need to establish common understanding and closer relationships among members of the audience

Rhetoric that takes the form of public speaking generally attempts to accomplish the following goals:

- Establish or reinforce relationships between members of the audience
- Encourage dialogue in the audience subsequent to the speech's conclusion, which contributes to shared understanding and solidarity
- Make listeners more attentive to the significance of their physical and social surroundings
- Provide a dramatic narrative which projects and clarifies long-term goals
- Highlight the importance of the most important available means to attain those goals
- Create a unified emotional response capable of moving and inspiring an audience

---

[7]McLuhan, *Understanding Media*, 50.

Perhaps the best way to appreciate the unique functions of a public speech is by experiencing the opposite—speeches that attempt to perform functions better performed by written or online communication. Particularly in organizational settings, so-called informative speeches are often given that really just summarize what is already written on paper. One has, during these speeches, the feeling that one should have just "sent a memo on that." Alternatively, people often launch into speeches that try to re-create the experience of seeing a movie or a video that is better shared by simply being forwarded electronically. The reaction to such speeches is the proverbial, "I guess I needed to be there." A public speech should never be used as a replacement for a medium of communication that can do the job better. But the inverse is also true. Given the ease of sending e-mails, we often assume that a quick message can perform the job that oral communication should do. But there are many times when we need to address people in person, either in a conversation or in a speech. Knowing *what* to say is important, but even more important is knowing *how* to say something.

Discussion: Think of a public speech you attended with friends or family. In that memory, what stood out about that experience that was separate from the content of the speech itself? How did that event of being there affect your interpersonal interaction before, during, and after the speech? Lastly, what was the most memorable moment of that experience: the speech itself or the situation surrounding the speech?

SPECIFIC CONTEXTS FOR PUBLIC SPEAKING

Following Aristotle's lead, we can define several specific contexts in which certain functions of public speaking are emphasized over others. For instance, Aristotle saw the law court as highlighting the ability for public speaking to address the past facts concerning justice and the forum as bringing out its capacity to determine the usefulness of future actions. Yet one should understand these categorizations not as absolute distinctions but as the identification of dominant tendencies. Certainly, speeches of law deal not only with past facts, but also the honor of the defendant and the prudence of the judicial decision. Thus, when identifying speeches of introduction, identification, deliberation, solicitation, commemoration, enrichment, administration, and advocacy, this only means to point out the dominant tendency of certain speech acts. Yet all speeches, in some way, *introduce, identify, deliberate, solicit, commemorate, enrich, administer,* and *advocate*. This is important to keep in mind when writing speeches in order to communicate in such a way that makes the best use of all the powers of language. Notably absent, then, is the speech of persuasion, precisely because **persuasion** is a function of every single one of these speeches. The only speech that does not persuade is one that is either meaningless or simply ignored.

Each of the speeches made in these contexts can be understood as a "genre" of speech. The function of a genre is to provide an audience with a framework of interpretation that situates any novelty within a stable and predictable structure that the audience can readily understand. Audiences attend and listen to public speeches at certain occasions with certain expectations of what they will hear and how they will hear it. For example, the political stump speech represents a certain genre, as does the religious sermon, the graduation speech, the parental lecture, the soapbox diatribe, the tearful public apology, the sales pitch, the friendly advice, the boss's reprimand,

and the coach's inspirational rant. When we encounter these types of speeches, we can expect to hear certain things while knowing that other parts will be left out.

A rhetorical speech **genre** represents a coherent and recognized arrangement of elements in a composition or discourse that is appropriate to certain occasions and which creates audience expectations that constrain and guide a speech's content, style, and delivery. When we go to a celebrity roast, for example, we *expect* that good friends of the "roastee" will all stand up to offer witty but biting remarks at his or her expense. To hear someone praise the host would be to violate the norms of appropriateness for the occasion—it would be to ignore the constraints of the speaking genre. Defining a genre in terms of its "familiarity with an audience" is thus crucial to understanding its rhetorical significance. In rhetoric, genres are not artificial academic categories for the purpose of attaching the correct label, but rather are practical tools that speakers can use to anticipate and control the reactions of an audience. Related to notions of appropriateness and occasion, speaking genres refer to what people *actually expect* (and prepare themselves to hear) when they attend a speech.[8]

Speeches of **introduction** disclose personal facts through narrative form for the purposes of establishing a productive and positive future relationship with an audience. In many ways, an introductory speech fulfills the same function as a conversation or interview. However, the context is different. Whereas conversations or interviews happen among a few people, speeches of introduction are given before a larger group. Introductory speeches thus emphasize perhaps the first dominant quality of public speaking: generally the establishing of a relationship between speaker and audience that is meant to endure beyond the meaning of the message itself. In introductory speaking, the important facts are not so much the words coming out of one's mouth, but the very fact that one has made the effort to be present before others.

There are two typical occasions for such speeches. First, introductory speeches are given by candidates for official positions vying for support or by those who have newly been assigned some official position and who wish to introduce themselves to a group. In these cases, speeches of introduction are meant to solicit support and establish credibility. Second, introductory speeches are given by members of a group who wish to establish friendly and trustworthy relationships with one another. The latter are frequently employed in settings where an impromptu group has been formed and a diverse group of strangers must start working or living together. The goal of introductory speeches in this context is to create trust and a feeling of cooperation.

Discussion: Almost all of us, at some point in our lives, have had to give an introductory speech (in school, at camp, at church, etc.) in which we select some "interesting fact" about ourselves to tell a group. Thinking back on that experience, what did you select? Was it effective in actually forming future relationships or did it backfire?

---

[8]The importance of expectation is emphasized by Karlyn Kohrs Campbell and Kathleen Hall Jamieson, who write that: "A genre is a group of acts unified by a constellation of forms that recurs in each of its members . . . External factors, including human needs and exposure to antecedent rhetorical forms, create expectations which constrain rhetorical responses. By the internal dynamic of fused elements also creates expectations which testify to its constraining force. Generic exemplars have an internal consistency." Karlyn Kohrs Campbell and Kathleen Hall Jamieson, "Form and Genre in Rhetorical Criticism: An Introduction," *Readings in Rhetorical Criticism,* ed. Carl R. Burgchardt (State College, PA: Strata Publishing Co., 1995), 403.

Speeches of **identification** invite diverse members of an audience to share a common identity that makes it possible for them to act as a unified group with common interests and values. These speeches are also called "constitutive rhetoric" because of their ability to constitute, or form, a coherent group or movement through symbolic representations.[9] This kind of speech is frequently used in athletic contexts for rallying "team spirit," in business contexts for generating employee loyalty, in interpersonal contexts for creating group unity, or in political contexts for forming political parties or movements, as when American revolutionaries like Sam Adams formed the "Sons of Liberty" or civil rights activists such as Huey Newton formed the "Black Panthers." Thus, the core function of the speech of identification is to create a sense of group participation and solidarity. Whereas introductory speeches deal with the relationship between speaker and audience, speeches of identification deal primarily with the relationships among audience members, with the speaker being secondary.

The occasion for such a speech is generally one in which a group of people, either strangers or a loosely knit group, feel it necessary to create a tighter bond in order to accomplish some task. The paradigmatic speech of identification is thus the coach's rallying oratory before the beginning of the game, consummated by the unified cheer, "Go, team!" These speeches gain even more power by being given in a particularly meaningful place that signifies this bonding. A football game speech made in a parking lot is different than one given in a locker room; a family reunion speech is more powerful made at the family farm than a rented hall; and patriotic speeches intended to bind people together into a political whole is often more effective when made before memorials, landmarks, or near significant battlefields. Of course, the function of identification holds for almost all speeches. But some speeches are clearly focused on creating that sense of common bond while others reinforce one already in existence.

Discussion: What was the most ridiculous "identification" you tried to make with your childhood friends growing up? Did you give yourselves a group name? What were the qualities you attributed to your group identity? Did you develop any practices or rituals to express those qualities in public?

Speeches of **deliberation** allow for a diverse group of speakers to address a common topic in sequence in order to develop a suitable judgment on that matter by comparing different perspectives. Deliberative speeches are similar to group introductory speeches insofar as they often require "turn taking." However, some introductory speeches can be performed solo, as with a speech by the new boss. A deliberative speech cannot occur if only one speaker is allowed. The essence of the deliberative speech, like those which occur in town halls, boardrooms, kitchen tables, courtrooms, and parliamentary bodies, is that it is delivered in support or in criticism of opposing views that are given a chance to present a case or respond to other speeches. A law court, for instance, would be much different if the prosecution and defense did not present their speeches alongside each other. This feature is important because it puts an audience in a deliberative frame of mind, where words, phrases, and arguments are in immediate juxtaposition of one another. A

---

[9]See Maurice Charland, "Constitutive Rhetoric: The Case of the Peuple Québécois," *Quarterly Journal of Speech* 73 (1987), 133–150.

deliberative speech thus requires a structured competitive environment that allows speakers to overcome objections and present defensible claims.

Contexts that call for deliberative speaking tend to occur when there exist clear divisions of opinion within a group or institution that cannot be resolved by further inquiry or polite conversation. The deliberative speaker often comes not with a mere "opinion" but with a specific point of view that is developed in relationship to competing arguments. However, the deliberative speaker differs from someone who is merely argumentative. Deliberation requires not only competition but also respect for rules of the deliberative forum and the institution or group that regulates it. In parliamentary bodies, arguments are directed not at the opposition so much as the uncommitted center, whose vote will determine the course of actual policy. Likewise, lawyers do not persuade one another, but they must respect the decision of the jury.

Therefore, deliberative speaking, to be successful, must not only provide a chance for the airing of different perspectives; it also must guarantee procedures of judgment based on a consideration of those arguments by an audience with respected authority, which may include the family, Congress, the jury, the board of directors, the stockholders, or the spectators. In short, deliberative speaking is called for when no consensus has yet been reached, when intractable divisions remain within a group, and when legitimate judgment must be made without appearing to force the issue or take sides. Deliberative speaking provides a method of coming to resolution such that all parties feel they have had a chance to be heard and considered before a decision is reached by a respected authority.

Discussion: One of the interesting qualities of a speech of deliberation is that it rarely works out as planned, because it is given in front of competing parties. Think of a family situation that called for a deliberative setting to arbitrate a conflict or make a joint decision. What did you ideally imagine would happen in preparation for this event and what actually occur?

Speeches of **solicitation** persuade a reluctant but deliberative audience to adopt some policy, object, process, or attitude based on the perceived rightness or utility of the subject matter. In other words, speeches of solicitation are same as deliberative speeches insofar as they present a case before an audience that has the authority to accept or reject what is being offered. The primary difference from deliberative speeches are that speeches of solicitation are typically made by a single speaker before an audience of one or many who either accept or reject the speaker's proposition rather than compare and contrast it with other points of view. In addition, in most cases, speakers are directly benefited by the audience's adoption of their judgment, as when a salesperson gets a commission, a fundraiser gets money for a cause, or a religious evangelist gains another faithful member. Thus, the challenge for most speeches of solicitation is to prove that adoption of the speaker's judgment also benefits the audience in specific ways as well.

The explicit goal of speeches of solicitation is to thus argue before a reluctant and skeptical audience for the mutual benefit in buying some product, adopting some policy, or changing some behavior favored by the speaker. There are two contexts for speeches of solicitation. The first context is the proverbial "door-to-door" sales pitch in which the speaker simply makes the same speech to whoever will listen. The audience here is almost always an individual or small group that may simply have time to spare and may be curious about what is being offered. Such solicitations are almost always failures, but they remain the only method for many people with few resources or established credibility to gain a foothold of support. The second context is a more formal presentation in which an organized group invites a speaker to make a case for something that they believe may actually benefit them. The latter is frequent in economic conditions in which businesses must adopt the most efficient products in order to compete efficiently. In both settings, however, the key aspect of speeches of solicitation is that the audience acts as the sole authority and judge and that the decision is usually one of "Yes" or "No" rather than a more nuanced opinion.

Discussion: Children are the hands-down masters of speeches of solicitation, in part because they know their audience (parents) so well, and that audience is always available. What was the most elaborate and successful speech of solicitation you made to your parents? What appeals did you make that appealed to their self-interest rather than just your own personal desires?

Speeches of **commemoration** make moral judgments about, and attribute values to, particular people, objects, or events important to the audience in a way that alters or reinforces their long-term attitudes toward those things. Commemorative speaking thus differs from other speech genres in its sense of speaking to historical time. We commemorate something when we want to remember and preserve it. Most often in our lives, commemoration happens when we wish to remember loved ones who have died and to preserve in our memories the celebrations and triumphs of our lives. Cultures, too, memorialize certain events, objects, or people that have played an important role in their historical development. The purpose of the commemorative speech is thus to create a shared sense of reverence and memory for things of common value, thus reinforcing the close bonds of members of a group by celebrating its best qualities.

The two central components of a commemorative speech are the *value*, which is an abstract and universal concept, and the *subject matter*, which is a specific and concrete thing. Either the value or the subject matter must then hold a special significance for the audience. An audience like the Veterans of Foreign Wars may hold the values of honor and sacrifice in high regard and will readily commemorate any citizen who upholds those values. But a family loves not values but people, regardless of values they might uphold or represent. The one starts with a value and then finds subject matter to praise; the other starts with subject matter and finds values with which to praise it.

Contexts for commemorative speech are either ritualistic, as with annual national holidays: or situational, as with weddings or graduations. Both, however, serve the same basic function. A commemorative speech brings people together to honor the values that unite them as a group and that are embodied in their members and their actions. Consequently, any group or institution that relies on the motivation of its members makes frequent use of commemorative speeches both to inspire excellence and create a shared sense of commitment. Even commemorating loved ones at a funeral binds people together in a uniquely powerful way by using their stories to create a sense of reverence and legacy. Thus, although speeches of commemoration often do not usually argue specific points, they create and reinforce the values on which people often rely upon when called to make concrete judgments in practice. In speaking to the past and future, they endeavor to create a lasting impression in historical time.

Discussion: Graduation speeches are often marked by a somewhat predictable nostalgia for the past and optimism for the future. Yet a commemorative speech is not just about offering general praise, but selecting very specific things to memorialize. In thinking about your high school experience, what do you think actually warranted commemoration?

Speeches of **enrichment** give entertaining instruction about objects, events, processes, or concepts that are consistent with the preexisting interests of an audience and that promise to benefit the audience members' lives in some way. The term *enrichment* is meant to bridge the supposed division between information and entertainment. There is no such thing as an "informative" speech that supplants the function of written forms of communication. Oral speech simply cannot even hope to mimic the logical complexity of efficiency of written explanations. Moreover, oral forms of communication always come with the expectation of being entertaining. All speakers are performers of some kind, and audiences expect them to be. *Enrichment* thus closer approximates the actual function of so-called informative speaking, insofar as it promises not just the facts but the facts which are both interesting to hear and beneficial to its hearer.

Speeches of enrichment are generally given in situations in which an audience has already acknowledged its lack of awareness about some problem or issue and has voluntarily attended an occasion to gain this knowledge in order to resolve a situation (like learning how to get a job in a bad economy), to satisfy curiosity (like learning about the latest discoveries of planets outside our solar system), or to enrich one's life (like learning how to appreciate good wine). A good speaker in this genre will base whatever is said on the audience's **interests**, which are things that people enjoy doing, want to know, or desire to attain. The speaker will present information in an entertaining, but *noncontroversial* manner such that he or she is not advocating a particular position. Once an audience feels that it is not being informed, but being manipulated or pushed, it will no longer receive the information as a gift for enrichment, but as an active solicitation.

The most common speeches of enrichment (outside of the formal classroom) occur either as public lectures (usually by academics, celebrities, or authors) or paid seminars concerning methods of self-help or self-advancement. The question in terms of the medium of communication, however, is, Why seek enrichment from a speech rather than a book or video? First, with respect to written instruction, a speech promises to condense the main points of a subject and present them in a smooth, understandable, narrative form that speaks directly to an audience's everyday experience. Although it clearly leaves out a great deal of detail, a speech nonetheless makes a subject more immediately interesting and relevant to one's life. Second, with respect to multimedia or online communication, a speech of enrichment makes it a *community experience* of sharing knowledge rather than an isolated or detached event. Attending a speech of enrichment is itself an experience, and often it includes the discussion after the fact with other interested members of the audience.

The situations that call for speeches of enrichment thus tend to have two qualities: (1) a clear and expressed interest on the part of an audience to hear the subject matter presented, and (2) a desire in that audience to gather together and hear a speech in order to make associations with other like-minded people. Not surprisingly, then, public lectures often serve an important community-building function, which is what makes their frequent setting in public libraries or public universities so appropriate.

Discussion: It is characteristic of public speaking that one person's enrichment is another person's solicitation. Can you recall an experience in which a speech was interpreted in two different ways by different members of an audience? What was the reason for this difference in interpretation in which one person felt enriched and the other manipulated?

Speeches of **administration** are delivered by officials of a group or institution to an audience whose presence is usually mandatory in order to justify policy decision and improve the procedures and communication structures of an organization. Although often sold as speeches of enrichment, administrative speeches are different because the information is not meant to serve preexisting, voluntary interests of the audience, but to implement decisions made by administrative authorities. The result is that speeches of administration, not by intent but by the lack of necessity, tend to be experienced more as a duty than a pleasure. Thus, even the same speaker and the same speech is received differently in an administrative context. Whereas a self-help speaker may be received with a lively and energetic response by an audience that pays to attend, that same speaker might receive only polite applause by an audience of employees who have had to take time out of their day to learn the power of networking.

The situation that calls for an administrative speech, as opposed to a memo, a manual, or a video, are those in which changes must be implemented or announced to everyone simultaneously in order to maximize efficiency and reduce the possibility for misunderstanding. Because everyone in an administrative speech receives the same information at the same time, any problems, objections, or questions can be aired by the audience at once and can receive the same answer from the administrative officials. Thus, function is particularly important when the information is bad news rather than good news. Lastly, administrative speeches often have the side-effect of making "ignorance" an insufficient excuse for not implementing new policies.

Discussion: Of all public speaking genres, speeches of administration are probably lowest on the bar of eloquence. What is the worst speech of administration you ever experienced? And was it even necessary? By contrast, have you ever experienced a good speech of administration?

Speeches of **advocacy** occur before generally sympathetic audiences and use explicitly persuasive techniques to challenge and change the recalcitrant beliefs, attitudes, and values of a larger, spectator public. Speeches of advocacy are significantly different from speeches of solicitation and deliberation because of the two-layered audience. In solicitation and deliberation, the audience being persuaded is typically present at the speech event and stands in judgment of the speaker, such as with the jury, the congressional committee, or the boardroom. With the exception of hecklers who attend primarily to disrupt the event, in speeches of advocacy, the people in attendance usually gather willingly to hear the speech because they already support the speaker's position, as with protest rallies, religious revivals, or political campaign events. Only *indirectly*—through written, online, or mass communication—does their message reach the larger public audience that they are criticizing and/or persuading.

Consequently, speeches of advocacy stand apart from the other speech genres due to the fact that they often have two distinct audiences. On the one hand, the speaker knows that the people immediately present seek not to be persuaded (for their attendance usually guarantees they agree with the general positions) but to have their preexisting beliefs, attitudes, and values reinforced and to have their sense of identification solidified with the other attendees. On the other hand, the speaker is aware that a larger public audience may be paying attention to what is being said at this event. A transcript of the speech may be distributed, a video may be produced, and sound bites and commentary may be reproduced in the news media and online. The more active persuasion thus occurs with this secondary, public audience that may know little about the actual views being presented or that may, in fact, be critical of them.

So why bother going through the process of making the speech? Why not just distribute a video of the speaker? First, the identification and reinforcement function of the speech for the supporters is a key component of maintaining the motivation and coherence of any group advocacy. However, this could be accomplished simply by speeches of identification closed to public view. So why the "publicness" of the speech? This is because its second function is to demonstrate the magnitude of support that this position has in certain publics that carries with it a sense of legitimization in a democracy. This explains the predictable disputes that arise regarding published tallies of how many people were in attendance at any particular street protest or social movement rally. Those numbers matter because they are a show of power, and with power come voice. In effect, speeches of advocacy gather like-minded people together to reinforce their beliefs and identify themselves as a group, and by doing so hope to produce a show of constituent support that justifies bringing their viewpoints to the attention and consideration of a larger public.

The context for speeches of advocacy thus occurs when a smaller public wishes to make its position heard by a larger public through the power of spectacle. Whereas speeches of identification and commemoration may help that smaller public form close bonds and establish long-term working relationships and attitudes, speeches of advocacy bring their perspective and arguments into the light of the public sphere. An effective speech of advocacy thus relies on having agencies of mass media to distribute news of the speech, which generates public attention and discussion about what was said and argued at the event. Thus, the effect of most public protest rallies is often determined by the level of press it generates after the fact. This is one reason why eloquent speaking that is quotable, and which generates a powerful but brief image, is crucial for producing the kind of media spectacle for which a speech of advocacy is intended.

The majority of speeches included in this textbook are speeches of advocacy. They are generally made before sympathetic audiences but are harshly critical of the larger public of which those audiences are citizens. Yet the fact that the excerpts appear in this book show the lasting effect of speeches of advocacy. Speeches that may have actually been heard by but a few people have such power that they become reproduced and talked about in written or online communications only to finally be discussed in oral speech again between friends and within communities. The important point to remember is that the effects of public speaking are not restricted to the speech act itself; it has a long past and extends into the future, a characteristic exemplified most powerfully by the oratory of Martin Luther King, Jr., who fully brought oratory into the age of electronic communication.

Discussion: What speeches of advocacy (which you did not attend) do you recall gaining significant attention by the media in your lifetime? What did they select about these events as important? By contrast, what speeches of advocacy that you directly experienced gained no media attention at all? Why the difference?

CONCEPT REVIEW

Speech	Situation	Methods
INTRODUCTION	An individual needs to establish a working relationship with a group.	Telling personal narratives that connect with the values and interests of that group.
IDENTIFICATION	An audience that already shares common interests wishes to develop a collective identity in order to better coordinate action and create a sense of group belonging.	Employment of symbols, myths, arguments, and narratives, which gives an audience a shared sense of history, goals, and direction.
DELIBERATION	Judgment by a respected deliberative body is called for on a topic despite the existence of differing opinions within that body.	Rational and emotional argumentation intended to support a position while providing counterarguments against other positions.
SOLICITATION	Based on perceived need, speakers with a vested interest in the judgment appeal to a deliberative body or individual to adopt a policy or object in the name of mutual self-interest.	Rational and emotional argumentation intended to make one's proposal seem beneficial while making possible counterproposals seem undesirable.
COMMEMORATION	An audience with shared values and interests comes together to praise something consistent with those values and interests.	The use of "grand" stylistic form to amplify the valued qualities in a subject matter and thereby reaffirm those values for the audience.
ENRICHMENT	An audience desires to broaden and pursue preexisting interests by seeking out speakers (and other audience members) capable of helping them achieve their aims.	Putting complex information into stylistically pleasing and interesting forms that speak directly to the needs and experiences of the audience.
ADMINISTRATION	Administrative officials seek to efficiently implement policy decisions and deliver facts to a subordinate audience.	Clearly articulating the facts and procedures being implemented, allowing time for discussion, and providing motivational justifications.
ADVOCACY	An identified group who shared political and social aims seeks to present their case to a larger public audience by creating a media event based around eloquent public speech.	Giving passionate and articulate oratory to an enthusiastic audience of supporters within a meaningful physical setting that is witnessed by members of the news media.

KEY WORDS

Administration   53
Advocacy   53
Commemoration   51
Decentralization   38
Deliberation   49
Deliberative speech   37
Enrichment   52
Epideictic speech   37
Feedback   41

Forensic speech   37
Genre   48
Icon   39
Identification   49
Immersion   39
Implosion   38
Interests   52
Introduction   48
Mass communication   45

Mosaic form   39
Online communication   43
Persuasion   47
Public speaking   45
Public speech   45
Solicitation   50
Tactile   41
Written speech   42

SUMMARY

In the Classical Age of Greece, public speaking remained the dominant form of communication for most public business. Today, the situation has changed. Yet despite the prevalence of on-line forms of communication in the modern age, both written and oral forms of communication continue to play a vital function in political and cultural life. Thus, Aristotle would have a far more complex job on his hands should he reappear in the twenty-first century to analyze the contexts, genres, and functions of persuasive communication. Yet his insights into rhetorical public speaking would remain relevant. They would need only be put into a wider and far more complex communicative environment marked not only by the specialized languages of written speech but also the iconic, mosaic, and mass-mediated forms of electronic technology.

The interplay between the three forms of communication is apparent in the history of the civil rights movement itself. Not only did this movement include public speeches like King's "I Have a Dream," delivered during protest rallies, but it also included written documents and media events. For instance, one of the most lasting documents of the movement was King's "Letter from a Birmingham Jail." Characteristic of the written medium, it was composed by King while sitting in solitude in a jail cell and intended to be considered in a reflective context. Unlike his speeches, which tended to derive their power from eloquence, the letter reads as a philosophical rumination, defining the goals and ethics of nonviolent protest and clarifying the distinction between a just and unjust law. By contrast, that same Birmingham protest featured graphic images of young African-American children being blasted with water hoses and chased by police dogs. Here, the message is contained within the image and made powerful by being conveyed instantly across the world on the television. In the following passage, Birmingham attorney David Vann comments on the persuasive power of the iconic images:

> It was a masterpiece [in] the use of media to explain a cause to the general public. In those days, we had fifteen minutes of national news and fifteen minutes of local news, and in marching only one block they could get enough news film to fill all of the newscasts of all the television stations in the United States.[10]

In Birmingham, then, we see the two media of written and electronic communication being utilized in different ways to support the aims of a social movement. The question is not whether one is more powerful than the other, but how each functions to maximize its own unique characteristics to move people to action.

---

[10]David Vann, quoted in Juan Williams, *Eyes on the Prize: America's Civil Rights Years 1954–1965* (New York: Penguin Books, 1987), 191.

The power of public speaking, of course, was uniquely on display in King's address at Holt Street Baptist Church. Here, King sought to introduce himself to his audience, to create a sense of identification to unite his audience as a movement, to commemorate the actions of Rosa Parks, to deliberate about the proper course of action, and to advocate for the cause of civil rights to a larger public audience. It is this last function, however, which perhaps was most important in determining the long-term success of the new movement. Although King knew he had to address the people gathered before him, he was also conscious that there was a larger audience to which he was speaking. He writes in reflection that he "was also conscious that reporters and television men would be there with their pencils and sound cameras poised to record my words and send them across the nation."[11] Central in speeches of advocacy, King recognized his speech would carry to wider publics well beyond the thousands of people who had come to hear it. Americans across the country might read about it in their newspapers. King thus had the two-fold task to inspire the gathering of people before him as well as to speak to those secondary audiences that would encounter the incident as a detached observer. Reporter Joe Azbell of the *Montgomery Advertiser* captures both qualities in his reflection on covering the event:

> The Holt Street Baptist Church was probably the most fired up, enthusiastic gathering of human beings that I've ever seen. I came down the street and I couldn't believe there were so many cars. I parked many blocks from the church just to get a place for my car. I went up to the church, and they made way for me because I was the first white person there . . . I was two minutes late and they were already preaching, and that audience was so on fire that the preacher would get up and say, "Do you want your freedom?" And they'd say, "Yeah, I want my freedom!" The preacher would say, "Are you for what we are doing?" and they'd say, "Yeah, go ahead, go ahead!" . . . and they were so excited . . . I've never heard singing like that . . . they were on fire for freedom. There was a spirit there no one could capture again . . . it was so powerful. And then King stood up, and most of them didn't know how he was. And yet he was a master speaker . . . I went back and I wrote a special column, I wrote that this was the beginning of a flame that would go across America.[12]

Later, reporter Bob Ingram of the *Montgomery Advertiser* recalled that Dr. King told him that the "*Advertiser* printing that on the front page on Sunday morning was a greater impetus for the success of the boycott than anything before."[13] In a news environment in which issues dealing with the African-American community were rarely covered by the white press, the appearance of the story on the front page of the *Advertiser* had an enormous influence—an influence made possible only because of the power generated by the speech event itself.

CHAPTER 2 EXERCISES

1. Examine the speaking context of your rhetorical artifact. What made oral speech a preferable method of communication in that situation? Also, examine its genre. When this speech was given, under which genre was it interpreted? Was there any difference in interpretation from critics or audience members?

2. Have one person select a passage from a famous speech. Type this text on an e-mail and send it to each student. The next day, print this text in a nice

[11]Available from Stanford University, http://www.stanford.edu/group/King/publications/autobiography/chp_7.htm (accessed on April 20, 2010).
[12]Joe Azbell, quoted in Williams, *Eyes on the Prize*, 73–74.
[13]Alvin Benn, "Bob Ingram," *The Montgomery Inquirer*, http://www.montgomeryboycott.com/profile_ingram.htm (accessed on April 20, 2010).

font and distribute it to the class on paper. Then have someone actually give this speech in class. What is the difference in how you receive each message?

3. Locate a social movement website and analyze its content. Does it use a mosaic form? What iconic images are present? What is the difference in how information is presented and experienced in contrast with print material or oral communication? Then find a speech made by someone connected by the movement and compare its content.

4. Compose and deliver an introductory speech to the class in the form of a haiku (three metrical phrases with 5, 7, and 5 syllables). How did the condensed phrasing alter your content? Now do the same exercise with a speech of enrichment.

5. Choose a very ordinary object. Now commemorate this object by attributing to it a very grand value that playfully exaggerates its importance. Did any of the speeches make you value these objects any differently?

6. To simulate the dual audience of speeches of advocacy, divide yourselves into four groups, one in each corner of the classroom. Come up with a fictional "identification" for yourselves; then write a brief speech of advocacy that is intended to further your cause. Then, taking turns, have each group arrange itself so that all members of the group are seated in the corner with their chairs facing the very center of the classroom. Choose a speaker from each group and have the speaker deliver the speech directly to his or her identified audience (such that speakers face their own group but have their backs to the rest of the class). Each speaker must deliver the speech with vigor and elicit a forceful response from his or her particular group. However, while one group is speaking, the other three groups should watch silently behind them while the identified audience should be cheering madly and looking only at the speaker. How does this experience change the feeling of the speech from both perspectives?

7. Divide yourselves into three groups: a pro group, a con group, and a jury. Select a topic of deliberation. Have the pro and con groups take affirmative and negative positions on this topic and present their case before the members of the jury, who may interrupt and ask questions at any time. After arguments are completed, have the jury make an honest verdict based purely on the cases presented to it. What was a factor in your decision?

The Rhetorical Situation

This section explores the components of a situation that makes an act of public speaking a form of rhetoric. However, the term "situation" should not be taken to mean only the *material* components of an environment. In rhetoric, one of the most important parts of a rhetorical situation is the audience. Moreover, an audience includes not just the collection of people in a room. The members of an audience have a past and a future, are part of larger communities of value, and are active and interconnected members of a public culture. In rhetoric, to speak to an audience is to establish a relationship in action that extends beyond the walls of the classroom or the auditorium. Consequently, establishing that relationship requires understanding where people have come from, where they want to go, and where you wish to take them.

The following two chapters thus provide more than just a conceptual vocabulary for audience adaptation; they also establish the preconditions for transforming a public speech into a rhetorical act. Knowing the rhetorical background gives a rhetor a broader historical, sociological, and political perspective on his or her speech act; identifying the rhetorical foreground helps a rhetor focus on specific problems that are forefront in the experiences of an audience; and understanding the motives of the participants enables a speaker to generate action. Most importantly, this section provides a method for selecting topics and constructing an argument that is rhetorical not just in appearance but in form and in function.

Rhetorical Foreground and Background

This chapter introduces rhetoric as a situated discursive act within a larger public context of deliberation about controversial and pressing issues. It expands the notion of "public speaking" beyond the walls of the classroom to encompass one's larger social and historical environment. The rhetorical situation is divided into rhetorical background, which provides the broader historical and social context of the speech and its audience, and rhetorical foreground, which represents those aspects stand out significantly to specific audiences in the immediate present. The rhetorical background includes components such as the Public Sphere, the Open Society, Status, Public Opinion, Convention, and Social Knowledge, while the rhetorical foreground includes the components Exigence, Practical Judgment, Audience, Constraints, Speaker, Occasion, Purpose, and Message. The most important of these concepts for rhetorical public speaking is attention to exigence, which focuses rhetorical public speaking on the shared problems that an audience wishes will be addressed in a timely manner.

In most of our daily lives, we take most of the aspects of our environment for granted. Like fish in water, we are rarely aware of the medium through which we are moving—and rightly so. If a fish was always dwelling on the water, it would undoubtedly have little energy left for eating and finding shelter. Our "critical" spirit usually arises whenever some **contingency**—some unexpected obstacle, perplexity, or problem—arises out of that environment stands out concretely before us and threatens to disrupt our lives in some way. The appearance of contingency makes us look critically at our previous choices in the assumption that the path we had earlier chosen may not, in fact, be the best way forward. According to John Dewey, this process of reflection, judgment, and valuation "takes place only when there is something the matter; when there is some trouble to be done away with, some need, lack, or privation to be made good, some conflict of tendencies to be resolved by means of changing conditions."[1]

Rhetoric is the creature of shared contingency. Thus, a **rhetorical situation** is one that occurs when public contingencies generate concern and uncertainty within a public audience and give force and effectiveness to persuasive discourse which encourages collective

---

[1]John Dewey, "Theory of Valuation," in *John Dewey: The Later Works*, vol. 13, ed. Jo Ann Boydston (Carbondale: Southern Illinois UP, 1988), 34.

action.[2] In rhetorical situations, contingencies are problematic aspects of a situation shared by a group of people who must collectively deliberate about which actions to take to resolve their common problem. Contingencies are experienced this way whenever people encounter shared obstacles without knowing for sure the nature of the problem or the way to proceed effectively. Aristotle summed this up best:

> The duty of rhetoric is to deal with such matters as we deliberate upon without arts or systems to guide us . . . The subjects of our deliberation are such as seem to present us with alternative possibilities: about things that could not have been, and cannot now or in the future be, other than they are, nobody who takes them to be of this nature wastes his time in deliberation.[3]

Of course, not all contingencies require rhetorical resolution. Many contingencies already have pre-established means of resolution that are generally accepted as effective. In such cases, we have a **technical situation,** which exists when we confront problems with a proven discourse and method to guide us. A technical situation does not guarantee a positive result, but it does resolve the uncertainty about how to proceed. For example, a person diagnosed with cancer faces a contingency—their health might go this way or that way. But most people treat cancer by following the advice of established medical authorities and pursue some combination of chemotherapy or radiation treatment. Although they do not know their fate, they know the course to pursue. Yet the same applies for one who might choose alternative methods of healing, such as prayer or herbal medicine. What makes a situation "technical" is not the prudence of the response, but the assurance that one knows the way forward. A situation only becomes "rhetorical" when the way forward is in doubt and multiple parties engage in symbolic persuasion to motivate cooperative action.

There are three major components to the rhetorical situation. The **rhetorical foreground** represents the specific and salient aspects of a common situation as it affects or interests some audience at a particular moment in time. The **rhetorical background** represents the larger environment that defines the historical and social context for any particular rhetorical event. And the **motives of the participants** stand for the various cognitive, emotional, and behavioral attitudes and responses that may influence their future beliefs, feelings, and actions. The next chapter will explore the concept of motives in greater detail. This chapter will focus on the relationship between the rhetorical foreground and background in any rhetorical situation.

---

[2]The literature on the rhetorical situation includes Lloyd Bitzer, "The Rhetorical Situation," *Philosophy and Rhetoric 1* (1969), 13–14; Richard E. Vatz, "The Myth of the Rhetorical Situation," *Philosophy and Rhetoric,* 6 (1973); Barbara A. Biesecker, "Rethinking the Rhetorical Situation from Within the Thematic of Difference," *Philosophy and Rhetoric,* 22 (1989), 110–130; Alan Brinton, "Situation in the Theory of Rhetoric," *Philosophy and Rhetoric,* 14 (1981), 234–248; Scott Consigny, "Rhetoric and Its Situations," *Philosophy and Rhetoric,* 7 (1974), 175–186; Kathleen Hall Jamieson, "Generic Constraints and the Rhetorical Situation," *Philosophy and Rhetoric,* 6 (1968), 162–170, 165–168; John H. Patton, "Causation and Creativity in Rhetorical Situations: Distinctions and Implications," *Quarterly Journal of Speech,* 65 (1979), 36–55.

[3]Aristotle, *Rhetoric,* 1357a.

THE RHETORICAL BACKGROUND

Knowing the rhetorical background provides a speaker with a broader perspective to more efficiently identify resources from which to draw when creating the speech and to better anticipate the possible long-term consequences after speaking. This background knowledge includes the public, the open society, the public sphere, status, public opinion, convention, and social knowledge. In analyzing these concepts, one should always keep in mind that these are largely *general* characteristics. Their purpose is to *set the stage* for a rhetorical act. It is the characteristics of the *rhetorical foreground* that gives a more concrete interpretation of what is specifically at stake in any rhetorical performance. However, we start with such general perspective to emphasize that any particular rhetorical act grows out of and responds back to a richer and more complex social environment.

The Public

The "public" forms the rhetorical background for any rhetorical speech act. In common interpretation, the public is thought to represent the total population of any national culture. However, a "public" is more than just a "mass." A **public** is a complex interaction of individuals that constitute a political culture. Defined in a functional way, a public is a group of citizens who recognize each other's interests and have developed habits of settling disputes, coordinating actions, and addressing shared concerns through common communication media. Therefore, what ultimately characterizes the American public in general is common participation within a political process. A public, then, comes about when a group of strangers come together for a common purpose that affects them all directly or indirectly. The **state** is thus distinct from the public insofar as it represents the instrument that the public uses to address consequences that it deems important enough to manage. In this sense, democracy is defined in terms of a state developed as a means for the public to regulate itself.[4]

However, if a state (in the name of one clearly defined public) formally excludes other publics, then **counterpublics** develop outside of and counter to the established mechanisms of the state. As Michael Warner writes, the discourse that constitutes a counterpublic "is not merely a different or alternative idiom, but one that in other contexts would be regarded with hostility, or with a sense of indecorousness."[5] Consequently, their rhetoric tends to be directed internally, toward group cohesion, rather than externally, at social persuasion. Yet the goal of a counterpublic is usually to form a genuine public able to express its will through legitimate public institutions and governing bodies. They exist as counterpublics only when this access is denied and they are forced to organize through alternative channels of communication. Once democratic reforms are initiated, they reclaim their status as one public among many.

The idea of the public influences rhetorical invention in three ways. First, rhetorical persuasion can produce visible and concrete changes in reality only if there is an audience capable of acting on its beliefs through organized channels.

---

[4]This notion of the public comes from John Dewey, *The Public and Its Problems* (Athens: Ohio University Press, 1927).

[5]Michael Warner, "Publics and Counterpublics," *Public Culture* 14.1 (2002): 49–90 (86).

Speaking to people who had opted out of collective social life may produce persuasion, but those persuaded people will have few means of acting upon that new belief in collaboration with others—unless they have been persuaded to participate in the public. Second, a functional definition of the public encourages a speaker to think of people as something other than a stereotyped ground of generic individuals who all think and feel the same thing. A functional definition of the public helps us realize that what binds people together is common interests in regulating social affairs and resolving common problems for the benefit of everyone—*despite* their obvious differences. Third, it reminds a speaker that there is almost always a plurality of "publics" that exist within any more generic "public." It is a relatively straightforward matter to adapt to the specific group of people who might be arranged in a room. It is quite another to interpret that specific group as an amalgam of overlapping publics joined together in a common space.

Discussion: Although we often think of ourselves as only a member of one ubiquitous "public," in reality we act within several smaller, overlapping publics. An easy test to determine whether or not you are a part of a public is to ask where you are involved in communication with an identified group, not because you share a particular interest, but because you all wish to solve common problems. For many people, then, deciding to act as a part of a public is an involuntary affair that occurs after being effected by a contingency. Given this criteria, when have you acted as part of a public?

The Open Society

When speaking one's mind in public, there are always boundaries about what can be said. What determines a public to be open or closed is how many and how high those boundaries are. Put simply, the **open society** is one in which facts are made available and judgments are made by its members through open discussion, criticism, and persuasion. Perhaps the highest practical manifestation of the ideals of an open society in American history is the First Amendment to the United States Constitution and the corresponding social knowledge it expresses concerning the values of free speech, religion, and assembly. To the extent that these notions stand for the democratic process of governance in which any citizen can speak his or her mind, demand disclosure of information, and have the authority to make judgments, they represent the ideals of an open society.

From the perspective of the open society, change is not a threat to be feared, but a process to be managed. Rhetoric helps us deal intelligently and sympathetically with change by considering and weighing all alternatives and points of view before committing ourselves to a course of action. Undoubtedly, many of these alternatives will be misguided if not downright dangerous or offensive. But the faith of proponents of the open society, like Aristotle, is that these views will all "come out in the wash," as it were. By airing all views in a vigorous public sphere, citizens can judge for themselves which perspectives are worth adopting and which are not; and if they turn out to be wrong, then their mistakes will be recorded in the public memory, called *social knowledge*. This view was perhaps best expressed by John Stewart Mill:

> If all mankind minus one, were of one opinion, and only one person were of the contrary opinion, mankind would be no more justified in silencing that one person, than he, if he had the power, would be justified in silencing mankind. Were

an opinion a personal possession of no value except to the owner; if to be ob-structed in the enjoyment of it were simply a private injury, it would make some difference whether the injury was inflicted only on a few persons or on many. But the peculiar evil of silencing the expression of an opinion is, that it is robbing the human race; posterity as well as the existing generation; those who dissent from the opinion, still more than those who hold it. If the opinion is right, they are de-prived of the opportunity of exchanging error for truth: if wrong, they lose, what is almost as great a benefit, the clearer perception and livelier impression of truth, produced by its collision with error.[6]

The contrast to the open society is, of course, the **closed society,** in which lead-ers are responsible for making decisions and suppressing opinions they feel to be unnecessary or dangerous. This distinction does not mean to imply that closed so-cieties are "evil" in any way. It simply means that a social group has decided that the best way to achieve certain ideal goals is to suppress dissent and enforce official doctrine; and usually, this official doctrine explicitly supports the noble ideals of security, unity, purity, and knowledge. The Puritan culture of early America was in many ways the paradigm of a closed society despite the fact that their ideals explic-itly sought to promote the establishment of the Kingdom of God on Earth. Thus, the distinction between an open and closed society is not found in the ideals or virtues they hold valuable; it has everything to do with the means by which a social group tries to achieve them. An open society believes that all views should be heard and facts exposed in order to allow the truth to be heard; a closed society believes that the truth can be heard only when we silence those offensive views which tend to drown it out.[7]

Discussion: We often assume that an open society is "good" and a closed society "bad." However, rarely are those ethical choices so clear cut. (An exception would appear to be a severe crisis, such as war.) What drawbacks might you see in a com-pletely open society? What benefits are there to be gained by making it more closed?

The Public Sphere

Even in a completely open society, there are times and places where rhetorical public speech is appropriate and those in which it is not. Determining the right time and place to make one's views heard is important so as not to allow issues of inappropriateness to obscure the content of one's message. The forum best suited for allowing people to speak and be heard by others about matters of public con-cern is called the public sphere. Gerard Hauser defines a public sphere this way:

> [A] discursive space in which strangers discuss issues they perceive to be of conse-quence for them and their group. Its rhetorical exchanges are the bases for shared awareness of common issues, shared interests, tendencies of the extent and

---

[6]John Stewart Mill, *On Liberty* (Indianapolis: Hackett Publishing, 1978).

[7]See Karl R. Popper, *The Open Society and Its Enemies*, Vol. 1, 5th ed. (Princeton, NJ: Princeton University Press, 1966).

strength of difference and agreement, and self-constitution as a public whose opinions bear on the organization of society.[8]

The public sphere is not to be confused with simply the "physical" place, such as one would think of the public forum in Classical Greece where people physically gathered to hear speeches. After all, in the modern age of mass communications, this space has become more abstract, including not only traditional venues such as the town hall, the city common, or the local café, but also more contemporary venues such as the newspaper, television, and the Internet. But even more important than whether or not space is physical or virtual is the issue of *how* such space is used. For G. Thomas Goodnight, the ability for democratic societies to address pressing problems rests on their ability to make use of a vibrant public sphere, for the deliberative "arguments in the public sphere necessarily pertain to the domain of probable knowledge—that kind of knowledge which, although uncertain, is more reliable than untested opinion or guesswork." In sum, "public argument is a way to share in the construction of the future."[9]

The public sphere designates the discursive, physical, and conceptual space in which citizens are able to exchange views on matters of public interest. "Conceptual space" means that space which exists not in our environment but in our attitudes. It deals with the conventions and expectations we share concerning when and where it is appropriate to discuss public issues. The Internet can be a powerful source of public debate, but as long as we imagine its use only in terms of e-mailing our friends, purchasing products, or entertaining ourselves, then it conceptually does not function as a public sphere. In other words, we not only have to *possess* the physical space with which to communicate with each other, but we should also *imagine* and make *use* of that physical space in order to address public issues using reasoned arguments that are understood and acted upon by average citizens.[10] This public sphere contrasts with three other types of communicative spheres:

- In the **technical sphere,** an elite group with specialized knowledge uses technical jargon to discuss narrow problems in a way that average citizens cannot understand. The technical sphere refers to those contexts in which it is appropriate for such specialists to engage in this communication for the purposes of solving some specific problem that cannot be addressed using everyday language.
- In the **personal sphere,** technical jargon is shunned in favor of a language which favors the expression of intimate feelings, experiences, and opinions. A diary, a confessional, a dinner table, a date, or a daytime talk show interview are all considered physical spaces in which we feel it appropriate to participate in the personal sphere.

---

[8]Hauser, Gerard. *Vernacular Voices: The Rhetoric of Publics and Public Spheres* (Columbia: University of South Carolina Press, 1999), 105.

[9]Goodnight, G. Thomas. "The Personal, Technical, and Public Spheres of Argumentation: A Speculative Inquiry in the Art of Public Deliberation," in *Contemporary Rhetorical Theory: A Reader,* ed. John Louis Lucaites, Celeste Michelle Condit, and Sally Caudill (New York: The Guilford Press, 1999), 251.

[10]On the origins of the idea of the public sphere, see Jürgen Habermas, *The Structural Transformation of the Public Sphere: An Inquiry into a Category of Bourgeois Society,* trans. Thomas Burger (Cambridge, MA: MIT Press, 1989).

■ In an **authoritative sphere,** the only views that are encouraged to be expressed are those which are sanctioned by an established authority. This does not mean that authoritative spheres are by nature oppressive. A church, for instance, is often not a space for open criticism of religious doctrine.

There is nothing essentially good or bad about any of these spheres. Each serves a function in its proper context. A technical sphere allows for detailed examination of a problem. A personal sphere provides emotional release and relational bonding. An authoritative sphere provides stability, unity, and direction. And a public sphere provides diversity of opinions in order to promote new ways of thinking and acting. A speaker should thus always be aware of the sphere in which he or she is speaking in order to best facilitate its goals or, if necessary, consciously disrupt its goals in order to set new ones. For instance, a child growing up in an authoritative sphere may find it necessary to break the norms of appropriateness and try to open up a public sphere around the kitchen table. A citizen listening to complex technical jargon in the midst of a public health crisis may demand to hear a concrete plan for action. And a friend listening to another dwell on feelings of self-pity and fear may demand that that person start trying to decide what to do with his or her life. Each of these interventions transforms one sphere into another such that rhetoric becomes free to be heard and considered by a public audience.

Discussion: Imagine a single physical location (for instance, a schoolyard, a bar, a front porch, a courtroom, a television studio) that might reasonably perform the functions of all four spheres, and describe the situation under which each sphere would come about. Then come up with specific forms of speech that might represent each of the four spheres.

Status

Complicating the issue of the open society and the public sphere is that no two issues are quite alike in their status; some issues are easier to bring out into the open than others. For example, few people would question a citizen's right to criticize a political leader in a democracy, but when that criticism also entails the threat of violence, it becomes something to condemn and suppress. This example, of course, merely represents extremes. Usually, issues fall somewhere in the spectrum between the commonplace and the taboo. Knowing where one's own sentiments might fall on that spectrum is thus crucial to know in order not only to adapt to any anticipated resistance, but also to take advantage of any expected support.

Status refers to the relative authority or marginality that particular ideas, words, or discourses possess within a community. It is how things are "ranked" on a scale from positive to negative. Those ideas, words, or discourse which are explicitly valued, respected, and/or embraced possess **authority,** whereas those which are widely condemned, ignored, and/or rejected are resigned to **marginality.** For example, Americans tend to grant authority (or high status) to ideas that support a free market economy, to words like *freedom* and *liberty,* and to the discourse of Christianity, while relegating to marginality (or low status) ideas that support state control of industry, to words like *fascism* and *tyranny,* and to the discourse of Satanism. Thus, to speak using the language of authority will generally guarantee a more positive response from a generic American audience than from one that employs the language of the margin. As Robert Hariman explains,

> [Just] as superior status is a condition of social privilege, so inferior status is a condition of social marginality, and we empower discourses by imposing a social order upon the world that relegates words, writers, and speakers to zones of centrality or marginality.[11]

Of course, status is never an absolute category and is always relative to a particular community. What has the authority for one might be marginal for another. What makes rhetorical public speech so challenging, then, is that it inevitably seeks to *change* the status of some idea, word, or discourse—whether it is marginalizing something that currently possesses authority or granting authority to that which is marginal. In this sense, every act of "dissent" is in actuality an effort to change the rhetorical status of something. At some point in American history, after all, people generally marginalized the ideas that women should be able to vote, that Native Americans had rights to their land, or that slavery was unjust. In each case, certain ways of talking about our world that we now find distasteful were favored while others that we now value were condemned. In each case, rhetoric was always at the center of this transition of status.

Discussion: Identify one common object, phrase, or habit in popular culture that has undergone a dramatic shift in status over the past two decades, moving it from "out" to "in" and vice versa. What has caused this shift? Has it been a good or a bad thing? Do you think there are advantages to staying in the margins, particularly with regard to the constant fear that artists have of "selling out"?

Public Opinion

Unlike status, public opinion represents what people generally hold to be true regardless of its comparative or hierarchical ranking. Status, for instance, helps determine whether astronomy or astrology has more credibility with the general public; public opinions determine how many people go to astrologists and whether they think that spending money on space exploration is worthwhile. **Public opinion** thus represents the percentage of people who hold certain views to be true. Often we see this portrayed in "opinion polls" that represent public opinion with a series of bar graphs and pie charts. While there are many flaws to such polls, not the least of which is the assumption that opinions are discrete entities that can be discerned by narrow questioning, they are nonetheless valuable to the extent that they show general trends of opinion.[12] Walter Lippmann defines public opinion this way:

> Those features of the world outside which have to do with the behavior of other human beings, insofar as that behavior crosses ours, is dependent upon us, or is interesting to us, we call roughly *public affairs*. The pictures inside the heads of these human beings, the pictures of themselves, of others, of their needs,

---

[11]Robert Hariman, "Status, Marginality, and Rhetorical Theory," in *Contemporary Rhetorical Theory: A Reader,* ed. John Louis Lucaites et al. (New York: The Guilford Press, 1999), 36.

[12]For an exploration of public opinion, see Carroll J. Glynn, Susan Herbst, Garrett O'Keefe, and Robert Shapiro, *Public Opinion* (Boulder, CO: Westview Press, 1999).

purposes, and relationship, are their public opinions. Those pictures which are acted upon by groups of people, or by individuals acting in the name of groups, are Public Opinion with capital letters.[13]

The important thing about public opinion from a rhetorical perspective is the fact that it represents the collective *opinions* of a public audience. An **opinion** is a conscious personal belief expressed as a commitment to a certain matter of fact or value. We might have opinions that television is a wasteland, that our neighbor's yard is a mess, that America's foreign policy is too isolationist, or that gay marriage is a sin. Public opinion is thus valuable for rhetoric in that it provides a starting point to approach an audience. It lets a rhetor know what truths they can take for granted, which ones they need to challenge, and which ones they need to promote.

The notion of public opinion clearly brings rhetoric into the realm of the mass media. After all, without the institutions of the news, people would hold vastly different opinions about national and global affairs. Consequently, the place to go to learn about the content of public opinion is not one's neighbor but to the television, the newspaper, and the Internet. This does not mean that individual citizens simply parrot what they see on the news media. Rather, it means that until an issue appears on the news media, it is impossible for any national public to hold an opinion about it at all. Rhetoric thus has a twofold relationship with the mass media. On the one hand, public speakers often seek to highlight an issue that has not gained national attention by giving a dramatic address in public view. On the other hand, by putting certain issues on the public agenda, the mass media encourages and even forces public speakers to address them. A savvy public speaker, of course, will find a way to make both happen to their advantage.

Discussion: Political historians always have great fun looking back at past public opinion and highlighting the ridiculous things that people have held to be true (e.g., that witches cause drought or that eating tomatoes will kill you). In a technological age, public opinion changes even more rapidly. What public opinions in your lifetime have you already seen undergo a rapid change? And which public opinions differ the most between different generations (e.g., grandparents and grandchildren)?

Convention

Matters of status and public opinion both are largely cognitive, intellectual affairs. To have an "opinion" about something, including how it should be ranked, necessitates having information about some object, event, or process. Ask adults to express their view of economics and they will generally be able to state their opinion (however informed or uninformed) about whether the current economic condition is in a good or bad state and then be able to rank certain economic perspectives as having more authority than others in dealing with the problems. But ask a young child about economics and he or she won't understand the question. What children *will* know is that if they give money to the corner merchant they will get candy in return, and that they should say "thank you" when that exchange occurs. In other words, they will be able to describe how things are generally done even if they can't necessarily form an opinion about it.

---

[13]Walter Lippmann, *Public Opinion* (New York: Simon & Schuster, 1922), 18.

The knowledge of the child in this regard represents knowledge of convention. **Conventions** are the accepted and established habits, norms, routines, traditions, and unspoken laws of a community. Whereas issues of status or public opinion are general statements of principle or belief embodied in the language of fact that can be determined true or false, convention simply refers to some habitual behavior and often has no similar truth value. For example, the facts that Americans drive on the right side of the road, make toasts at weddings, tailgate at football games, love fast food, shake hands in greeting, and vote for a new president every four years all represent conventions of American culture. These are the habits that make up our everyday lives and rarely come to be matters of opinion on which we must take a stand. Often we do not recognize things like these as conventions unique to our culture because we never have been exposed to anything different. We assume this is just the "way things are done." Consequently, conventions form a very important background for any rhetorical act for three reasons:

- Conventions make up the substance of *appropriateness*. Like the social norms that make it acceptable for comedians to mock members of their audience, for politicians to flatter them, and for parents to discipline them, conventions establish the "ground rules" for any speech act that occurs in a public context. Violating these ground rules, while sometimes necessary, generally makes it more difficult to garner support from one's audience.
- Conventions provide cultural resources from which to draw when attempting to persuade an audience that a certain course of action is consistent with its own values and traditions. Often this is accomplished using analogical reasoning or metaphor in which the rhetor draws parallels between conventions that are already established and the new behavior that is advocated. For example, by analogical reasoning, the convention that encourages families to balance their checkbooks every month can be used by politicians to justify enforcing balanced budgets for government institutions.
- Conventions often embody the very problems that cause a rhetorical situation in the first place. Especially as cultures change, older habits and traditions come to represent outdated ways of doing things that actually inhibit social progress. For example, the American love of driving large automobiles has become more and more an issue of concern as air pollution and the cost of energy increase. By using rhetoric, citizens can question the value of conventions that earlier might simply have been accepted as part of the social fabric.

Discussion: Nothing makes one more aware of one's inherited conventions than travel. When have you traveled somewhere only to find that a convention you assumed was "universal" was not? And where did you encounter an unexpected convention of another culture and find it more appealing than your own? After returning home, did you then try to change the conventions of those around you?

Social Knowledge

Social knowledge, in many ways, represents a fusion of the concepts of status, public opinion, and convention. **Social knowledge** signifies a culture's conventional wisdom and practical judgment as expressed in maxims, generally held beliefs, and value judgments. In other words, social knowledge represents what we might call *common sense*. Like status, social knowledge tells us what is better and worse; like public opinion, it tells us the acknowledged facts of the world; and like convention, it is something that has become habit—a kind of "second nature"—to a culture. Social knowledge thus signifies an attitude that is almost universally held by a wide number of people and has been passed down through generations and reaffirmed through history. Consequently, social knowledge is the most durable and most hard to change of any of the qualities of the public. It represents the collective judgments of a social group that are the result of past experience and which guide beliefs and behaviors in future situations. Aristotle offers an amusing example of social knowledge in the form of maxims:

> The maxim is a general statement and people love to hear stated in general terms what they already believe in some particular connection: e.g., if a man happens to have bad neighbors or bad children, he will agree with any one who tells him, "Nothing is more annoying than having neighbors," or, "Nothing is more foolish than to be the parent of children."[14]

A maxim need not be such a trivial affair, however. For example, we often think back to the horrors of World War II to have affirmed the social knowledge that one should not appease dictators in order to win their favor. But this attitude, in fact, had already been present in America going at least back to the American Revolution. Social knowledge is thus the product of historical social learning. It is the reservoir of lessons from the past that have been preserved in values and maxims and can be applied—and, most importantly, adapted—to future unforeseen situations. This cumulative nature of social knowledge is explained by Thomas Farrell. He writes:

> [As]individual problems are encountered and, through the frustrating incrementalism of human decision-making, managed or resolved, new problems emerge; and with these, new knowledge may be attributed, based reasonably upon the collective judgments which have previously been made.[15]

Rhetoric thus has a twofold relationship with social knowledge. In the first case, it draws from the pool of social knowledge to justify actions. Thus, a rhetor draws from available social knowledge to authorize a similar action in the present, as when the refusal to appease tyrants is used to justify the next military action. In the second case, rhetoric helps create new social knowledge in response to new situations. Here, a rhetor responds to a conflict by advancing a novel judgment that attempts to modify or replace some aspect of social knowledge using the strength of persuasion. Thus, one might argue that while it is bad to appease tyrants, it is worse to appease friends lest they become tyrants themselves.

Discussion: Most of the time, we encounter social knowledge as so many clichés to which we do not pay much attention, particularly when repeated to us by our friends and family. However, often we encounter situations when what had seemed

---

[14]Aristotle, *Rhetoric*, 1395b.

[15]Farrell, Thomas, "Knowledge, Consensus, and Rhetorical Theory," in *Contemporary Rhetorical Theory: A Reader*, ed. John Louis Lucaites, Celeste Michelle Condit, and Sally Caudill (New York: The Guilford Press, 1999), 147.

a meaningless cliché suddenly takes on real significance. When have you had an experience where some aspect of social knowledge suddenly took on a new meaning?

A fine historical example that encompasses all of the elements of rhetorical background is Thomas Paine's famous 1776 revolutionary pamphlet, *Common Sense*. That year, the American colonists were still torn about whether or not to break from Britain. Finally, in order to rally the full support of the American public to the cause of independence, Paine's anonymously published pamphlet was destined to become one of the most influential single rhetorical artifacts in the nation's history. The very title of the pamphlet indicated that Paine's strategy was to appeal to the elements of the rhetorical background that seemed to his audience should simply be "common sense." For Paine, however, the nature of this common sense had not yet been fully recognized, hidden as it was by various forms of bias, ignorance, and false reasoning. Hence, in his opening passage, he admits that his goal is to alter *public opinion* by use of arguments disseminated in a *public sphere* that appeal to the rational ideals of an *open society* despite being in conflict with *convention*. He writes:

> Perhaps the sentiments contained in the following pages, are not YET sufficiently fashionable to procure them general favour; a long habit of not thinking a thing WRONG, gives it a superficial appearance of being RIGHT, and raises at first a formidable outcry in defense of custom. But the tumult soon subsides. Time makes more converts than reason.

Paine's comment that "time makes more converts than reason" encapsulates the importance of the rhetorical background. For it is easy to get frustrated when persuasion does not happen overnight, despite what appear to be "unshakeable" arguments rallied for a cause. Attention only to the particulars of the foreground always seems to make rhetorical success contingent on immediate success. But the existence of a rhetorical background, which is slow to change but more enduring, gives some solace that what might lose the battle may win the war. This, at least, is the faith which bolsters the ideals of the open society based on the notion that even popularly held wrongs eventually give way to more substantial and reliable rights. In effect, Paine has faith that time will alter the *status* of his discourse from one of marginality to authority.

One of his "common sense" arguments dealt with the nature of government. Born out of the common experience of many American colonists who fled monarchical rule in Europe to seek a new and independent life in the "New World," a social knowledge began to develop that saw government as little more than a necessary evil that should be kept to a minimum and then cast off and replaced when a burden. Paine sought to formalize this social knowledge in his pamphlet in order to justify an act of revolution. In fact, for Paine, "revolution" was perhaps the wrong word. If a government was simply an external mechanism for keeping the peace, people had the right to develop whatever mechanism they desired. This decision only led to war when the leaders in charge of the government denied this legitimate right of the people. For Paine, only when the American public came to embrace this "right" would they fully support war as a means of freedom. He draws from and establishes this social knowledge as follows:

> Some writers have so confounded society with government, as to leave little or no distinction between them; whereas they are not only different, but have different

origins. Society is produced by our wants, and government by our wickedness; the former promotes our happiness positively by uniting our affections, the latter negatively by restraining our vices. The one encourages intercourse, the other creates distinctions. The first is a patron, the last a punisher.

Society in every state is a blessing, but government, even in its best state, is but a necessary evil; in its worst state an intolerable one; for when we suffer, or are exposed to the same miseries by a government, which we might expect in a country without government, our calamity is heightened by reflecting that we furnish the means by which we suffer! Government, like dress, is the badge of lost innocence; the palaces of kings are built on the ruins of the bowers of paradise. For were the impulses of conscience clear, uniform, and irresistibly obeyed, man would need no other lawgiver; but that not being the case, he finds it necessary to surrender up a part of his property to furnish means for the protection of the rest; and this he is induced to do by the same prudence which in every other case advises him out of two evils to choose the least. Wherefore, security being the true design and end of government, it unanswerably follows that whatever form thereof appears most likely to ensure it to us, with the least expense and greatest benefit, is preferable to all others.

If one were to sum up this social knowledge, it might be "government, even in its best state, is but a necessary evil; in its worst state an intolerable one." This basic maxim, once accepted, forms the basis of public opinion with respect to the matter of revolution. Paine, in effect, is asking his audience whether or not the government of British rule is necessary or intolerable. The social knowledge does not provide a particular answer to this question, but it does provide the criteria by which to make that particular judgment—even if that judgment may be opposed by all the conventions of the colonial life that had developed as a British colony.

Lastly, Paine's intent is not only to appeal to a public which exists (English colonists), but to generate a new form of a *public* (American citizens). In his conclusion, he thus appeals for his audience to cease using terms like "Whig" and "Tory," which refer to the political parties that bore allegiance to the British crown. Instead, he wants to bring into being a new form of a public:

On these grounds I rest the matter. And as no offer hath yet been made to refute the doctrine contained in the former editions of this pamphlet, it is a negative proof, that either the doctrine cannot be refuted, or, that the party in favor of it are too numerous to be opposed. WHEREFORE, instead of gazing at each other with suspicious or doubtful curiosity, let each of us hold out to his neighbor the hearty hand of friendship, and unite in drawing a line, which, like an act of oblivion, shall bury in forgetfulness every former dissension. Let the names of Whig and Tory be extinct; and let none other be heard among us, than those of a good citizen, an open and resolute friend, and a virtuous supporter of the RIGHTS of MANKIND, and of the FREE AND INDEPENDENT STATES OF AMERICA.[16]

Here is thus the ideal culmination of his rhetorical efforts—the constitution of a new public, a new nation, committed to the ideals of an open society, guided by a social knowledge grounded in principles of liberty, and committed to cultivating conventions that put those principles in practice in everyday life. How well the history of the

---

[16]Thomas Paine, "Common Sense" (1776) <http://www.ushistory.org/paine/commonsense/index.htm> (Accessed on 23 April 2010).

United States has lived up to Paine's ideals is an open question. What is undeniable is that Paine's rhetoric still continues to reverberate today, lodged firmly in public memory and embedded in the social knowledge reaffirmed continually in political discourses that cross all partisan boundaries. Paine's words have, in fact, become "common sense."[17]

THE RHETORICAL FOREGROUND

The rhetorical foreground describes those aspects of a situation that "stand out" from the background. These aspects include not only the problem or contingency at hand, but also the components of the specific speech situation in its relative immediacy. Expanding on the model initially posed by Lloyd Bitzer, these include an exigence, practical judgment, an audience, constraints, a speaker, an occasion, a purpose, and a message. Although each of these aspects emerges out of the rhetorical background, the nature of the contingency gives them a distinct individuality that demands our focused attention. However, as we shall see, each also reflects something of the rhetorical background that is significant. It is thus important to keep the foreground-background relationship in mind when dealing with even the most pressing contingency.

Exigence

What dominates the foreground of any rhetorical situation is the presence of an exigence. Defined in a general sense, an **exigence** is an experience of a contingency that makes us feel a combination of *concern* and *uncertainty*. A specifically *rhetorical* exigence is more than just the existence of a pressing problem, however. A **rhetorical exigence** must be a public issue that generates concern and uncertainty and which can be resolved in part through rhetorical persuasion. This means that the outcome of any problematic situation must have consequences that affect other people besides the speaker. Largely *personal* concerns, like your clogged sink, are not necessarily proper issues to address in rhetorical discourse because they usually have no essential interest for a public audience. However, they may become *public* concerns when their effects touch the lives of other people, such as when your clogged sink prevents you from providing meals for the homeless shelter. And they may become *rhetorical* concerns when their resolution requires the persuasion of an audience, such as when fixing the sink requires an increase in public spending for social services that in turn requires harnessing public support. In short, a rhetorical exigence arises when a practical problem experienced by a large number of people is accompanied by a desire to solve that problem, but a consensus about the most appropriate course of action is lacking.

One of the effects of the presence of shared experience from an exigence is to cause things otherwise in the background to come to the foreground. By "foreground," we mean two things. First, being in the foreground means being forefront in our minds, such that we pay attention to and dwell on certain details in our environment. For example, following the detonation of the first atomic bomb, the complexities of atomic physics, once addressed only in the isolated rooms of the

---

[17]For more on Paine's "Common Sense," see David C. Hoffman, "Paine and Prejudice: Rhetorical Leadership through Perceptual Framing in Common Sense." *Rhetoric & Public Affairs* 9.3 (2006), 373–410.

research university or engineering firm, become matters of public concern. It was "on people's minds." This means they achieve what Chaim Perelman and L. Olbrechts-Tyteca call **presence.** As they explain:

> It is not enough indeed that a thing should exist for a person to feel its presence . . . Accordingly one of the preoccupations of a speaker is to make present, by verbal magic alone, what is actually absent but what he considers important to his argument, by making them more present, to enhance the value of some of the elements of which one has actually been made conscious.[18]

Not only does rhetoric make issues present to people's consciousness, but it also brings people physically present before each other and the speaker. In rhetorical public speech, the second "foreground" effect is to bring people out of their homes to be present together in one place to deliberate about and discuss matters of public concern. The speaker's responsibility is thus to address these people and their concerns directly. A way of summing up the relationship between an exigence and the rhetorical foreground, then, is to say that a shared problem brings people together in the same space to address the issues that are present in their consciousness.

The concept of a rhetorical exigence can be difficult to grasp because there is often no agreement about the nature or even the existence of a particular problem. Indeed, convincing people that there *is* an exigence is often one of the most significant challenges to any speaker. Consequently, it is helpful to distinguish between two kinds of rhetorical exigence relative to the different nature of consensus and uncertainty. With an **uncontested exigence,** an audience achieves consensus as to the nature of the problem but is uncertain as to the solution. In such cases, a speaker concentrates on advocating some solutions over others. It is in these situations that rhetorical persuasion is the most powerful, for the audience is already predisposed to act in some way. With a **contested exigence,** by contrast, rhetorical public speech addresses a problem about whose very reality remains in doubt for an audience. In such cases, a speaker has to work to persuade people of the nature of the exigence before proposing a solution.

Of course, sometimes people recognize a problem but still fail to act. In these cases, rhetoric must heighten the sense of urgency while trying to develop a common plan of action. For instance, in March 2003, the African nation of Sudan erupted into a Civil War when militants attacked government forces, claiming that they were being oppressed by the Sudanese government in the western region of Darfur. The government responded with a campaign of aerial bombardment in support of ground attacks on the general population by a militia called the Janjaweed that it had recruited from local tribes. By 2006, at least 200,000 people had been killed by such militias and about 2.5 million people had fled their homes to live in crowded and unsafe refugee camps. Although widely condemned by the international community as "genocide," by the end of 2006 little had been done to stop the killing.

On December 14, 2006, actor George Clooney spoke at the United Nations Security Council to address the need for action on what was a globally uncontested

---

[18]Chaim Perelman and L. Olbrechts-Tyteca, *The New Rhetoric: A Treatise on Argumentation* (Notre Dame, In: The University of Notre Dame Press, 1969), 117.

exigence and yet had produced little concerned action. He says:

> I'll make you two promises: The first is that I'll be brief; and the second is that I won't try to educate you on the issues of Darfur and the regions around it. There's nothing I can say that you don't already know. You know the numbers. You know the urgency. And you know how bad this is likely to get.

By acknowledging the universal agreement that the violence in Darfur is a problem, Clooney allows himself to skip over trying to "prove" his case in order to concentrate on making a more emotional and ethical plea for action. He continues:

> I'm here to represent the voices of the people who cannot speak for themselves. And from our side, we're not so naive either. We know how difficult a task this is. We understand how many issues are in front of you this moment, each needing great care and attention. But you are the U.N. and this is a task that you have been given. You have to decide what's most urgent. You have responsibility to protect.

Here, Clooney points out the uncertainty that is at the heart of any exigence—the contingencies that resist any easy answer or resolution. Yet he also places the burden upon finding that answer on that particular public called the United Nations. Finally, he goes on to appeal to the shared social knowledge, proven in large part by the global experience of the Holocaust, that responsible nations cannot stand by while genocide occurs. He concludes:

> In the time that we're here today, more women and children will die violently in the Darfur region than in Iraq, Afghanistan, Palestine, Israel, or Lebanon. The United States has called it "genocide." For you it's called "ethnic cleansing." But make no mistake: It is the first genocide of the 21st century. And if it continues unchecked it will not be the last.
>
> Now, my job is the come here today and to beg you on behalf of the millions of people who will die—and make no mistake; they will die—for you to take real and effective measures to put an end to this. Of course it's complex, but when you see entire villages raped and killed, wells poisoned and then filled with the bodies of its villagers, then all complexities disappear and it comes down to simply right and wrong. It's not getting better. It's getting much, much worse. And it is only the international community that can help us.[19]

Clooney's effort is to take a recognized problem and rally the energies of a diverse number of parties to come to a solution. This task is difficult enough when people agree about the nature of the problem; imagine the added challenge of having to convince an audience that a problem even *exists*. This was the situation that faced Patrick Henry in 1995. Following the Boston Tea Party of December 16, 1773, the British Parliament passed a series of acts intended to suppress the rebellion in Massachusetts. In May of 1774, General Thomas Gage arrived in Boston with four regiments of British troops. For the next two years, uncertainty spread as to whether Britain was preparing for a full-scale war on the colonies or whether tensions could be resolved through political petition and deliberation. When the Virginia Convention met in 1775, many delegates remained unsure if the exigence of a possible war really existed, clinging to the hope that the British government would rely on sensible reasoning instead of force.

---

[19]Available from *The American Rhetoric.* <americanrhetoric.com> (Accessed on 23 April 2010).

However, Patrick Henry firmly believed that war was imminent, and in his famous speech "Liberty or Death," he set out to resolve any doubt about the reality of the contested exigence even while acknowledging the limits of his own knowledge. For Henry, one had to act on the best available knowledge to avoid disastrous consequences, and his knowledge led him to the conclusion that the British were about to attack. This view was not, however, in the majority. Other "gentlemen" did not see such a threat. To convince them, Henry tries to highlight certain aspects of the rhetorical foreground with what he calls the "lamp of experience" in the hopes of illuminating them regarding the nature of the threat. He says:

> For my part, whatever anguish of spirit it may cost, I am willing to know the whole truth—to know the worst and to provide for it. I have but one lamp by which my feet are guided; and that is the lamp of experience. I know of no way of judging of the future but by the past. And judging by the past, I wish to know what there has been in the conduct of the British ministry for the last ten years, to justify those hopes with which gentlemen have been pleased to solace themselves and the House?

One of the reasons for "solace" was a friendly reception of a petition submitted to the British by the American diplomats. But Henry then points to the contrary evidence that shows how, despite conciliatory remarks by the British, they were, in fact, preparing for war. He continues:

> Is it that insidious smile with which our petition has been lately received? Trust it not, sir; it will prove a snare to your feet. Suffer not yourselves to be betrayed with a kiss. Ask yourselves how this gracious reception of our petition comports with these warlike preparations which cover our waters and darken our land. Are fleets and armies necessary to a work of love and reconciliation? Have we shown ourselves so unwilling to be reconciled that force must be called in to win back our love? Let us not deceive ourselves, sir. These are the implements of war and subjugation—the last arguments to which kings resort. I ask gentlemen, sir, what means this martial array, if its purpose be not to force us to submission? Can gentlemen assign any other possible motives for it? Has Great Britain any enemy, in this quarter of the world, to call for all this accumulation of navies and armies? No, sir, she has none. They are meant for us; they can be meant for no other. They are sent over to bind and rivet upon us those chains which the British ministry has been so long forging.[20]

Was Henry right to say that war was inevitable? The way history played out, it may be impossible to ever know. This issue of whether an exigence really exists or in what capacity it exists is the most difficult one for any participant in a rhetorical situation to resolve. Just as nobody wants to be the "Boy Who Cried Wolf," the fate of the ostrich who buries his head in the sand is no better. But contingencies force these decisions upon us. The ethical lesson is that in rhetorical situations, we are responsible for making the best practical judgment with limited information.[21]

Discussion: *Tenacity* is defined as the dogged determination to pursue the same course of action despite evidence that it may not be the right one. Often, we respond

---

[20]Suriano, 1.

[21]For more on Henry's speech, see Judy Hample, "The Textual and Cultural Authenticity of Patrick Henry's 'Liberty or Death' Speech," *Quarterly Journal of Speech* 63.3 (1977), 298–310.

to exigencies by tenaciously treating them as technical situations, only to find that our preferred method actually makes the situation worse. When has that happened to you, and how were you convinced to adopt a new method of dealing with the problem?

Practical Judgment

Once an exigence becomes universally recognized, the immediate question becomes "What do we do?" The answer to this question always involves a **practical judgment**, which is the act of defining a particular person, object, or event in terms of a general category for the purposes of making a practical decision. In other words, practical judgment tells one what kinds of things are in his or her environment and what to do in response to them. A practical judgment involves the relationship among a *thing,* an *idea,* and an *action.* For example, I wake up at night and hear a tapping sound (thing). Fearful that it is a burglar (hypothetical idea), I get up and discover it is just the rattling of the air conditioner (conclusive idea). I then decide to go back to sleep (action). As indicated by this example, usually our practical judgments are absorbed into the habits and conventions of our everyday life. We do not need to think consciously about whether we should respond to a stop sign (thing), by associating it with the command to stop (idea), and then stopping (action). We just stop. But when we are learning to drive, all of these practical judgments must be consciously taught and enforced through instruction.

As indicated by the discussion of exigence, practical judgment takes on rhetorical qualities when we are unsure about what kind of judgment to make. Should we view British soldiers in Boston as "peacekeepers" or "oppressors"? Should we view the violence in Darfur as "genocide" or "civil war"? In each case, rhetorical conflict involves the struggle to advance one judgment over another and thereby encourages forms of action on the basis of that judgment. One of the key challenges of any rhetoric public speaker is to promote their version of practical judgment and thereby provide the meanings for any contingency that will make an audience prefer certain options over others.

One event that called upon Americans to make a practical judgment was the case surrounding enigmatic figure John Brown, the radical abolitionist who seized the federal armory at Harper's Ferry in the hope to use the approximately 100,000 rifles and muskets to arm slaves and create a violent rebellion against slavery in the South. When he was captured by federal forces and put on trial, he heated up the debate over slavery leading up to the Civil War. The issue of practical judgment involved whether or not Brown was a "prophet" and "hero" or whether he was "insane" and a "traitor."

Realizing the importance of determining the meaning of Brown's legacy, Transcendentalist writer and philosopher Henry David Thoreau delivered his speech, "A Plea for Captain John Brown," at Concord, Massachusetts, on October 30, 1859, just two weeks after the raid. One of the issues Thoreau raises is the relationship between law and practical judgment concerning how Brown's actions should be defined under the legal code. Should we simply obey the "letter" of the law and act as if all cases are the same, or should we use our individual practical judgment to decide on the particularity of his case? Indeed, should citizens be able to obey their own practical judgments in opposition to the legal judgments of a government? Thoreau appears to favor the individual in both cases:

> Any man knows when he is justified, and all the wits in the world cannot enlighten him on that point. The murderer always knows that he is justly punished; but when a government takes the life of a man without the consent of his conscience, it is an audacious government, and is taking a step towards its own dissolution. Is it not possible that an individual may be right and a government wrong? Are laws to be enforced simply because they were made? or declared by any number of men to be good, if they are not good? Is there any necessity for a man's being a tool to perform a deed of which his better nature disapproves? Is it the intention of lawmakers that good men shall be hung ever? Are judges to interpret the law according to the letter, and not the spirit? What right have you to enter into a compact with yourself that you will do thus or so, against the light within you? Is it for you to make up your mind,—to form any resolution whatever,—and not accept the convictions that are forced upon you, and which ever pass your understanding?

The idea that it is "for you to make up your mind" is the essence of practical judgment in the context of a rhetorical situation, whether one be a member of the jury, the judge, or just a common citizen. In the case of John Brown, Thoreau advocated not necessarily for his life, but for his legacy. He wished the American public to embrace his cause and make the practical judgment that rebellion against a state is justified if done for the sake of granting liberty to a people in bondage. He goes on:

> I am here to plead his cause with you. I plead not for his life, but for his character,—his immortal life; and so it becomes your cause wholly, and is not his in the least. Some eighteen hundred years ago Christ was crucified; this morning, perchance, Captain Brown was hung. These are the two ends of a chain which is not without its links. He is not Old Brown any longer; he is an angel of light.[22]

The idea that Brown is "an angel of light" embodies the thrust of Thoreau's practical judgment. His hope was that, in dying, Brown would nonetheless leave behind a more entrenched practical judgment that slavery was an evil to be abolished—a legacy that was complicated by Brown's violent methods.[23]

Discussion: Although we might not intuitively associate practical judgment with leisure, it is in our social relationships and choices of pleasure that we often make the most important practical judgments—whom we should associate with, where we should go, what we should consume, how we should act. What was the worst practical judgment you made in such an environment? Did it have lasting negative consequences? How did it affect your future judgments?

---

[22]Henry David Thoreau, "A Plea for Captain John Brown," 1859, <http://www.transcendentalists. com/thoreau_plea_john_brown.htm> (Accessed on 23 April 2010).

[23]For more on Thoreau's praise of Brown, see Paul D. Erickson, "Henry David Thoreau's Apotheosis of John Brown: A Study of Nineteenth Century Rhetorical Heroism," *Southern Communication Journal* 61.4 (1996), 302–311.

Audience

In the rhetorical background, the **audience** exceeds the people immediately present in the room. The background audience represents the larger publics who might eventually be influenced by the speaker's words in some way or another, just as a politician might address the "American People" even though he or she is speaking immediately to a gathering of the VFW. But for someone seeking to influence people to act within a timely manner about a shared problem, there is a limit to relying on such generic conceptions of audience. Although this background audience is important when considering long-term effects of any situated speech act, it lacks the specificity and detail that provides a speech its unique character, energy, and focus.

The audience of the rhetorical foreground helps provide the concreteness and particularity which balances the more universal qualities of the background audience. In its most basic form, the foreground audience is the **situated audience**, or the audience that physically exists together in a particular place and time to hear a message. The situated audience includes all those people in the boardroom, the gymnasium, the stadium, or the street. Clearly, many of these people can be defined in terms of their membership in various publics. But added to these more general characteristics are the specific experiences they all share as participants in a shared space. For example, many people still make it a point to say they "walked with Dr. King" during the March on Washington. This shared experience made the reception of the speech different for those watching the speech at home. For someone watching the television or listening to the radio, these words are interpreted metaphorically, as a statement concerning the progress toward civil rights. But for those who had literally just completed marching, there is added a sense of having actually walked down the streets, possibly holding hands with others, as a physical demonstration of involvement and support. Clearly, those sitting in their living rooms or listening on car radios also are part of the audience; but they inhabit the spectrum somewhere between the situated audience and the background audience.

Complicating this picture even more is the concept of the **target audience**, or that group of people who are both able to be persuaded and capable of acting in such a way to help resolve the exigence. The target audience is more of an "ideal" than either the background or the situated audience. It stands for the best possible group of individuals who might hear a speech. This ideal target audience is not, as one might suppose, the people with whom you already agree. Such an audience would guarantee a supportive response, but little persuasion (and therefore little productive action) would occur since they would already agree with you. A target audience more accurately represents a group of people who have the ability to solve a problem through collective action but who are not already predisposed to act, meaning that they must be persuaded to do so. In speeches of advocacy, for instance, the target audience often is precisely the one watching the event on television, in which case the situated audience acts as part of the message.

Identifying a target audience beforehand is crucial to sculpting a message that actually produces social consequences by influencing those people in the best position to initiate change. Sometimes that audience may be a single person, such as when groups try to make their local representative or senator change his or her vote on a crucial issue by large-scale petition campaigns. Other times that audience may be a whole community or population, such as when attempts to influence politicians through accepted channels fail and one decides to initiate social change through the collective action of the public.

One resource for audience analysis is the analysis of **demographics.** Largely through survey and statistical methods, audiences can be analyzed in terms of gender, race, age, income, disabilities, mobility, educational attainment, home ownership, employment status, and location. In politics, terms like *soccer mom* and *NASCAR dad* are often used as shorthand for people who share certain demographic characteristics, and political messages are tailored around them. Of course, demographic analysis is often complicated by the fact that audiences belong to many demographics at once. Therefore, one often speaks to only one facet of an audience's demographic while ignoring others. A political candidate who knows that he or she needs the votes of a certain demographic, for instance, will speak to a mixed audience *as if* everyone in it were members of that demographic. Consequently, teenagers in a county dominated by retirement communities might show up to a campaign rally only to hear the candidate speaking about Medicare, prescription drug prices, and Social Security; and this is by design. Because teenagers are generally a tiny proportion of the voting block, candidates rarely mention issues related to their lives. They do not make up the target audience, even though they might be physically present *in* the audience.

One excellent example of a speaker who targeted her audience was African-American writer and political activist Maria Stewart. Shockingly, before September 1832, no African-American woman had ever delivered a public lecture. They were a marginalized group, denied access to the public sphere by the norms of convention and the social knowledge concerning matters of race and gender. So it must have been a surprise to her diverse audience, including men and women, both black and white, when she stood up in Boston's Franklin Hall to give a speech (despite the fact that the meeting was being sponsored by the women of the African-American Female Intelligence Society!). What made her speech even more provocative is that she spoke directly to the black women in her audience, targeting them (rather than men) as the primary agents of social change because of their power as mothers to influence and educate their children. Her strategy of speaking directly to women, in their roles as mothers, is announced early on in the speech. Challenging their sense of despair and resignation, she appeals to them:

> Oh, do not say you cannot make anything of your children; but say, with the help and assistance of God, we will try. Perhaps you will say that you cannot send them to high schools and academies. You can have them taught in the first rudiments of useful knowledge, and then you can have private teachers, who will instruct them in the higher branches. It is of no use for us to sit with our hands folded, hanging our heads like bulrushes lamenting our wretched condition; but let us make a mighty effort and arise.

Once her target audience has been announced, Stewart then goes even further by speaking about the men as if they were not even present; and not only are they absent, but they are placed in a role even more helpless than what the women may have previously thought about themselves! This further seeks to empower the women by placing the burden of their family's future upon their shoulders. She says:

> Look at our young men smart, active, and energetic, with souls filled with ambitious fire; if they look forward, alas! What are their prospects? They can be nothing but the humblest laborer, on account of their dark complexion; hence many of them lose their ambition and become worthless . . . Look at our aged sires, whose heads are whitened with the frosts of seventy winters, with their old wood saws on their backs. Alas, what keeps us so? Prejudice, ignorance and poverty.

Lastly, Stewart appeals to the social knowledge concerning the courage of the American pilgrims to endure hardship. By looking to the past, she hopes to find an inspiration for the present. She also adeptly uses an agricultural metaphor of cultivating the soil, knowing that such labor was also done by women during the Colonial Era. She concludes:

> But ah! Did the pilgrims, when they first landed on these shores, quietly compose themselves, and say, "The Britons have all the money and all the power, and we must continue their servants forever?" Did they sigh and say, "Our lot is hard; the Indians own the soil, and we cannot cultivate it?" No, they first made powerful efforts to raise themselves. And, my brethren have you made a powerful effort? Have you prayed the legislature for mercy's sake to grant you all the rights and privileges of free citizens, that your daughters may rise to that degree of respectability which true merit deserves, and your sons above the servile situations which most of them fill?[24]

The combination of criticism, challenge, and plea signals that Stewart's audience had the capability to change and the power to alter the situation for the better, but needed a final push to actually become motivated to action.[25]

Discussion: Imagine that you were going to advocate a national policy that provided fully paid college tuition for all Americans. First, who would be the target audience for such a policy? In other words, who has the power to influence this decision? Who is willing to be persuaded but is not already committed to the policy? Second, given the fact that you can't speak to all audiences directly, what situated audience might you address that would indirectly influence your target audience?

Constraints

In a more ideal world, the response to every exigence would be swift and unimpeded. Once identified as a problem, our solutions would immediately be universally adopted and energetically applied. However, most of our proposed solutions do not go so smoothly. We encounter **constraints**, which are obstacles that stand between us and the attainment of our interests. Sometimes these constraints are physical things, like when our car doesn't start or when we hit traffic on the road. Sometimes they are personal things, like when we dislike our job so much that it is hard to get ourselves

---

[24]Safire, 679.

[25]For more on Maria Stewart's role in abolitionism, see Jacquiline Bacon, "'God and a Woman': Women Abolitionists, Biblical Authority, and Social Activism," *Journal of Communication & Religion* 22.1 (1999): 1–39.

out of bed. And sometimes they are other people, like when our co-workers resist your suggestions about how to streamline an office's business practices. Anything that restrains or inhibits movement toward a desired end functions as a constraint.

In rhetoric, constraints are defined in relationship to interests or ends that require rhetorical persuasion to achieve. **Rhetorical constraints** are therefore those obstacles that must be overcome in order to facilitate both the persuasive and practical effects desired by the speaker. By "persuasive" effects, we mean those effects which make people think and act differently than they did before the speech. Constraints relating to persuasive effects are thus called **internal constraints,** referring to the beliefs, attitudes, and values of an audience that must be changed if persuasion is to occur. For example, convincing a population to support tax on junk foods to cut down on child obesity may require challenging the **belief** that obesity is not a social problem, changing the pervading attitude of resisting higher taxes, and dissociating the eating of junk food with the value of personal choice and freedom. Unless these internal constraints can be modified, they will lead to the rejection of the proposal. (More about beliefs, attitudes, and values will be found in Chapter 4).

However, a public speaker who actually desires to make a lasting change in actual conditions must also consider **external constraints,** which are the people, objects, processes, and events that may physically obstruct any productive action even if persuasion of an audience has occurred. A *person* acting as a constraint is someone who cannot be persuaded and who possesses the power to obstruct your goal, such as the governor who threatens a veto of your bill. An *object* is defined here as any tangible and enduring thing that tends to resist change while having constant influence on an environment, such as the presence of vending machines in schools (a "physical" object) or laws which gives school's financial incentives to place them in schools (a "legal" object). An *event* that is a constraint is a tangible but ephemeral thing that occurs at a specific point and time and has a distinct beginning and end, such as a sudden downturn in the economy which makes new taxes unpopular. Lastly, a *process* represents a sequence of events that must be followed in order to bring something to conclusion. As a constraint, such a process might be a lengthy and burdensome petition process by which any changes in tax laws require years of persistent effort.

Any of these external constraints may impede successful social action even *after* an audience has been persuaded to act. Consequently, public speakers who fail to account for external constraints may recommend a course of action, only to find it to be impossible to implement later, thereby wasting everyone's time and energy. Successful speakers should always consider all possible constraints before creating and delivering rhetorical discourse. Ignoring constraints often ruins any possibility of instigating effective social action. On the one hand, if external constraints are ignored, a speaker risks appearing ignorant about the "realities" of the situation. On the other hand, ignoring internal constraints is the common flaw of all "technical" discourse that believes that the only thing needed for persuasion is accurate facts and reasonable solutions. The most effective speaker combines elements of both types of discourse by adapting his or her language to both types of constraints.

One provocative analysis of the internal constraints of an audience is found in Audre Lorde's speech, "The Transformation of Silence into Language and Action," given at the 1977 convention of the Modern Language Association. In this speech, Lorde's persuasive intent is a general one—to get her target audience of African-American women to make their voices heard. Drawing from her social experience as an

African-American, a woman, and a lesbian, Lorde draws on her experience living in the "margins" of society and explores the challenges of speaking from a position of marginal social status. In this opening paragraph, she addresses the fear she perceives in her audience that makes it resistant to hearing her message. She begins with a challenge:

> What are the words you do not yet have? What do you need to say? What are the tyrannies you swallow day by day and attempt to make your own, until you will sicken and die of them, still in silence? Perhaps for some of you here today, I am the face of one of your fears. Because I am woman, because I am Black, because I am lesbian, because I am myself—a Black woman warrior poet doing my work—come to ask you, are you doing yours?

With this internal constraint called into the open, Lorde doesn't rest content with simply trying to tell them to get over it. Instead, she tries to analyze its causes and explain its existence. Interestingly, she attributes the internal constraints on her audience (the fear of speaking out in public) to external constraints (sexism and racism) that have kept them silent. For Lorde, these external constraints are real, and challenging those constraints comes with great risk. So there is reason to be afraid. She continues:

> And of course I am afraid, because the transformation of silence into language and action is an act of self-revelation, and that always seems fraught with danger . . . In the cause of silence, each of us draws the face of her own fear—fear of contempt, of censure, or some judgment, or recognition, of challenge, of annihilation. But most of all, I think, we fear the visibility without which we also cannot truly live.

So far, nothing Lorde has said has amounted to anything persuasive. She has, in fact, appeared to simply reinforce their fears. Yet then she tries a new strategy, which amounts to the fact that their fears, however legitimate, do not accomplish anything. Scared or not, they will all suffer the same fate. So why not suffer with courage and pride and strength?

> And that visibility which makes us most vulnerable is that which also is the source of our greatest strength. Because the machine will try to grind you into dust anyway, whether or not we speak. We can sit in our corners mute forever while our sisters and ourselves are wasted, while our children are distorted and destroyed, while our earth is poisoned; we can sit in our safe corner mute as bottles, and we still will be no less afraid.[26]

Lorde's message thus balances sympathy for internal constraints and recognition of external constraints in her effort to be "realistic" about the situation while still hopeful that her audience can collectively change some aspect of that situation to make the lives of its members better. Striking this balance makes an audience both enlightened and inspired.[27]

Discussion: In the previous discussion question, you were asked to consider the target audience for a policy of universal college tuition funding. Let us now say you are an opponent to this policy. What internal and external constraints would you highlight to inhibit the possibility of such a policy?

---

[26]Joy Ritchie and Kate Ronald, *Available Means: An Anthology of Women's Rhetoric(s)* (Pittsburgh: University of Pittsburgh Press, 2001), 301.

[27]For more on Lorde's speech, see Lester C. Olson, "On the Margins of Rhetoric: Audre Lorde Transforming Silence into Language and Action." *Quarterly Journal of Speech* 83.1 (1997), 49–70.

Speaker

As indicated by all the examples used so far, the **speaker** in rhetorical public speech is something more than just a person who says words in the presence of others. A rhetorical public speaker is called a **rhetor,** meaning a conscious instigator of social action who uses persuasive discourse to achieve his or her ends. Being *conscious* implies that a rhetor is not simply one whose speech happens to have consequences. All acts of communication have the potential to influence people and events, but rhetorical public speech is unique in having been created specifically for that purpose. That is what makes it an art rather than a product of luck. Being an *instigator* then means that a rhetor intentionally behaves in such a way as to cause others to think and feel in new and different ways. We instigate not only when we prompt, originate, and begin something, but also when we do so in the presence of others who may be reluctant to follow. An instigator makes people act in such a way they might not otherwise have done if not prodded to do so. Finally, what is instigated is a *social action,* meaning that the effects of a rhetor's *persuasive discourse* are determined by how they alter and affect the behaviors of other people with respect to some *end,* or some goal or interest that functions in response to an exigence. A rhetor thus represents a person willing to stir, motivate, challenge, and even confront an audience in order to make its members think and act in such a way that addresses a shared problem.[28]

A speaker who was certainly aware of his persona as a rhetor was Albert Einstein in his speech "The Menace of Mass Destruction" given to the United Nations General Assembly on November 11, 1947. During World War II, the physicist Einstein had tried to leverage his scientific credibility in a letter in 1939 to President Franklin D. Roosevelt recommending that the United States develop an atomic weapon before Germany in order to prevent a Nazi victory in Europe. However, after seeing the subsequent devastation wrought by use of atomic weapons, Einstein became a proponent of disarmament. In fact, he became so firm in his belief that we need to ban such weapons that he felt it should be treated as a technical situation—that since we already knew what to do, we should just get to work developing and applying a procedure. What he found, however, was that the international community was hardly of one mind; that instead of a technical situation, the world was in the midst of a rhetorical one in which different parties were arguing about the real nature of the contingency as well as what to do about it. Frustrated, Einstein tried to create a sense of urgency by comparing the problem of atomic weapons with a technical situation of a plague that demands coordinated action by scientists to come up with a technical solution:

> Everyone is aware of the difficult and menacing situation in which human society—shrunk into one community with a common fate—finds itself, but only a few act accordingly. Most people go on living their everyday life: half frightened, half indifferent, they behold the ghostly tragicomedy that is being performed on the international stage before the eyes and ears of the world. But on that stage, on which the actors under the floodlights play their ordained parts, our fate of tomorrow, life or death of the nations, is being decided.

---

[28]For the relationship between rhetoric and citizenship, see Robert Asen, "A Discourse Theory of Citizenship," *Quarterly Journal of Speech* 90.2 (2004), 189–211.

It would be different if the problem were not one of things made by man him-self, such as the atomic bomb and other means of mass destruction equally menac-ing all peoples. It would be different, for instance, if an epidemic of bubonic plague were threatening the entire world. In such a case conscientious and expert persons would be brought together and they would work out an intelligent plan to combat the plague. After having reached agreement upon the right ways and means, they would submit their plan to governments. Those would hardly raise serious objec-tions but rather agree speedily on the measures to be taken. They certainly would never think of trying to handle the matter in such a way that their own nation would be spared whereas the next one would be decimated.[29]

Throughout this speech, an audience is made conscious of Einstein's unique role as a speaker. His status as a world-renowned scientist and respected humanist allows him the freedom to compare the utopian world of rational deliberation with the corrupt and inefficient sphere of political haggling and compromise. This is a speech only a person like Einstein could give, and knowledge of that fact brings forward the unique character of his persona.

Discussion: Despite what we might tell ourselves, almost never do we actually verbalize everything that is on our minds that we wish to say. Indeed, we often fail to do so even when we consciously prepare ahead of time. Can you think of a time where you held back saying something that, in retrospect, you wish you would have said? Why do you think you held back? Was it an internal or exter-nal constraint?

Occasion

Rhetoric as a form of public speaking specifically refers to rhetoric that occurs at a specific time and place shared by both speaker and audience. The **occasion** is the spe-cific setting shared by speaker and audience whose circumstances constrain the form and appropriateness of what is said. It is a concrete "happening" consistent with tra-ditional situated conceptions of oratory. A narrow focus on such "face-to-face" en-counters may seem archaic in the Internet age. However, the emphasis on occasion is not meant to downplay the importance of electronic forms of communication that often diminish if not eliminate considerations of space and time. It is simply to say that rhetorical public speech, in its specificity to occasion, makes it a different, more complex, and more powerful genre of communication that calls for its own analysis.

For example, only with respect to occasion do we understand how the actual en-vironment in which we speak constrains the *form* and *appropriateness* of what we say. We would not expect, for example, the same person to make the same speech at a church service, a political rally, a family dinner, a graduation ceremony, or a protest march. This is because we associate each of these different contexts with different standards of *appropriateness* that influence the *form* of a speech, meaning the way a speech is structured and delivered. Appropriate speech is a sign of competence and respect, and an appropriate speaker considers the audience's needs and desires as determined by the occasion and takes care to account for them in a speech. An

---

[29]Suriano, 177.

inappropriate speaker, by contrast, tends to think only of his or her own self-interest and displays ignorance or even contempt for the expectations of the audience.[30]

Yet the importance of occasion goes deeper than simply constraints on form and appropriateness. Even an Internet blog, after all, has *some* such constraints. The importance of occasion for rhetorical public speech is that it demands that we be *physically present* in the same space at the same time as other people. As explored in Chapter 2, this characteristic makes rhetorical public speech a *tactile* event, meaning one that focuses our entire being on the *feeling* of a situation. When we are physically present with others within the same occasion, attention is more focused on one thing, making one's words have that much more significance while also making us that much more anxious. Speaking at an occasion thus makes one's words generally have more of an immediate impact. The power of occasion is its tendency to focus attention and interest on a single subject and allow speakers to utilize all their emotional, intellectual, creative, and physical capacities to persuade an audience.

The power of occasion is demonstrated in the testimony of Susan B. Anthony before a court of law. Anthony still appears on the face of some dollar coins, but it is not as well known that she also was convicted of a crime—the crime of casting a ballot in the 1872 presidential election which happened during a time when women could not vote. On June 19, 1873, after having been denied the opportunity to say a word in her defense, she stood before Judge Ward Hunt after her lawyer appealed the guilty verdict. This excerpt from her interaction with the judge demonstrates how occasion and appropriateness influence the performance of situated rhetorical discourse. The fact that her words were spoken in resistance to the formal requirements of a defendant and the direct commands of the judge make her words much more powerful. Imagine, for instance, the courage it must have taken to respond to the judge as she does in this exchange:

JUDGE HUNT   (Ordering the defendant to stand up) Has the prisoner anything to say why sentence shall not be pronounced?

MISS ANTHONY   Yes, your honor, I have many things to say; for in your ordered verdict of guilty, you have trampled under foot every vital principle of our government. My natural rights, my civil rights, my political rights, my judicial rights, are all alike ignored. Robbed of the fundamental privilege of citizenship, I am degraded from the status of a citizen to that of a subject; and not only myself individually, but all of my sex, are, by your honor's verdict, doomed to political subjection under this, so-called, form of government.

The image of Anthony facing down the judge adds visual and perceptual elements to her language that would be lacking if she had simply sent him a letter in the mail. It also offers the opportunity for the immediate back-and-forth between judge and defendant as he attempts to end the trial and she insists on extending it. They continue:

JUDGE HUNT   The Court cannot listen to a rehearsal of arguments the prisoner's counsel has already consumed three hours in presenting.

---

[30]For the Sophistical view of appropriateness, see John Poulakos, "Toward a Sophistic Definition of Rhetoric," in *Contemporary Rhetorical Theory: A Reader,* ed. John Louis Lucaites, Celeste Michelle Condit, and Sally Caudill (New York: The Guilford Press, 1999).

MISS ANTHONY   May it please your honor, I am not arguing the question, but simply stating the reasons why sentence cannot, in justice, be pronounced against me. Your denial of my citizen's right to vote, is the denial of my right of consent as one of the governed, the denial of my right of representation as one of the taxed, the denial of my right to a trial by a jury of my peers as an offender against law, therefore, the denial of my sacred rights to life, liberty, property and . . .

JUDGE HUNT   The Court cannot allow the prisoner to go on . . . The Court must insist the prisoner has been tried according to the established forms of law.

MISS ANTHONY   Yes, your honor, but by forms of law all made by men, interpreted by men, administered by men, in favor of men, and against women; and hence, your honor's ordered verdict of guilty, against a United States citizen for the exercise of "*that citizen's right to vote,*" simply because that citizen was a woman and not a man . . . As then, the slaves who got their freedom must take it over, or under, or through the unjust forms of law, precisely so, now, must women, to get their right to a voice in this government, take it; and I have taken mine, and mean to take it at every possible opportunity.

JUDGE HUNT   The Court orders the prisoner to sit down. It will not allow another word. . . . (Here the prisoner sat down.)

Interestingly, the judge, apparently bewildered by Anthony's rhetorical assault, falls back on the authority of the occasion to render her silent. The judge, in effect, tries to reinforce the ethics of an authoritative sphere despite Anthony's efforts to use the courtroom as a public sphere (and thereby violating legal convention). In an almost comedic turn, however, he immediately demands the opposite in order to finish the procedure:

JUDGE HUNT   The prisoner will stand up. (Here Miss Anthony arose again.) The sentence of the Court is that you pay a fine of one hundred dollars and the costs of the prosecution.

MISS ANTHONY   May it please your honor, I shall never pay a dollar of your unjust penalty. All the stock in trade I possess is a $10,000 debt, incurred by publishing my paper—The Revolution—four years ago, the sole object of which was to educate all women to do precisely as I have done, rebel against your man-made, unjust, unconstitutional forms of law, that tax, fine, imprison and hang women, while they deny them the right of representation in the government; and I shall work on with might and main to pay every dollar of that honest debt, but not a penny shall go to this unjust claim. And I shall earnestly and persistently continue to urge all women to the practical recognition of the old revolutionary maxim, that "Resistance to tyranny is obedience to God."[31]

---

[31]Zinn, 130.

The power of occasion, in this case, was to focus attention on Anthony's testimony, which was then recorded and distributed in subsequent newspapers and pamphlets. Without the trial, public attention would not have been focused on her protest. It is for this reason that social activists often seek court trials in order to give them the occasion to get their voice heard. Finally, note how Anthony appeals to the social knowledge of the American Revolution to justify her own resistance to American law. Because she consciously attends to the rhetorical background, she is able to speak beyond the immediate particulars of her exigence and occasion. She speaks to a broader public, including the public of today.[32]

Discussion: Holidays and reunions are unique in their ability to create occasions which are shared by people who otherwise communicate from a distance. At these events, we often find ourselves communicating differently with others, even if we had maintained close contact via telephone or e-mail. How does the power of occasion at holidays alter what is said and how it is said between friends and family? Did you ever find yourself expressing something you had not expected to say, simply because of the occasion?

Purpose

Fully understanding the importance of occasion, however, requires discerning the nature of the shared purpose that brings people together in one place. The **purpose** for rhetorical public speech represents the reason for and circumstances under which an occasion occurs. To be clear, the purpose is not the purpose of the *speaker;* it is the purpose for the *event* that brings speaker and audience together. Purpose establishes common expectations among members of a diverse public that helps direct their attention and focus. The purpose of the occasion for Anthony's speech was, for instance, to determine her guilt or innocence according to the laws of the state. The purpose therefore establishes the norms of appropriateness for what to say in any occasion.

However, the constraints of appropriateness are not fixed rules or absolute responsibilities. They are norms of behavior usually established through cultural tradition and social habit. In everyday life, following the dictates of appropriateness as determined by the purposes of the occasion is the easiest way to get our voice heard. Anyone preparing for a job interview quickly realizes the importance of saying the right thing in the right way in order to get what one wants. Yet sometimes norms of appropriateness are so narrow as to be oppressive. In the case of Anthony's trial, for example, she was not allowed even to defend herself, for it was not considered proper at that time for a woman to speak during the formal proceedings. What is considered appropriate might not equate with what we consider ethical or moral. It is simply what is expected. It is up to rhetors to judge whether their conformity to or violation of these constraints helps enable the productive resolution of some larger problem.

Most often, of course, we gather at an occasion for the purpose of feeling a part of a larger community. Ceremonies and celebrations are some of the more enjoyable occasions we attend, for it offers a chance to be inspired, to remember, and to share. One

---

[32]For more on Anthony's significance as a public speaker, see Elaine E. McDavitt, "Susan B. Anthony, Reformer and Speaker," *Quarterly Journal of Speech* 30.2 (1944), 173–180.

such occasion occurred on May 21, 1944, during "I Am an American Day" in New York's Central Park. The purpose of the occasion was to celebrate the ideals of American citizenship and the unified character of a diverse nation enriched by the thousands of immigrants who arrived at its shores. Held when the specter of World War II still loomed over the nation, the keynote speech was delivered by Judge Learned Hand, one of the most distinguished American legal minds of his generation who served as presiding judge of the Second Circuit Court of Appeals from 1939 to 1951. His brief address so captured the spirit of the occasion that the text was quickly printed and put into anthologies. In his introduction he speaks directly to this shared purpose:

> We have gathered here to affirm a faith, a faith in a common purpose, a common conviction, a common devotion. Some of us have chosen America as the land of our adoption; the rest have come from those who did the same. For this reason we have some right to consider ourselves a picked group, a group of those who had the courage to break from the past and brave the dangers and the loneliness of a strange land. What was the object that nerved us, or those who went before us, to this choice? We sought liberty; freedom from oppression, freedom from want, freedom to be ourselves.

By referencing this "common purpose," Judge Hand establishes the common ground on which his audience stands. Many of them immigrants, he unites them in their diversity by citing a general desire for "liberty." Yet he does not simply rest content with reaffirming a preexisting belief. His rhetorical message is that immigrants coming to America should not expect the law or the constitution to automatically guarantee their freedoms. His point is not to distrust the government, but rather to trust the government only insofar as it reflects the genuine spirit of liberty within its people:

> What then is the spirit of liberty? I cannot define it; I can only tell you my own faith. The spirit of liberty is the spirit which is not too sure that it is right; the spirit of liberty is the spirit which seeks to understand the mind of other men and women; the spirit of liberty is the spirit which weighs their interests alongside its own without bias; . . . And now . . . in the spirit of that America for which our young men are at this moment fighting and dying; in that spirit of liberty and of America I ask you to rise and with me pledge our faith in the glorious destiny of our beloved country.[33]

The message of Judge Hand's speech is that the spirit of liberty is found in the ability of fallible citizens to work together in sympathy and trust for a common end. For the thousands of American citizens who had gathered in Central Park to feel part of a common culture, Judge Hand knew enough to speak directly to them rather than praise a distant group of laws, men, Constitutions, institutions, or rights. And this keen attention to the rhetorical foreground also gave his words the energy and life that made it attractive to the publics who occupied the rhetorical background.[34]

Discussion: It is one thing to be a part of an occasion whose purpose is made obvious ahead of time. Going to a baseball game, a graduation, or a cookout has a clear purpose. But sometimes the purposes of an occasion are intentionally unclear, as in the

---

[33]Safire, 271.

[34]For more on Learned Hand, see his biography, Gerald Gunther, *Learned Hand: The Man and the Judge* (Cambridge, MA: Harvard University Press, 1998).

paradigmatic "secret meeting" that only gives a place and time. When have you been a part of an occasion in which people either did not understand the purpose or had very different interpretations of what the purpose was to be? What happened as a result?

Message

Each of the concepts this chapter has examined are ultimately useful in the *art* of rhetoric only in the construction and interpretation of the *message* that is delivered in the context of the rhetorical situation. The **message** in rhetorical public speech is spoken language delivered for the purposes of persuading an audience to think, act, and feel in ways different than it already does. That a rhetorical message must make an audience do this may seem obvious from all that has been said, but it is important to always keep in mind when thinking about what makes rhetorical public speech specifically *rhetorical*.

To learn rhetorical public speech is to learn how to simultaneously challenge and motivate an audience, to make its members both uncomfortable and inspired. For only when we are dissatisfied with where we are do we consider somewhere else, and only when we desire somewhere else do we move away from where we are. The art of rhetorical public speaking in this way is the art of encouraging *movement*, just as democracy represents the deliberative process by which we decide where and how to move. Even an audience that only has its preexisting beliefs and attitudes reinforced still is moved in terms of its degree of commitment and motivation. Without this spirit of movement, a message is not really rhetorical. This is important to consider in developing your own speech as you go. If no one is capable of being moved by your speech, then it does not belong to the category of rhetorical public speaking.

One of the ironies of the word "rhetoric," of course, is that it is often used to refer to the use of pretty sounding, but largely empty, words. What this kind of "mere rhetoric" refers to is actually a kind of discourse designed largely to escape responsibility by making promises that were never meant to be kept. However, this kind of speech is the very antithesis of rhetorical public speech, for it is directed, not toward moving anything, but rather toward evading something. Unfortunately, being able to distinguish between what is and is not genuine rhetorical public speech, designed to honestly make a change in the world, unfortunately cannot be determined simply by looking at a speech in isolation. It must be judged in light of the subsequent actions and speeches by the same rhetor.

It was exactly this lack of commitment to one's words that caused the population of Native Americans to doubt the credibility of American leaders during the period of Westward expansion. One of the most tragic series of events in American history involves the seemingly unending sequences of broken promises by American presidents to guarantee the sovereignty of native lands. This sense of frustration and despair is evident in the words of Chief Joseph, leader of the Nez Perce tribe, delivered in Washington, D.C., after he met with President Rutherford B. Hayes, among others, concerning the plight of his people who had been forced off their lands. His account shows the frustration of having his genuine rhetorical appeals being met with empty promises. He narrates his experience as follows:

> At last I was granted permission to come to Washington and bring my friend
> Yellow Bull and our interpreter with me. I am glad I came. I have shaken hands

with a good many friends, but there are some things I want to know which no one seems able to explain. I cannot understand how the Government sends a man out to fight us, as it did General Miles, and then breaks his word. Such a government has something wrong about it. I cannot understand why so many chiefs are allowed to talk so many different ways, and promise so many different things . . . [T]hey all say they are my friends, and that I shall have justice, but while all their mouths talk right I do not understand why nothing is done for my people.

Chief Joseph then uses a synonym for "mere rhetoric," being the phrase "good words." For Joseph, the American diplomats and generals all spoke very well, but their words became meaningless as soon as they were spoken. He continues:

> I have heard talk and talk but nothing is done. Good words do not last long unless they amount to something. Words do not pay for my dead people. They do not pay for my country now overrun by white men. They do not protect my father's grave. They do not pay for my horses and cattle. Good words do not give me back my children. Good words will not make good the promise of your war chief, General Miles. Good words will not give my people a home where they can live in peace and take care of themselves. I am tired of talk that comes to nothing. It makes my heart sick when I remember all the good words and all the broken promises. There has been too much talking by men who had no right to talk.[35]

What Chief Joseph expresses is not distaste for rhetoric, but a demand for it. He wishes to hear words that people intend as forms of action, as ways of dealing with a problem by altering peoples' beliefs and behaviors. Unfortunately for Joseph, too many constraints, both internal and external, stood in the way of seriously stemming the tide of American expansion, thereby frustrating his own rhetorical efforts to save his people.[36]

Discussion: Give a recent example of a politician or public figure who engaged in "mere rhetoric" and one who actually used rhetoric to promote action. Do you think there are any ways to tell when a rhetor is engaging in one or the other beforehand? In your everyday experience, how can you judge when people are sincere about their words and when they are speaking just to avoid responsibility?

CONCEPT REVIEW

Rhetorical Background		
CONCEPT	DEFINITION	EXAMPLE
THE PUBLIC	A group of people who participate in a common deliberative forum to address shared problems.	"Every American has a responsibility to address the crisis of global warming, for all of our actions affect each other on this earth."

[35]Zinn, 147.

[36]For more on Chief Joseph, see Merrill D. Beal, *I Will Fight No More Forever: Chief Joseph and the Nez Perce War* (Seattle: University of Washington Press, 1966).

THE OPEN SOCIETY	The degree to which any public allows criticism and free inquiry about matters of controversy.	"It is in the spirit of free inquiry that I call for a transparent and sustained debate about our environmental policy. We cannot let back-room deals determine whether our planet lives or dies."
THE PUBLIC SPHERE	A place considered appropriate for discussing and arguing about matters of public interest.	"Perhaps this speech may get drowned out by the latest celebrity gossip on the late news, but I would hope that your reporting of this event will respect the American people enough to put this matter on the public agenda."
STATUS	The relative level of respect that an audience has for any particular way of talking about the world.	"I know that, generally, environmentalism still does not have the authority that economic arguments possess, but we are now seeing environmentalism becoming not a threat to economic growth but its engine."
PUBLIC OPINION	The gauge of what percentage of a public believes certain things to be true or false.	"The old belief that we have to choose between plants and people has given way to the belief that we are more profitable when we care for our world rather than exploit it."
CONVENTION	The reflection of the accepted habits and rituals that relate to a certain issue.	"I understand that we have become accustomed to cheap gas and easy energy. But our habits of consumption do not match the constraints of the new era. We must change lest we perish."
SOCIAL KNOWLEDGE	The "common sense" maxims and morals related to an issue.	"In World War II, we came together as a nation to sacrifice for the common good. Why cannot we harness that same spirit to fight the threat of global climate change?"

Rhetorical Foreground

CONCEPT	DEFINITION	EXAMPLE
EXIGENCE	A shared problem that causes an audience concern and uncertainty.	"The challenge of global warming is real. A scientific consensus has emerged, and now it is time to act before it is too late."
PRACTICAL JUDGMENT	The classification of a problematic issue as a certain "type" of thing that encourages certain practical reactions.	"We were told global warming was just a natural fluctuation of temperature. We were told it was a hoax. But it is real."
AUDIENCE	The people who need to be moved to action and who have the capability of generative change.	"It is up to you, the citizens of this country, to press your representatives to action. They will not do it by themselves."

CONSTRAINTS	The obstacles, both internal and external, which stand in the way of successful resolution.	"We know that there is still doubt about whether it exists. We know that special interests are rallied against action. We know that even if we possess the will, that we still need better technology and enormous financial investment to make the necessary changes."
SPEAKER	The rhetor who advocates a certain position.	"I had once been a skeptic myself. But when fires ravaged by town after years of drought, I could no longer sit still. I must do this as a father for the sake of my children."
OCCASION	The event which brings people together in the same space.	"Thus, we have come on Earth Day to Central Park, this beautiful place of sanctuary...."
PURPOSE	The shared reason for the occasion.	"...to create a common motivation to fight for environmental sustainability and champion the new green economy."
MESSAGE	In rhetoric, a speech which alters people's beliefs, attitudes, or actions.	"Many of you agree with our goals but have yet to invest your time, energy, and money. Yet we must sacrifice to reach our end."

KEY WORDS

Audience 79
Authoritative sphere 66
Authority 66
Closed society 64
Constraints 81
Contested exigence 74
Contingency 60
Conventions 69
Counterpublics 62
Demographics 80
Exigence 73
External constraints 82
Internal constraints 82
Marginality 66

Message 90
Motives of the participants 61
Occasion 85
Open society 63
Opinion 68
Personal sphere 65
Practical judgment 77
Presence 74
Public 62
Public opinion 67
Public sphere 64
Purpose 88
Rhetor 84
Rhetorical background 61

Rhetorical constraints 82
Rhetorical exigence 73
Rhetorical foreground 61
Rhetorical situation 60
Situated audience 79
Social knowledge 69
Speaker 84
State 62
Status 66
Target audience 79
Technical situation 61
Technical sphere 65
Uncontested exigence 74

SUMMARY

Considering the rhetorical background that frames any rhetorical public speech provides a speaker with the broader perspective that is necessary for any sustained effort at persuasion. This perspective not only expands the spatial horizon beyond the immediate physical context, but it also extends the temporal horizon so that it speaks to the past and looks toward the future. For example, simply thinking in terms of a larger

"public" makes even one's immediate audience representatives of a larger social group with a shared history. The concepts of status, public opinion, convention, and social knowledge can then be used to interpret the general characteristics of people—even individuals—insofar as they belong to that social group.

This does not deny a person's individuality by any means; it simply helps place people within the "big picture," which by nature tends to speak in generalities. Concepts like the open society and the public sphere then give instruction about when and where and how one might speak within that society. One must simply remember that the qualities of the rhetorical background should never be taken to represent anything more than convenient and pragmatic shorthand that ultimately proves the worth of those qualities within the successful act of rhetorical persuasion. In the end, all groups and individuals are unique and exceed the capacity for such broad generalizations. But these generalizations are necessary starting points nonetheless, for they help us look beyond the immediate moment and give us perspective. As Roman orator Cicero observed long ago, audience adaptation requires a great deal of labor beyond just adapting to what the members of an audience might be thinking, feeling, and saying in the present:

> We must also read the poets, acquaints ourselves with histories, study and peruse the masters and authors in every excellent art, and by way of practice praise, expound, emend, criticize, and confute them; we must argue every question on both sides, and bring out on every topic whatever points can be deemed plausible; besides this we must become learned in the common law and familiar with the statutes, and must contemplate all the olden time, and investigate the ways of the senate, political philosophy, the rights of

allies, the treaties and conventions, and the policy of empire; and last we have to cull, from all the forms of pleasantry, a certain charm of humor, with which to give a sprinkle of sale, as it were, to all of our discourse.[37]

Although we are far from Ancient Rome, the same principles apply. For example, even the controversy over whether or not to ban cigarettes in public places forces us to consider the *convention* of smoking outside the front door of a building on lunch break, *public opinion* concerning the danger of secondhand smoke, the *status* of the discourse of individual rights over the discourse of the public good, and the *social knowledge* concerning the risks of granting the state the power to regulate personal habits. In addition, one also knows that society is completely *open* to debating issues of smoking, and that *public spheres* concerning this issue often appear over the metaphorical "water coolers" at work. In other words, as any successful speech only emphasizes a handful of themes and examples, once the significant aspects are determined, a speaker can proceed with some degree of confidence that the important bases have been covered.

Let us take a hypothetical example of a speech written on taxing fossil fuels in order to fund green technologies that help the environment. A methodological approach to analyzing the rhetorical background might look like this:

What is the problem at issue?	Whether or not to raise the gas tax in order to raise revenue and encourage conservation
What convention resists change?	American love of cheap gas and big cars
What convention favors change?	American love of the great outdoors
What aspect of public opinion supports a tax?	Fossil fuels are pollutants. They are also running out.
What aspect of public opinion rejects a tax?	Higher prices are bad for the economy.
What ideas, words, or discourses are vying for higher status in this debate?	Regulation vs. Volunteerism / Environmentalism vs. Free Market Forces
What social knowledge supports a tax?	That American ingenuity will develop new solutions once they are given the incentive.
What social knowledge rejects a tax?	The high prices during the 70s oil embargo led to an economic recession.

[37]Cicero, 221.

What marks this analysis as a "background" is that it speaks only to the most general tendencies of the American public. Speaking to a group of environmentalists or oil executives would clearly require more specific adaptation and knowledge. But more general tendencies are, again, important to keep in mind if your speech is to "carry" beyond the immediate occasion. Even if it is never rebroadcast, the members of the audience might refer to your arguments in future conversations of their own. If you do not provide them a language with which to address the attitudes of the "average" American, you will limit your influence to a small group of people. This may be satisfactory if all you wish to influence is oil executives. But usually citizens are in the business of persuading other citizens. And this persuasion takes something more than a single speech delivered in a closed boardroom. As the environmental movement over the past century has proven, instigating social change usually requires a sustained effort across many different occasions and contexts.

However, the more significant challenge for any rhetor who seeks lasting social change is to be able to address the *unique* and *pressing* character of the problem in the *present*. The considerations of the rhetorical foreground thus link us to the concrete characteristics of our present surroundings that help balance the more universal characteristics of our larger social and historical environment. Attention to exigence, practical judgment, audience, constraints, speaker, occasion, purpose, and message gives a speech its energy and life. Whereas the rhetorical background helps to identify the general aspects of a somewhat generic American audience, the rhetorical foreground puts us in a specific place and time. Imagine, for example, that this speech will be made (as most of your speeches will be made) to an audience of university students in a classroom setting. These are some possible starting considerations of the rhetorical foreground:

Who is the audience for the speech?	University students mostly between ages 19 and 25, many of whom own cars and many of whom work to help pay their way through college
What are the exigencies at issue?	The future health of the environment that students will inherit / The need to spur ingenuity in the economy to compete with foreign auto makers / The rising gas prices that students can't afford
What are some constraints to imposing a gas tax?	Reluctance on part of lawmakers to raise taxes / Unwillingness of cash-strapped students to pay now for unknown future benefits / The idealistic belief that ingenuity should not be forced from above / The lack of clear alternative fuels or technologies
What is the occasion for the speech?	A public speaking classroom
What is the purpose of the occasion?	To present and hear public speeches from members of the class for a grade
Who is the speaker?	One of the class members who has chosen a topic he/she cares about
What is the message?	To persuade other students to overcome resistance to taxes in order to promote the greater good
What practical judgment is required?	That tax policy is a progressive means toward achieving a healthy environment

The above list of foreground characteristics is thus actually far from complete, as it consists only of the most generic qualities that are usually unique to public speaking classes. Giving it more life is contingent upon the student's analysis of his or her own class. Many times, for instance, public-speaking classes are restricted to certain majors, like engineers or nurses or business majors. Other times, classes are all men, or all women, or have a higher or lower average age than others. And any university will generally be filled with students who share a common experience growing up in the state or city in which the university is situated. In any case, it is always more beneficial to adapt to the audience that is actually present rather than a fictional one.

Let us return to Dr. King's speech at Holt Street Baptist Church to examine how he highlights aspects of the rhetorical background and foreground to give energy and focus to a speech that might have otherwise spoken in vague generalities about the fight for civil rights. In terms of considering the rhetorical background, King first knew that the very cause of the controversy surrounded the propriety of the **convention** that black citizens had to sit in the back of the bus. Second, he recognized his speech would carry to wider **publics** well beyond the thousands of people who had come to hear it. Americans across the country might read about it in their newspapers. Third, he chose a Baptist church to function as a **public sphere**, drawing on the traditions of the African-American church that often freely addressed social and political issues. Fourth, he understood the competing **status** between the discourses of militancy and nonviolence. Fifth, he sought to emphasize the **social knowledge** derived from the Christian tradition of "loving thy enemy" in order to promote nonviolence as a method of social change. Sixth, he knew that if violence occurred, American **public opinion** would immediately turn against their cause. With these issues in mind, he proceeded with the speech, beginning with these words:

My friends, we are certainly very happy to see each of you out this evening. We are here this evening for serious business. We are here in a general sense because first and foremost we are American citizens and we are determined to apply our citizenship to the fullness of its meaning. We are here also because of our love for democracy, because of our deep-seated belief that democracy transformed from thin paper to thick action is the greatest form of government on Earth.

What is striking about King's words is their sheer generality. Despite all the energy and intensity of the moment that would encourage a speaker not only to address the specifics of the bus boycott and of racial segregation and division, but also to emphasize the specific and unique qualities of the public gathered together in that space, King addresses members of the audience in their most abstract form—as "American citizens." In effect, King speaks to them not as people distinct or different *from* the general public, but as representatives *of* that public. By doing this, he appeals to the most deep-seated social knowledge to which all Americans tend to profess—that democracy when enacted by its citizens represents the greatest form of government on Earth. This does not require that statement to be empirically true in fact; for rhetorical persuasion, it only requires that a public generally holds this statement to reflect a shared commitment to certain values and goals.

What makes King's words so powerful and lasting, therefore, was that he recognized the importance of understanding his specific speech in the context of the larger rhetorical background that would ultimately determine the success or failure of the civil rights movement. By doing so, he helped bring that social knowledge about democracy one step closer to actual fruition in practice. Yet, of course, King and his audience were also there for a more particular reason accounted for by the nature of the rhetorical foreground. He continues:

But we are here in a specific sense, because of the bus situation in Montgomery. We are here because we are to get the situation corrected. This situation is not at all new. The problem has existed over endless years. For many years now Negroes in Montgomery and so many other areas have been inflicted with the paralysis of crippling fears on buses in our community. On so many occasions, Negroes have been intimidated and humiliated and impressed—oppressed—because of the sheer fact that they were Negroes. I don't have time this evening to go into the history of these numerous cases. Many of them now are lost in the thick fog of oblivion, but at least one stands before us now with glaring dimensions.

The reference to the bus boycott represents the specific exigence that concerned his audience of African-American citizens enough to organize an occasion at Holt Street Baptist Church to pursue their common purpose. But King also notes that this specific exigence is simply one manifestation of the larger oppression that has existed in the rhetorical background for years. What, then, made the issue of segregation on the busses take center stage? King explains:

> Just the other day, just last Thursday to be exact, one of the finest citizens in Montgomery—not one of the finest Negro citizens but one of the finest citizens in Montgomery—was taken from a bus and carried to jail and arrested because she refused to get up to give her seat to a white person . . . Mrs. Rosa Parks is a fine person. And since it had to happen I'm happy that it happened to a person like Mrs. Parks, for nobody can doubt the boundless outreach of her integrity. Nobody can doubt the height of her character, nobody can doubt the depth of her Christian commitment and devotion to the teachings of Jesus. And I'm happy since it had to happen, it happened to a person that nobody can call a disturbing factor in the community. Mrs. Parks is a fine Christian person, unassuming, and yet there is integrity and character there. And just because she refused to get up, she was arrested.

Despite the fact that King denies that Rosa Parks is a "disturbing factor in the community" due to her Christian devotion, it was the action of Rosa Parks that functioned as the "disturbance" which sparked the bus boycott. Her specific act of civil disobedience, and the subsequent overreaction by the authorities, embodied the problem of racial oppression so acutely that it could no longer be tolerated. By pulling her into the foreground in his speech, then, King speaks to the specific qualities of the exigence that gives it a dramatic character; at the same time, however, King still remains focused on the larger problems of civil rights that this problem represents. Note how he already is looking forward from the perspective of the future concerning the legacy of their act of civil protest in the face of oppression:

> As we stand and sit here this evening and as we prepare ourselves for what lies ahead, let us go out with a grim and bold determination that we are going to stick together. We are going to work together. Right here in Montgomery, when the history books are written in the future, somebody will have to say, "There lived a race of people, a *black* people, 'fleecy locks and black complexion,' a people who had the moral courage to stand up for their rights. And thereby they injected a new meaning into the veins of history and of civilization." And we're gonna do that. God grant that we will do it before it is too late.

One might distinguish between the rhetorical foreground and rhetorical background simply by saying that they represent the same moment as seen up close and from a distance. The rhetorical foreground represents a more proximate space and a shorter frame of time, whereas the rhetorical background looks to broader horizons in both space and time. In other words, the rhetorical foreground attends to the problem of the bus boycott in Montgomery in 1955; the rhetorical background attends to the problem of civil rights in America in the 20th century. These should be thought of as two ends of the same spectrum, however. Again, the challenge for any rhetor is to be able to move fluidly along that spectrum, always keeping both ends in mind in any rhetorical act.

CHAPTER 3 EXERCISES

1. Analyze your rhetorical artifact according to the table provided in the summary.

2. Identify a convention in your immediate environment that annoys you. Explain why it bothers you in terms of its consequences. Then violate this convention. Explain what happens and how you feel.

3. As a class, come up with a major historical event in the nation's history. Have everyone privately draw a historical lesson from this event and present it as a brief commemorative speech. How are these lessons the same or different?

4. Find an actual written text or speech created by what you would consider a "marginal" group. Read out this text loudly in class and discuss why you think it is marginalized. Do you think its marginalization is justified?

5. Find an example of a public statement made by a public figure that was interpreted as inappropriately "crossing spheres" in the sense of employing the discourse of one sphere (i.e., private, public, technical, authoritarian) within the discourse of another. What were the consequences of this action?

6. Bring in a common object that has no mysterious or controversial aspects (e.g., a fork, a rock, a hat). Then make a new practical judgment about this object (however hypothetical or fanciful) in front of the class in order to make them approach it differently in the future.

7. Remember a time you experienced a "contingency" as a child. (This does not have to be rhetorical.) Tell the story of your experience, trying to make it as vivid as possible so that your audience feels what you felt. The purpose here is to try to embody the *feeling* of contingency.

8. Find a print advertisement for some product. Who do you think is the target audience? What cues point you to this conclusion?

9. Like the examples in the book, think of an exigence that can take different forms according to the situation. Describe your exigence as a personal problem, a public problem, and a rhetorical problem. What factors determine it to be one or the other type of problem?

10. Invent a new "crisis" that might face your community or the country as a rhetorical exigence. What would be the constraints to resolving this exigence rhetorically? Then create a short impromptu speech proposing a solution.

11. Think of an "occasion" with which you are very familiar and which recurs frequently. What are the rules and expectations (in terms of communication) at such an occasion? Can you think of a time when such things were violated? What were the consequences?

12. Recall an experience when somebody unexpectedly tried to persuade you with a particular "message" during a conversation. How did you feel when you realized you were not simply engaging in friendly banter? How did you react?

Persuasion and Motivation

The previous chapter dealt with external aspects of a rhetorical situation—the people, objects, processes, and events that constitute a situation that makes people amenable to being persuaded. The purpose of that chapter was to encourage public speakers to look beyond the confines of their immediate context and direct their words toward shared problems and future possibilities. This chapter deals with internal aspects of a rhetorical audience—the psychological processes and motivational influences that guide people's attention, interest, and decisions. These include belief, reason, value, feeling, emotion, memory, imagination, and attitude. If the first two chapters provide ways of identifying the subject matter and purpose of a speech, this chapter identifies the psychological substance that a speaker must later form by means of ethos, logos, pathos, and style.

The most successful rhetor is one who not only draws on the knowledge of the rhetorical background and foreground, but who also uses that knowledge to understand the possible motives of a public audience. This understanding can then be used in developing a message that channels his or her latent or preexisting motivations toward a common end. For example, Dr. King developed his speech at Holt Street Baptist Church knowing that he would be speaking to an audience highly motivated to seek an end of racial justice and equality in Montgomery. He also knew, however, that a high percentage of his audience might have been motivated to pursue violent means to pursue this end. His challenge was to channel the desire for justice while suppressing and/or transforming the natural impulse to fight fire with fire. His creative rhetorical solution was to advocate for nonviolent acts of civil disobedience that allowed for resistance without destruction.

When talking about the motives of an audience, it is important not to think of a motive or motivation as something purely subjective, cognitive, and internal. Often, we think of motives as something "inside" of us that only occasionally finds expression in words or deeds. Yet the reality is, we cannot have a motive apart from a situation that calls us to act and make a choice. A **motive** refers to the interests, impulses, habits, conventions, and desires that function as incitements to action within particular situations. The most important aspect of this definition is the fact that motives are situational characteristics which include the relationship between situation and actor.[1]

---

[1]For an explanation of Burke's theory of motive, see Andrew King, "Motive," *American Communication Journal* 1, no. 3 (1998).

For example, most people try to obey the law and live a respectable life by following the rules. Perhaps they have developed a habit of returning lost items, thus providing a motive that gives them satisfaction. Yet have them stumble across a wallet full of money, and they suddenly find themselves in moral conflict. The motive to do the "right thing" and turn the money into the police now has competition with the motive to take the money for oneself. If this decision appears easy in the abstract, put yourself in this situation with two more situational details: the fact that you know the man who dropped the wallet is a despicable character, and the fact that you just lost your job and can't afford Christmas presents for your two children. Now the motivation to keep the money is not driven by selfish greed, but by a combination of wanting to punish an enemy and reward your family.

We can easily perceive how situations in which there is a clash of competing motives easily become rhetorical situations. In the case of the wallet, simply add the presence of other friends with different opinions to the situation and you now have what is, in effect, a rhetorical situation in microcosm. By contrast, if the person who finds the wallet has no need of money and finds pleasure in "doing the right thing," then there is no real motivation to keep the money and hence no reason to debate about what to do. The only debate concerns the method of how the wallet should be returned.

Rhetors entering into rhetorical situations must first identify what motivations are at odds with one another and then decide which motives to bolster and which ones to suppress. In the case of the wallet, one friend wishing you to keep the money would amplify your sense of duty to your children while diminishing your sense of guilt on stealing the money. Another friend, believing you should return it, might diminish the short-term gain of buying Christmas presents while amplifying the long-term sense of guilt on allowing personal desires to license a criminal act. In both cases, the persuasive method of the rhetor is the same:

1. Examine all the possible motivations at work in a situation.
2. Focus on those motives that are most likely to influence a decision either way.
3. Decide which motives to amplify and which motives to diminish in order to move someone toward a preferred action and move away from others.

Amplification exaggerates something, makes it "larger than life," and forces it to stand out as important and significant. Likewise, **diminution** reduces something, pushes it into the background, and makes it insignificant and trivial. It is important to observe, however, that amplification does not necessarily make something "good," nor does diminution make something "bad." After all, any time one seeks to rally energy against a common threat, this threat must be amplified as something evil and worth confronting ("This will be the mother of all battles against the Great Satan."). By contrast, to practice humility in the face of praise is to diminish what is widely respected as a good and virtuous ("I am no hero. I am just following the values of the nation."). Whether something is great or small stands not for its worth but for how much attention we call to it when making a decision.

Motivation became subject matter of *philosophical* interest with the Greeks when rhetors began making careful observations of how different audiences reacted to different forms of language. This philosophical study matured with Aristotle when he distinguished between appeals to ethos, pathos, and logos. For

Aristotle, audiences were motivated by respect for the speaker (**ethos**), by emotional affection or dislike (**pathos**), and by the strength of reason and evidence (**logos**). This study of motivation then took a "scientific" leap during the Age of Enlightenment when the new study of psychology was used to explain the phenomenon of persuasion. Rhetorician George Campbell, for example, wrote that the function of rhetoric is "to enlighten the Understanding, to please the Imagination, to move the Passions, or to influence the Will." The novelty behind this definition was the application of the recently discovered mental "faculties" to the study of rhetoric. Much like different departments within a modern corporation, these faculties existed in our minds as discrete units, each with their unique process and function. So when we wanted to think about ideas, we called on the Understanding (sometimes called Thought or Reason); when we felt like stimulating our body, we sought out the Passions (sometimes called Emotions or Feeling); when we pondered the unknown, we appealed to the Imagination; and when we wanted to act, we rallied the Will. The most successful rhetoric engaged all the faculties at once. We argued logic to the Understanding, aroused the Passions through visual examples, used fantastic possibilities to excite the Imagination, and moved the Will through imperatives to action.

Modern psychology has complicated this tidy picture so that not much remains of these mythical "faculties" in the specialized discourses of contemporary science. Nonetheless, there is a certain intuitive appeal and practical function of thinking in these terms when they are used as *actions* rather than *things*. Entities called the Understanding, the Passions, the Imagination, and the Will may not exist, but we still *think, feel, wonder,* and *act*. As such, there is still valuable truth in these early treatises in rhetoric such that their advice remains largely applicable—the successful rhetor should appeal to *all* of our motivations as they actually exist, not just the one he or she arbitrarily declares to be the best. To adopt any other approach is to simply speak to the empty air.

The concepts in this chapter—belief, reason, value, feeling, emotion, imagination, and attitude—will provide a framework to help provide a more complex and concrete representation of an audience or public in order to assist in motivating them to action. Clearly, there is an enormous ethical responsibility on the part of the speaker who employs such motivational tools. When people's motivations are directed toward goals that serve primarily the self-interest of the speaker at the expense of the audience, we call such persuasion **manipulation**. This is the kind of persuasion in which one promises the moon, only to send someone off with a bag of useless rocks. Yet, as many of our examples show, the study of motivation has also produced some of the greatest and most inspirational works of art. The ethical ideal that guides the art of rhetoric is to motivate an audience to seek out and strive for a higher good than it may have naturally sought on its own.

BELIEF

Nothing is easier than starting an argument with someone. All one needs to do is contradict someone else's stated belief on an issue that the other person cares about. It doesn't even matter if one actually knows anything about the issue, because disagreement simply requires turning a "yes" into a "no" or vice versa. In other words, the reason why issues of belief are usually the causes of rhetorical argument is because beliefs are so clearly formulated and expressed in statements of fact that can be easily communicated and therefore easily refuted. Take the following statements of belief, for instance:

> *God exists.*
> *The United States is a model democracy.*
> *Dogs make better pets than cats.*
> *Slavery is evil.*
> *Drinking water makes for healthy joints.*
> *My mother is an excellent cook.*
> *You look attractive dressed in black.*
> *Homosexuality is a private choice.*
> *Abortion is murder.*
> *Guinness is good for you.*

All of these are **beliefs** because they represent logical relationships between specific things and more general ideas. For example, "Dogs make better pets than cats" is a belief because it associates a thing (dogs) with a general idea (good pets). The sheer simplicity of this formulation makes it easy to grasp and, therefore, easy to respond to without a great deal of reflective thought. To start an argument, then, one need only reject that belief ("Dogs *do not* make good pets") or challenge it with an opposite belief ("*Cats* make *better* pets than dogs."). Once this clash of beliefs is established, argument begins.

Why do we react so quickly and defensively to such challenges to our beliefs? Why should I care whether or not another person feels the same way I do about cats and dogs? One major reason is that our beliefs represent more than isolated bits of information that we store in our brain; our beliefs form the basic components of our understanding about our world. As we mature, we constantly accumulate more and more associations that function as building blocks of cognition which help us build a larger and more complex framework of meaning. This belief structure is often referred to as an **ideology**, defined here neutrally as simply a network of interlocking beliefs that provide a comprehensive interpretation of one's world.[2] This belief structure serves an important function—it provides us stability that helps provide us comfort and security in an uncertain world. A belief in the superiority of dogs as pets justifies someone living in a house with five of them and exhausting a great deal of physical and emotional energy to take care of them. Refute that belief in dogs, and suddenly all that effort seems wasted.

Of course, not all beliefs are created equal. If our belief structure represents a kind of house in which we live, some material is *stronger* than others (i.e., "all humans are mortal" is a stronger belief than "I will live until 90"), certain bricks *corrode* and need to be *replaced* (i.e., "cigarettes are harmless" is replaced by "cigarettes are carcinogens"), and sometimes a whole structure needs to be *torn down*

---

[2]*Ideology* also has a more negative definition as a false or misleading discourse used to control and manipulate a population. This textbook uses the neutral definition for lack of a better term to refer to a coherent set of beliefs that guide practical behaviors.

(e.g., "the world is flat") or *added* (e.g., "we now have the power to destroy all life on earth"). Following this metaphor, much of our process of learning, curiosity, doubt, reflection, and criticism is based on our efforts to make our belief structure more complex, stable, beautiful, and practical.

Beliefs can be characterized by four things: existence, weight, salience, and valence. **Existence** refers to the fact that a person holds a belief about something. For example, it would be impossible for a young child to have a belief about global warming. He or she might be able to repeat a phrase overheard from a parent but would not actually be able to *act on* or *explain* that phrase. The point is that a belief only exists when it has *practical meaning* for a person and can be applied in some situation. **Weight** is how much credibility we give to certain beliefs. For example, we all give great weight to the fact that human beings are mortal, but agnostics will give little weight to assertions about the existence of an afterlife because they don't think it can be shown to exist, one way or the other. **Salience** describes how strongly we feel about a belief compared to other beliefs, particularly in certain situations. For example, during a hurricane, my belief that the safety of my family is the most important thing in my life is more salient than my belief that red wine is good for my heart. Lastly, **valence** describes how well a certain belief fits into my larger worldview or ideology. For a Catholic, the belief that the Pope is an authority on biblical scripture has a "positive" valence, whereas for a Lutheran, that same belief has a highly "negative" valence. In other words, valence describes (and, more importantly, *predicts*) whether or not a particular belief plays well with your other beliefs.[3]

Predictably, when another person tries to shake this structure or knock out some of its supporting material, we naturally resist. If we have lived our lives believing certain things to be true, it literally disrupts our world to find those beliefs to be wrong. This is because the opposite of belief is **doubt**, and as Charles Sanders Peirce long ago pointed out, the feeling of doubt is unpleasant. He explains:

> Doubt is an uneasy and dissatisfied state from which we struggle to free ourselves and pass into the state of belief; while the latter is a calm and satisfactory state which we do not wish to avoid, or to change to a belief in anything else. On the contrary, we cling tenaciously, not merely to believing, but to believing just what we do believe. Thus both doubt and belief have positive effects on us, thought very different ones. Belief does not make us act at once, but puts us into such a condition that we shall behave in a certain way, when the occasion arises. Doubt has not the least effect of this sort, but stimulates us to action until it is destroyed.[4]

The reason every new generation is typically more willing to question traditional beliefs is simply because it has not yet built a stable belief structure—hence it has nothing to sacrifice. The rest of the population, however, may have much to lose by altering even the smallest belief, even if it happens to be wrong.

---

[3]See Martin Fishbein and Icek Ajzen, *Belief, Attitude, Intention, and Behavior* (Reading, MA: Addison-Wesley, 1975); Daniel J. O'Keefe, *Persuasion: Theory Research*, 2nd ed. (Thousand Oaks, CA: Sage, 2002).

[4]Charles Sanders Peirce, "The Fixation of Belief," *The Philosophy of Peirce: Selected Writings*, ed. Justus Buchler (New York: Harcourt, Brace, and Co., 1950).

Because nothing we consciously do is wholly detached from our belief structure, all rhetorical disputes necessarily involve some controversy over belief. Any rhetor stepping into a controversy must therefore be cognizant of all the relevant beliefs that might be associated with any particular problem or issue. A debate about whether sexual preferences are wholly "private" affairs, for instance, is also tied up with whether or not one believes that homosexuality is genetic, whether "God" condemns it, whether the homosexual "lifestyle" is harmful, or whether sexual preference falls under the category of a civil right. Any single belief is thus like a doorway to a mansion with many different rooms. It is easy to walk in the door, but if one doesn't wish to get lost, it is important to know ahead of time the many corridors and rooms that one might stumble into during the course of his or her stay.

Let us take the somewhat counterintuitive belief, "War is the health of the State." This belief was advanced by social critic Randolph Bourne during the period of the World War I. While many of his intellectual friends flocked to support American use of force to help win the war for democracy, Bourne remained steadfastly opposed to war as a method of resolving political disputes. He argued, to the contrary, that war ultimately functioned as a means of social control that undermined the democratic spirit. In his essay "The State," which was left unfinished at his untimely death in 1918, Bourne articulates his belief that even a war for democracy ends up supporting the elements of the state that are wholly undemocratic. He writes:

> War is the health of the State. It automatically sets in motion throughout society those irresistible forces for uniformity, for passionate cooperation with the Government in coercing into obedience the minority groups and individuals who lack the larger herd sense. The machinery of government sets and enforces the drastic penalties; the minorities are either intimidated into silence, or brought slowly around by a subtle process of persuasion which may seem to them really to be converting them.[5]

By "the State," Bourne does not mean a whole society, civilization, or nation; he also does not mean a "democratic" state. He means the formal institutions of governance that are manipulated by those already in power. How is war then "healthy" for the State? It provides the sense of crisis that justifies means of coercion and suppression (whether by force or propaganda) which would otherwise be resisted in times of relative peace and stability. In other words, war licenses the transformation of an open society into a closed society in the name of self-preservation and necessity. Yet this effort is never wholly completed, precisely because people's individual beliefs are never easy to change overnight. Bourne continues:

> Of course, the ideal of perfect loyalty, perfect uniformity is never really attained. The classes upon whom the amateur work of coercion falls are unwearied in their zeal, but often their agitation instead of converting, merely serves to stiffen their

---

[5]Howard Zinn and Anthony Arnove, *Voices of a People's History of the United States* (New York: Seven Stories Press, 2004), 298.

resistance. Minorities are rendered sullen, and some intellectual opinion bitter and satirical.[6]

In other words, those who disagree with the State often still remain in disagreement. In effect, they attribute a low weight and negative valence to the claims made by State officials. Indeed, their resistance to State beliefs often becomes even stronger. But because free expression is limited, this resistance often is not heard in the public sphere. It either festers in silence or finds outlet in "underground" expression that rarely reaches more than a small audience. Thus, despite being in opposition to State beliefs, the salience of the issue diminishes as people realize they are powerless to change anything. Therefore, the attainment of at least a superficial uniformity is still achieved if only by people giving up and remaining silent. He concludes:

> But in general, the nation in wartime attains a uniformity of feeling, a hierarchy of values culminating at the undisputed apex of the State ideal, which could not possibly be produced through any other agency than war. Loyalty—or mystic devotion to the State—becomes the major imagined human value. Other values, such as artistic creation, knowledge, reason, beauty, the enhancement of life, are instantly and almost unanimously sacrificed, and the significant classes who have constituted themselves the amateur agents of the State are engaged not only in sacrificing these values for themselves but in coercing all other persons into sacrificing them.[7]

The nature of *values* will be discussed in the following pages; but what is significant about Bourne's argument with respect to belief is the idea of producing an ideological "hierarchy" that, like a pyramid, produces a fixed structure of beliefs that are all interconnected and supportive of the aims of the State. War, in other words, encourages people to construct and adopt belief systems (thereby giving them existence) to which they all attribute the same weight, salience, and valence.[8]

Discussion: Take any common belief that almost everyone thinks is obvious—for instance, "The sun is a star" or "Human beings are mortal" or "This pencil is yellow." Now challenge that belief. In defending its "truth," how many other beliefs are connected to that fact that you then have to modify? When do you reach a point where you can no longer defend your claim?

REASON

If beliefs represent the building blocks of our frameworks of understanding, reasoning represents the process by which we arrange and rearrange those blocks in order to make a better structure. From the perspective of reason, rhetoric means

---

[6]Ibid.

[7]Ibid.

[8]For more on Bourne, see Casey Nelson Blake, *Beloved Community: The Cultural Criticism of Randolph Bourne, Van Wyck Brooks, Waldo Frank Lewis Mumford* (Chapel Hill: University of North Carolina Press, 1990).

more than the act of attacking or advocating some belief in the assumption that persuasion will happen automatically. Any change in belief requires the rebuilding and repair of a whole belief structure (or ideology), which means that rhetors should be careful to make such reconstructions as easy and fluid as possible. It is not enough to tell someone that he or she needs to knock out a wall and put in a bay window. One also needs to provide the materials and methods to assist in the hard work of rebuilding.

Reason is the capacity to manipulate symbols for the purposes of creating practical frameworks of belief. We thus employ reason whenever we are "rebuilding" our ideological belief structures in some way. Reason tells us what to keep, what to take away, what to add, and how to add it. To possess reason is thus different from possessing intelligence. **Intelligence** is possessed by any animal with the capacity to "size up" a situation and act skillfully in order to accomplish some immediate goal. Many animals are highly intelligent and can solve many complex situational problems. One only has to watch a seeing-eye dog crossing a busy street or a chimpanzee using tools to get ants out of a hole in order to respect the intelligence in the animal world. But solving immediate problems using physical tools is different than solving abstract problems using conceptual tools. Dogs can cross the street, but they cannot design better streets. Chimpanzees can find ways to eat ants, but they cannot study entomology. Reason signifies this ability to address far-reaching problems by consulting and revising our symbolic "maps" that guide our actions.

The meaning and significance of "reason" changed dramatically over the course of the Classical Greek experience. For the Sophists, reason was connected with logos, or argument, and was concerned with the critical use of thought and language to resolve practical problems. Training in reason thus focused on the practice of **dissoi logoi**, or "double argument," which in effect was like debate training for lawyers. Students would learn to argue both sides of a case in order to see an issue from every angle so as not to be "tripped up" by an opponent. Success in reasoning thus amounted to a competitive victory. Plato naturally found this practical interpretation of reason offensive. For him, reason was not a tool; it was that part of the soul in charge of controlling the appetites and directing the spirit toward the good life. Finally, Aristotle had a scientific view of reason that advocated inquiry into empirical facts that could then guide practical judgment. In sum, for the Sophists, reason was a lawyer's competitive muscle; for Plato, reason was a priest's moral guide; for Aristotle, reason was a scientist's tool of measurement.

All agreed, however, that reason was a skill that needed to be cultivated. Although they all identified the potential for reason as an inherent component of human nature, they also acknowledged that all people don't reason in the same way with the same frequency about the same things. Today, we determine a person's capacity to reason in a specific situation by the presence of *motivation* and *ability*. First, we engage in serious reasoning only when some exigence motivates us to modify some part of our system of belief. Consequently, insofar as we can get through our lives applying our preexisting beliefs and performing our habits, we have little imperative to reason about anything. This does not mean we don't "think"; it only means that we don't seriously challenge and transform our structure of belief to accommodate a new problem. The *frequency* of our reasoning is thus related to how often situations demand that we do so. Second, although we all have the capacity to reason, our actual ability to reason is partly a product of conscious art. Like learning how to solve a puzzle, the ability to reason is enhanced through the practice, skill, and training we often get through formal education. Generally speaking, the higher level of education an audience has received, the easier it will be for that audience to follow a long and complex train of reasoning.[9]

An ideal audience, then, is that who has both the *motivation* and the *ability* to resolve a shared problem by transforming some aspects of its belief structure through the sometimes difficult process of reason. In such a case, rhetors have both a captive and an attentive audience. However, most audiences are not this ideal. On the one hand, audiences may be motivated to solve a problem but are impatient for a solution and/or unable to sit through a long treatise. On the other hand, members of an audience may have the ability to use reason but are in a situation in which they lack or are uninterested in a problem and prefer to occupy their energies in a different way.

A sensitive public speaker will always be prepared to overcome these internal constraints to persuasion. If an audience possesses ability but lacks motivation, then a good deal of the speech will involve making the subject appear interesting to audience members' lives and relevant to their interests. If an audience lacks ability but possesses motivation, then more attention will be paid to visualizing the issues using examples and concrete words that highlight the main points without getting bogged down in details. And if an audience lacks both, then a rhetor has probably done something wrong in selecting an appropriate topic for the occasion.

Historically, one issue that inevitably motivates an entire nation to reason is the choice of whether or not to declare independence from some larger state authority. The prospect of revolution affects almost every belief that guides people's lives because revolution inevitably culminates in a war that disrupts almost everything stable they have come to know—including their very identity. It should come as no surprise, then, that even the American Revolution was preceded by a lively public debate about the wisdom of such an act. On the side of the Loyalists, who sought to retain connection with Britain was William Smith who wrote a series of newspaper letters "To the People of Pennsylvania" using the name "Cato," referring to a figure from Roman history who had defended the Republic against Julius Caesar. In the third of these letters published on March 23, 1776, in *The Pennsylvania Ledger,* Smith defends the following position:

> I have, in my second letter, freely declared by political creed, viz.—"That the true interest of America lies in reconciliation with Great Britain, upon Constitutional Principles, and that I wish it upon none else." I now proceed to give my reasons for this declaration. It is fit, in so great a question, that you should weigh both sides well, and exercise the good sense for which the inhabitants of these Colonies

---

[9]The use of "reason" here equates with what is known as the "central processing route" within the Elaboration Likelihood Theory. For more on this, see Richard Petty and John Cacioppo, *Communication and Persuasion: Central and Peripheral Routes to Attitude Change* (New York: Springer-Verlag, 1986).

have been hitherto distinguished, and then I shall be under no apprehensions concerning the pernicious, though specious plans, which are every day published in our news papers and pamphlets.[10]

An obvious part of Smith's persuasive strategy here is to praise the reasonableness of his audience. He does this for three purposes: (1) to create a sense of goodwill; (2) to warrant the airing of both sides of an issue; and (3) to imply that it will prove its rational character once they consent to his superior reasoning in the fact of his "specious" competition. Smith states the risks of following this method of reason:

> The people generally judge right, when the whole truth is plainly laid before them; but through inattention in some, and fondness for novelty in others, when but one side of a proposition is agitated and persevered in, they may gradually deceive themselves, and adopt what cooler reflection and future dear-bought experience may prove to be ruinous.[11]

The sentiment expressed here by Smith ironically coincides with that written by Paine in "Common Sense." Both men acknowledge that when all sides are not heard (as in a closed society), people eventually come to accept the common view largely out of habit. Also, both men hope that the ability to engage in rational reflection, allowing one to "step back" and get a broader view of things, will help to avoid disaster and achieve progress. So what kind of perspective might be gained by stepping back with Smith? He paints the following picture by drawing out the rational consequences of proclaiming revolution before America has proven to the world that independence is warranted:

> We could neither hope for *Union* nor *Success* in the attempt. We must be considered as a faithless people in the sight of all mankind, and could scarcely expect the confidence of any nation upon earth to look up to heaven for its approving sentence. On the contrary, every convulsion attendant upon revolutions and innovations of government, untimely attempted or finally defeated, might be our portion; added to the loss of trade for want of protection; the consequent decay of husbandry, bloodshed and desolation; with an exchange of the easy and flourishing conditions of farmers and merchants, for a life, at best of hardy poverty as *soldiers* or *hunters*.[12]

For those eager revolutionaries reading Smith's pamphlet, the author's challenge is to replace the belief that revolution will bring Union and Success with the belief that war will produce bloodshed and desolation (thereby changing the latter from a negative to a positive valence while giving it greater weight and salience). To do so, Smith carefully diagnoses the present condition and constructs a vision of a potentially disastrous future. Reason thus represents the process of transforming our belief structure to help us better navigate the terrain of a future environment.

---

[10]Ronald Reid and James Klumpp, *American Rhetorical Discourse* (Long Grove, IL: Waveland Press, 2005), 131.

[11]Ibid.

[12]Ibid.

Discussion: Often the superficial source of a disagreement (like the superiority of cats over dogs, or vice versa) is actually about some other unspoken belief. For instance, if one believes that dog owners are more honest than cat owners, or that cat owners are more sensitive than dog owners, then the argument is really not about which *pet* is better but about which *person* is better for owning a particular pet. What petty disagreement have you had that, after rational reflection, you realized was really about something else entirely?

VALUE

If beliefs and reason represent the materials for and the method of building a structure of belief, values represent the guiding ideals that those structures are supposed to embody or represent. Take for example, the values of beauty, truth, virtue, courage, justice, love, knowledge, and pleasure. Now think of literal buildings or institutions that we associate with these values. You probably thought of some of the following (in no particular order): churches, museums, courts, laboratories, universities, bars, military academies, and the family home. The fact of our ready association with buildings with certain values demonstrates the "ideal" nature of a value. As opposed to belief, which always deals with a relationship of fact, values are almost never true or false. Rather, values are either present or not present. Love is present when a mother hugs her child and courage is present when she fights for her.

Values, in other words, stand for stable ideals that give structure to our beliefs and guide our behavior across a variety of situations. For example, we establish our relationships on the basis of love and loyalty, our careers on the basis of professionalism and competence, and our communities on the basis of justice and freedom. These values then function as a common reference point for us to gauge whether or not our activities and beliefs are "living up to" our values. Is ours a *loving* relationship? A *just* society? A *virtuous* faith? Whenever we think consciously about values, we tend to think in these general terms that ask us to examine all our actions as a whole and judge whether or not they have met an acceptable standard.[13]

We often think values play one of two functions in rhetoric. Rhetors appeal to *positive* values that act as goals toward which we aspire (e.g., "We shall seek liberty") while using *negative* values to repel us from certain actions or beliefs (e.g., "Do not follow the path of evil"). This strategy (which we will later examine as a form of polarization) is supposed to help us avoid temptation and seek the path of righteousness. However, this is a somewhat simplistic way of using values, because most people do not view themselves as ever following a path of evil. Consequently, telling a crowd to seek the good and avoid the bad is thus usually interpreted as saying, "Keep doing what you are already doing." A thief who steals from the rich, for instance, may not see himself as a thief, but as a moral agent of social justice in the manner of Robin Hood. So on encountering a rhetor preaching righteousness, this thief would emerge feeling quite content that he or she is seeking exactly that.

One should thus think of values in rhetoric not in terms of aiding in a struggle of good against evil, but rather as *helping to choose between two opposing goods*. In

---

[13]For more on values, see Milton Rokeach, *Understanding Human Values* (New York: Free Press, 1979); Nicholas Rescher, "The Study of Value Change," *Journal of Value Inquiry* 1 (1967): 12–23.

fact, most exigencies not only involve a *practical* uncertainty, but also a *moral* one. Exigencies often involve moral dilemmas in which we are forced to choose between two competing, but equally important, values. For example, a parent who must decide whether to stay at home with a young child or to return to work is not struggling between good and evil. He or she is trying to decide whether the good of personally nurturing a child (expressed in the values of love and intimacy) outweighs the goods of career advancement (power and ambition) and the material necessities for supporting a family (wealth and prosperity). Likewise, members of a public who are asked to go to war may be torn between giving unqualified support to the campaign (patriotism and loyalty), resisting enlistment into the military (self-preservation and independence), or questioning the benefits of the war (prudence and restraint). Rhetoric usually follows from this dilemma simply because when people are torn between competing values, they often seek out advice from others to make a decision. It is in these contexts that rhetoric takes on a heightened significance and power.

From this discussion, it should be apparent that values are not simply empty abstractions. For John Dewey, values operate as forms of practical judgment and are meaningful when understood as ends-in-view or as future goals that guide our present behaviors in anticipation of achieving those goals. An **end-in-view** is like a blueprint to a house being built rather than someone's vision of a dream home that exists only as a fantasy. For a value to have meaning, then, it must function to direct our behavioral choices on the basis of intelligent judgment between means and ends rather than just obedience to a code of action. In this sense, a value is not something that stands opposed to "facts;" quite the opposite: A value functions as a form of measurement through a direct engagement with the causes and consequences of one's actions in the long-term.

Values are clearly "general" categories, but it is their generality and flexibility that precisely gives values to their power. Values are durable ideals that we apply in many different situations in order to guide our actions. For example, the United States Military Academy teaches its West Point cadets to value "duty, honor, country." These are not simply empty words. These values sit atop a hierarchy of values in any dedicated army cadet. They are the ideals the army uses to determine whether or not they are living up to the standards of their social group, a consideration that is of the utmost importance to any military unit as they go into battle. In other words, only insofar as each soldier can count on the other to uphold these values can they ultimately depend on each other to act consistently in response to shared challenges and responsibilities. This was the point of General Douglas MacArthur in his classic speech, "Duty, Honor, Country," given on May 12, 1962. He begins by defining these values as ideals and goals:

> *Duty, Honor, Country*: Those three hallowed words reverently dictate what you ought to be, what you can be, what you will be. They are your rallying points: to build courage when courage seems to fail; to regain faith when there seems to be little cause for faith; to create hope when hope becomes forlorn.[14]

Implicit in MacArthur's definition is that the values of duty, honor, and country serve a practical purpose; they make certain choices seem more appealing and correct than

---

[14]Douglas MacArthur, "Duty, Honor, Country," *American Rhetoric,* at americanrhetoric.com (accessed on April 26, 2010).

others when conflict arises. Given their reality, then, MacArthur refutes skeptics who would see these values as mere puffery:

> The unbelievers will say they are but words, but a slogan, but a flamboyant phrase. Every pedant, every demagogue, every cynic, every hypocrite, every troublemaker, and I am sorry to say, some others of an entirely different character, will try to downgrade them even to the extent of mockery and ridicule.[15]

From a skeptical perspective, for instance, values like these might be viewed as mere advertising tools or empty words. However, for MacArthur, instilling these values has a genuine practical effect. He explains:

> But these are some of the things they do. They build your basic character. They mold you for your future roles as the custodians of the nation's defense. They make you strong enough to know when you are weak, and brave enough to face yourself when you are afraid. They teach you to be proud and unbending in honest failure, but humble and gentle in success; not to substitute words for actions, not to seek the path of comfort, but to face the stress and spur of difficulty and challenge; to learn to stand up in the storm but to have compassion on those who fall; to master yourself before you seek to master others; to have a heart that is clean, a goal that is high; to learn to laugh, yet never forget how to weep; to reach into the future yet never neglect the past; to be serious yet never to take yourself too seriously; to be modest so that you will remember the simplicity of true greatness, the open mind of true wisdom, the meekness of true strength. They give you a temper of the will, a quality of the imagination, a vigor of the emotions, a freshness of the deep springs of life, a temperamental predominance of courage over timidity, of an appetite for adventure over love of ease. They create in your heart the sense of wonder, the unfailing hope of what next, and the joy and inspiration of life. They teach you in this way to be an officer and a gentleman.[16]

This long list of benefits demonstrates how such simple terms can encompass a great deal of meaning. Obviously, different people will usually apply values in different ways in particular situations; but the fact that these people will all profess the same values in speech, despite their differences in practice, demonstrates their rhetorical potential.

Discussion: It is common that a group of people may participate in the same event and yet value that participation differently. Think of a shared experience involving many different people and try to list ten different relevant values that might be applicable. How would participating in that event on the basis of each value alter one's behavior?

FEELING

The "structural" metaphor we have used to describe the relationships among beliefs, reason, and values breaks down once we start talking about feelings, emotions, memory, imagination, and attitudes. The first three concepts (beliefs, reason,

---

[15]Ibid.
[16]Ibid.

and values) deal with how we piece together a stable picture of our environment and determine our place within it largely through acts of mental cognition. These three concepts also separate us most clearly from other biological organisms. Other mammals, like dogs, dolphins, and chimpanzees, can act intelligently in the world they know and can live sympathetically with other creatures within that world. But they cannot, through belief and reason, imagine a world that they do not know, nor can they, through values, consciously weigh the long-term consequences of their actions in reference to some larger ideal. Only human beings can perform these tasks, which is due to our unique ability to use language and symbols to communicate to each other about our experiences without having to replicate that experience.

However, once we begin talking about things like feelings (used here as a synonym not for *emotions* but for *sensations*), we begin to discuss those qualities that we *share* with other animals.[17] For example, human babies are not born into the world with beliefs and values. Indeed, we arrive with hardly any cognitive thought at all. As babies, we begin with very primitive attitudes, called *instincts,* along with the capacity for *feeling*. A **feeling** is a sensory response to some environmental stimulation or physical state. A baby feels pain, pleasure, cold, warm, hungry, full, sleepy, and awake. Feelings make up the substance of our perceptual world, and they are what we share with all other conscious beings. We may not know what goes on in our dog's mental life, but we can understand why he or she likes to run, eat, snuggle, and play.

Feelings are the basic elements that physically connect us with the world around us. Feelings make us aware of our surroundings. This biological need and love of sensorial feeling never goes away. When we see lizards sunning themselves on rocks, cats sleeping on a blanket, ducks splashing in pond, or eagles soaring in the sky, we always imagine what it would feel like if we were in their position. That is why we go to the beach, curl up on the couch, jump in puddles, and go hang gliding. A world without feeling would thus be barren and lifeless, for it would cut us off from the simple joy of being a part of the natural world.

In rhetoric, feelings usually come secondhand through the language. But the magic of language is that it can arouse in us the same kinds of feelings we might get if we were actually present in a situation. Rhetoric thus arouses feelings primarily through the effective use of style. The pleasure of poetry, in particular, often derives from its use of striking perceptual language that helps us *feel* more intensely in the perceptual rather than the emotional sense, even if we do not know what those feelings might mean. For members of an audience to recall the dark smell of hot coffee, the gentle coo of a newborn, the sharp taste of sour lemons, the grating moan of a bagpipe, or the needle sting of ice down their backs may not necessarily have any direct persuasive affect, but at the very least it makes the speech more enjoyable to *hear* because it makes them *feel*. The spoken description of a thing is thus roughly analogous to seeing something approaching from a distance. Both react not to the actual presence of something, but to the imagined presence of that thing as if it were actually there. The emphasis on feeling in rhetorical discourse

---

[17]Feeling is thus connected to the concept of "affect," which encompasses all kinds of pleasant and unpleasant feelings. For the relationship between affect and emotion, see Nico H. Frijda, "Varieties of Affect: Emotions and Episodes, Moods, and Sentiments," *The Nature of Emotion: Fundamental Questions*, ed. Paul Ekman and Richard J. Davidson (Oxford, UK: Oxford University Press, 1994), 69–67.

helps focus attention on details by making an audience feel as if it were actually present, thus heightening the aesthetic sensibility. Steve Whitson and John Poulakos note, for instance, that:

> Aesthetic rhetoric focuses on the human body as an excitable entity, an entity aroused by language. In as much as the ears can be bribed, the nose infiltrated, the skin raised, the tongue stimulated, and the eyes stopped at the surface of things, the task of aesthetic rhetoric is to speak words appealing to the bodily senses. In carrying out this task, it substitutes the sounds, the smells, the textures, the flavors, and the sights of the world with a sensual language that surpasses them.[18]

Sometimes, these details can be images of disaster or horror intended to make audiences feel disgust at certain conditions that the rhetor hopes to change, as one might describe images of poverty, pollution, or disease. Other times, details can be beautiful and inspiring, similar to how tourist advertisements always try to make us feel as though we were relaxing by the pool in the sun. The latter approach was taken by Henry Ward Beecher, who in the nineteenth century was a popular liberal Congregationalist clergyman who used the pulpit to argue for social reforms such as women's suffrage and the abolition of slavery. He also was a student of nature who believed that one could find God through euphoric natural experiences. One such experience he had while climbing a mountain in Switzerland led to what he called a "vision," which he reproduced in a January 15, 1866, sermon at Plymouth Church in order to convey to his audience the euphoric feelings that came upon him. He says:

> I shall never forget the half day that I spent on Gorner Grat, in Switzerland. I was just emerging from that many-formed crystal country (for Switzerland is one vast multiform crystal), and, coming up through the valley of the Rhone, and threading my way along the valley of the Visp, I arrived in the evening at Zermatt, in a perfect intoxication of delight. I lay that night and dreaming of the morning till it broke on me, and we directed our footsteps up the mountain; and after climbing two or three hours, we reached the top of Gorner Grat.[19]

The narrative here is simple so far, with only the striking image of Switzerland as a "multiform crystal" standing apart from what appears to be an ordinary account of a person preparing to ascend a mountain. Yet this story creates a sense of anticipation for what is to come. Beecher then continues:

> It is a barren rock, with snow only here and there in the cracks and crevices; but, oh, what a vision opened upon me as I cast my eyes around the horizon! There stood some fifteen of Europe's grandest mountains. There was Monte Rosa, Lyskamm, Breithorn, Steinbock, Weisshorn, Mischabel, and, most wonderful of all, Matterhorn, that lifts itself up thirteen thousand feet and more and is a square-cut granite rock, standing like a vast tower in the air, and all of it apparently, from basis to summit, rising right up before you. And there was Gorner Glacier, a great river of ice, always moving, but never seeming to move. Down

[18]Steve Whitson and John Poulakos, "Nietzsche and the Aesthetics of Rhetoric," *Quarterly Journal of Speech* 79, no. 2 (1993), 131–145.

[19]William Safire, *Lend Me Your Ears: Great Speeches in History* (New York: Norton, 2004), 496.

from the sides of these mountains flowed ten distinct glaciers beside. I swept the horizon and saw at one glance these glorious elevations, on whose tops the sun kindled all the melodies and harmonies of light.[20]

Several images now compete for the audience's attention—a barren rock covered with snow, a horizon dotted by all the great mountains of Europe, a single-cut rock towering into the air, a frozen river of ice, and above it all the sun kindling it all with a glimmering and rhythmic play of light. These physical feelings all then culminate in what Beecher hopes to be a religious feeling that makes one transcend from the material to the spiritual. He concludes:

I was alone. I disdained company. I was a son of God, and I felt eternity, and God, and glory.[21]

To appreciate the importance of taking the time to generate feelings in rhetorical discourse, imagine if Beecher had simply gotten right to the point: "On climbing Gorner Grat, I felt one with God." This is certainly a true statement, but without the slow generation of feeling in an audience, it does not generate any movement. It simply becomes a flat diary entry that speaks of Beecher's private experience. By using the language of feeling to make that private experience something capable of being shared, he generates a motivation in the audience to replicate that experience.[22]

Discussion: Think of a radio advertisement that attempts to generate desire or repulsion through graphic description. What words do they use to generate feeling? What did they make you visualize in your imagination? And to what objects were they connected? Did they make you want to purchase (or not purchase) the product?

EMOTION

If Beecher's descriptions of Gorner Grat represent feelings, his final revelation represents an emotion. Whereas a feeling can simply be a sensation, such as the feeling of being burned when touching a hot stove, an emotion is something more complex that relates to our entire reaction to that sensation, such as fear of being burned. In other words, emotions are different from feelings because they are not simply bare "happenings" without any necessary meaning. **Emotions** are dramatized feelings that orient us to things within our immediate environment that stand out as significant. Calling them "dramatized feelings" recognizes that emotions are related to feelings because they both happen "inside us" and are connected to our physical states. When we feel *scared*, we literally *feel* scared—our hair rises, our muscles tense, and our stomachs turn. But being scared is more than just these feelings. They are *dramatized* feelings, meaning that they occur only because we play

---

[20]Ibid.

[21]Ibid.

[22]For more on Beecher's influence, see Daniel Ross Chandler, "Henry Ward Beecher," *Religious Communication Today* 6 (1983), 1–10.

out scenarios in our imaginations that show us getting mugged by a stranger, eaten by a lion, or yelled at by a superior.

These dramatized feelings, in turn, only exist in relationship to people, objects, or events that immediately surround us (even if they are just in our imagination). This makes emotions different than **moods**, which tend to be pervasive qualities of a person's personality that affect their cognitive processing in all situational contexts (as when a "depressed" person always interprets things differently than one who is an "optimist"). Emotions, by contrast, are always specific. We love some*body* and we fear some*thing*. Emotions do not simply exist in a void. They are always responses to some aspect of our environment.[23]

Consequently, emotions can be effectively divided into ones that *attract* us to things and ones that *repel* us from them. **Attracting emotions** draw us positively closer to somebody or something; we associate such positively valenced emotions (for good or bad) with love, curiosity, pity, generosity, envy, or greed. **Repelling emotions** push us negatively away from somebody or something; we associate such negatively valenced emotions with anger, fear, shame, or cowardice. Emotions can exist without a corresponding action, however. We may love somebody and yet never talk to them, and be angry at those who we must, by necessity, obey. But the lasting presence of such repelling emotion usually makes us try to get out of that situation; just as attracting emotions usually push us toward something. We can usually resist the influence of emotions in the short term; in the long term, however, enduring emotions will almost always prevail.[24]

The power of rhetorical discourse is often based upon its ability to harness this motivational power of emotions to encourage new beliefs and actions. A rhetor who wishes an audience to reject something will inspire repelling emotions, while attracting emotions will be directed toward the object of the rhetor's preference. Usually, both of these effects are produced by loading up certain objects with positive or negative feelings. One of the basic strategies of advertising, for instance, is simply to show a product in association with pleasurable sensations (attractive people, a clean house, fresh breath, a healthy body) while associating its competitor with negative sensations (ugly people, a dirty apartment, bad breath, disease). These feelings then are bundled together in a particular way to make us desire or fear certain products and consequences. We then imagine ourselves owning this product through an imagined drama that culminates in us being popular, powerful, healthy, and wealthy. Our emotional attachment to this vision then leads us to buy a product.

It is evidence of the strong relationship between rhetoric and the emotions that a large part of Aristotle's *Rhetoric* is taken up simply with a definition of the various emotions, including calmness, anger, friendship, enmity, fear, confidence, shame, shamelessness, kindness, unkindness, pity, indignation, envy, and emulation. Aristotle also offers a very modern definition of emotions. For him:

---

[23]Richard J. Davidson, "On Emotion, Mood, and Related Affective Constructs," *The Nature of Emotion: Fundamental Questions,* ed. Paul Ekman and Richard J. Davidson (Oxford, UK: Oxford University Press, 1994), 51–55.

[24]For a review of different perspectives on emotion, see Randolph R. Cornelius, *The Science of Emotion: Research and Tradition in the Psychology of Emotions* (Saddle River, NJ: Prentice Hall, 1996).

> The emotions [*pathē*] are those things through which, by undergoing change, people come to differ in their judgments and what are accompanied by pain and pleasure, for example, anger, pity, fear, and other such things and their opposites. There is need to divide the discussion of each into three headings. I mean, for example, in speaking of anger, [one should describe] what is their state of mind when people are angry, and against whom are they usually angry, and for what reasons.[25]

An emotion, for Aristotle, is thus the psychological feeling of pain or pleasure associated with a contextual judgment about something in one's environment. Emotions are thus the opposite of something that can occur in the privacy of one's heart or consciousness. Emotions are public affairs that connect us to the public world of shared experiences. His advice for rhetors is thus to try to represent a type of experience that might bring forth an emotion, like when an orator who wishes to make an audience angry describes his adversaries as "possessed of such qualities as do make people angry."[26] In short, we shouldn't tell people to be angry; we should show them the people, actions, and events that have such qualities that tend to bring about anger.

Rhetorical strategies to attach attracting and repelling emotions to certain political policies and practical judgments are not so different from selling products. Repelling emotions are associated with the undesired policy, and attracting emotions are associated with the path advocated by the rhetoric. Take, for example, the speech given by Rania Masri, founder of the Iraq Action Coalition, which was formed to criticize the strict sanction policy against Iraq following the end of the 1991 Gulf War. These sanctions were placed on Iraq for the purpose of constraining Saddam Hussein's government, but they included not only weapons, but also materials for general civilian use. For Masri, the result was that many of the sanctions harmed ordinary Iraqis. In her September 17, 2000, essay in *The News and Observer,* she relies on an emotional argument to get her audience to feel compelled to help Iraqi civilians by sympathizing with their miserable conditions:

> Imagine what it feels like to live for 10 years under sanctions and bombardment. You're in Basra, Iraq's southern-most city. It's morning and 120 degrees in the shade. The electricity is off three hours out of every six. You're thirsty, but the tap water is unsafe to drink. You're hungry, but the monthly food ration has almost run out, and all that is left is some rice and tea. Your 8-year-old son has started screaming in fright again, as he does every time a fighter jet flies overhead. He is scared of the bombs that have been dropped almost daily. Your 4-year-old daughter is suffering from diarrhea, as a result of the dirty drinking water, and the doctor has said the simple medicine needed to cure her is not available. Most likely, your little girl will die in your arms. This story is replayed in homes throughout much of Iraq.[27]

The strategy of "putting yourself in someone else's shoes" is characteristic of arguments that rely on emotional impulse to move people to action. Masri graphically

---

[25]Aristotle, *On Rhetoric: A Theory of Civic Discourse,* trans. George Kennedy (Oxford: Oxford University Press, 1991), 1378a.

[26]Aristotle, *Rhetoric,* 1380a.

[27]Zinn and Arnove. *Voices of a People's History of the United States,* 581.

describes the sights, sounds, feels, and smells of everyday life in Basra, creating a picture of misery that would make anyone feel a combination of horror and pity. The repelling emotions that Americans felt toward Saddam Hussein are thus balanced by the attracting emotions we feel toward this struggling parent who simply wants to save her child. Suddenly, a moral decision now appears based on a competition of values—shall we pursue justice and seek to overthrow the regime, or follow the path of mercy and allow resources to reach these poor people? Masri clearly advocates for the second choice:

> Sanctions supporters claim this siege on Iraq is required to ensure that Iraq is disarmed. Even if true, how can we permit this continued killing of children through disease and malnutrition? And how can we continue this policy—or remain silent about this tragedy—when former weapons inspectors have repeatedly documented that Iraq is already disarmed?[28]

Note how Masri slips into reasoning here at the end, moving effortlessly from the emotions of sympathy to a logical argument intended to refute the rationale for sanctions in the first place. If she had started with such reasoning, her efforts at persuasion would probably have ended before they began. But by starting with emotions, her audience is more willing to consider such reasoning. And this was no coincidence. In a reflection on her years as a social activist, Masri said she learned that "it is not enough to inform. It is not enough to communicate information in the form of facts, statistics, and knowledge. In rousing people from inaction to movement, I have realized that it is necessary to communicate with emotion, to personalize it, and to infuse it all with a belief, an honest belief, that we do have the ability to create positive change."[29] Emotional language, in other words, makes reasoning and action possible by providing *motivation*.

Discussion: Most modern advertising is based almost exclusively on the power of emotions. One industry that makes dramatic use of emotions in its ads is the pharmaceutical industry, particularly in advertisements in which nothing explicit is actually said about the product. Think of a television advertisement campaign for a popular drug. What emotions are at play, attracting and repelling, in this campaign?

IMAGINATION

Imagination is the counterpart of memory (as discussed in Chapter 1). Whereas memory deals with the interpretation of what has been, imagination deals with the invention of what might be or might have been. Memory thus brings the past into the present, whereas imagination projects the present into the future. Like memory, imagination is creative, but it does not create something out of nothing. **Imagination** represents the capacity to consider new possibilities in light of what is familiar or actual. For instance, children who are asked to draw whatever is in their imagination

---

[28]Ibid.

[29]Rania Masri, "Teaching Amid Despair: Global Warming and Israeli Wars on Lebanon," *Environmental Communication* 1, no. 2 (2007), 236–242.

almost always draw exaggerated images of what is closest to them—their house, their pets, their parents, and themselves. The difference is that they draw their house in the clouds, their pets as dragons, their parents as kings and queens, and themselves as superheroes. Imagination is never just the old or the new—it is the new amid the old, the extraordinary beside the ordinary.

Our capacity for imagination is perhaps of even greater significance than our capacity for reason. Reason allows us to create complex systems of belief that help us navigate through a complex world. The sciences are perhaps the greatest achievement of reason that human beings have created. But it is imagination that gives us the ability to imagine a world beyond our experience, to think about what might happen tomorrow, or across the world, or in the house next door. Certainly, our everyday actions involve imaginary construction. We look forward to Christmas shopping because we imagine drinking hot chocolate and opening presents by a roaring fireplace. But our sciences require imagination, too. To think about what happens across the universe, or thousands of years into the past, or within the tiniest atom, requires great leaps of imagination. This is, after all, why children love dinosaurs. This link between imagination, reason, science, creativity, and aspiration is emphasized by John Dewey:

> The aims and ideals that move us are generated through imagination. But they are not made out of imaginary stuff. They are made out of the hard stuff of the world of physical and social experience. The locomotive did not exist before Stevenson, nor the telegraph before the time of Morse. But the conditions for their existence were there in physical material and energies and in human capacity. Imagination seized hold upon the idea of a rearrangement of existing things that would evolve new objects. The same thing is true of a painter, a musician, a poet, a philanthropist, a moral prophet. The new vision does not arise out of nothing, but emerges through seeing, in terms of possibilities, that is, of imagination, old things in new relations serving a new end which the new end aids in creating.[30]

Another way of describing imagination in a rhetorical sense is through the lens of possibility. In short, to persuade someone is by definition to get that person to imagine a new possibility. In rhetoric, this new possibility is called the **possible**, which represents the visualization of a future state of affairs that does not yet exist but could be brought into existence through the actions of an audience.[31] Imagination gives us the capacity to envision the possible; and rhetoric portrays it in such a way as to make it seem probable and preferable. On a personal level, the possible might be used to give your daughter an image of diving safely into the pool as she stands frightened on the high dive. On a political level, the possible might be used to inspire in the public a desire for a free society where all men and women are equal and free. In both cases, imagination is necessary if people are to consciously take a risk in the hope that some better future might await them. Without imagination, we would never advance except by luck.

---

[30]John Dewey, *A Common Faith* (New Haven: Yale University Press, 1934), 49.

[31]For more on the Sophistical notion of possibility, see John Poulakos, "Rhetoric, the Sophists, and the Possible," *Communication Monographs* 51 (1984), 215–226.

The key to making the possible more than just the ordinary but less than the utopian is the proper balance of the old with the new. To emphasize only the old is simply to reproduce what already exists, but to promote only the new is to make the leap of persuasion too great. One must encourage people to take a step into the unknown while still retaining a foothold on familiar ground. Rhetors should always make a careful study of what conditions to hold constant and which to modify when seeking to appeal to the imagination. Hold too much constant, and nobody is encouraged to move very far. Hold too little constant, and the distance seems so far that nobody moves.

An example of imagination in practice is the work of one of the most famous and influential architects in America, Frank Lloyd Wright. Known for his "organic" style of design that sought to create structures that grow out of the environment in which they are built, Wright was also an intense critic of traditional and institutional forms of architecture. An iconoclast of sorts, Wright believed that invention always occurred in the margins, outside of the stultified habits of convention. For him, imagination was the possession of an individual rather than an institution. Accordingly, he rejected efforts to make the government responsible for innovation, feeling that the government is always hostile to anything truly innovative. To make this point, he uses the simile of the "floo floo bird" that always flew backward; an example relies on the imagination of the audience to envision such an absurd creature:

> The cultural influences in our country are like the floo floo bird. I am referring to the peculiar and especial bird who always flew backward. To keep the wind out of its eyes? No. Just because it didn't give a darn where it was going, but just had to see where it had been. Now, in the "floo floo" bird you have the true symbol of our government architecture—too, and in consequence, how discredited American culture stands in the present time. All the world knows it to be funny except America. . . .
>
> This thing, which we call America, as I have said, goes around the world today. It is chiefly spirit but that spirit is reality. Not by way of government can we find encouragement of any help. No, we can have nothing by way of official government until the thing is at least ten years in the past.
>
> What can government do with an advanced idea? If it is still a controversial idea, and any good idea must be so, can government touch it without its eye on at least the next election? It cannot. I know of nothing more silly than to expect "government" to solve our advanced problems for us. If we have no ideas, how can government have any?[32]

Rhetorically, Wright appeals to the imagination in the idea of a bird who flies backward in order to reflect and admire the past. This simile then acts as a criticism of the lack of imagination in government architecture. Hence, he appeals to the imagination of individuals as a means of denying its existence in another institution.

Discussion: Think of all the imaginary fantasy worlds that you have encountered in fiction and television throughout your life. What characteristics of these worlds were typically held "constant" with what we already know (e.g., that all aliens in

---

[32]Safire, *Lend Me Your Ears: Great Speeches in History*, 617.

Star Trek looked liked humans)? And which characteristics did we assume would be changed (e.g., that the planets in *Star Trek* always had a different color)? Why did some things always change and some always stay the same?

ATTITUDE

Despite the importance of all the concepts so far examined—belief, reason, value, feeling, emotion, memory, and imagination—the concept of attitude is the single most important motivational consideration for a rhetorical public speaker. What distinguishes attitude from everything else is that it is the only concept linked to a recurrent type of behavior. With all the other concepts, their relevance to action is indirect. A person can hypothetically believe, reason, feel, remember, and imagine without ever moving a muscle. To have an attitude, however, means to act in a particular way in response to a particular stimulus. Attitudes are thus essentially public affairs; one can usually hide a belief or emotion, but attitudes must express themselves in action to be genuine attitudes.

Attitudes are habitual practical responses toward the people, objects, and events in our everyday environment based on likes and dislikes. For example, that I like to sit and watch the sun set, that I am scared of the dark, that I am suspicious of my neighbors, that I get nervous speaking in public, that I like my pizza with pepperoni, and that I am favorable to supply-side economic policies are all expressions of attitude. To have an attitude means that whenever something is present, a consistent response will follow—I will wait for the sun to set before going inside, I will sleep with the light on, I won't lend money to the guy next door, my stomach will turn during speech day, I will always order pepperoni, and I will usually vote for tax cuts. If any of those actions do not follow, then I do not possess a genuine attitude.[33]

In short, attitudes are most fully expressions of the body. Part of training young children is to cultivate in them the attitudes toward adults, other children, food, toys, strangers, cars, and all of the other components of their environment. Only later do we give the "reasons" for these attitudes in the hopes that they will not just habitually behave certain ways but consciously *choose* to behave those ways. But the important part of the attitude is not the conscious explanation, belief, or value that lies behind it; the defining characteristic of an attitude is the *actual habit* of acting in certain ways in response to certain things. As Kenneth Burke explains, an attitude represents "an implicit program of action" and emphasizes that the "body is an actor; as an actor, it participates in the movements of the mind, posturing accordingly."[34] Attitudes are therefore things that are intrinsically active, public, and shared. We exhibit attitudes as ways of adapting to problems and stabilizing our lives. Rhetoric can thus be considered as a tool for bringing our attitudes in better alignment with our environment.

---

[33]For more on attitudes, see Phil Erwin, *Attitudes and Persuasion* (Sussex, UK: Psychology Press Ltd., 2000); Carolyn Sherif, Muzafer Sherif, and Roger Nebergall, *Attitude and Attitude Change: The Social Judgment-Involvement Approach* (Philadelphia: W.B. Saunders Company, 1963); Icek Ajzen and Martin Fishbein, *Understanding Attitudes and Predicting Social Behavior* (Englewood Cliffs, NJ: Prentice Hall, 1980).

[34]Kenneth Burke, *The Philosophy of Literary Form* (New York: Vintage, 1957), 117, 125.

Attitude is of utmost importance in any rhetorical act. As any genuine problem can only be resolved by acting differently than we acted previously, our attitudes embody our habituated actions; any lasting changes must be expressed in an observable shift in attitudes. For example, ending racial discrimination in America requires not only altering our attitudes toward civil rights legislation, but also altering our attitudes toward other people. Part of the problem following Reconstruction was that the laws were changed, but the underlying racial attitudes remained in place. Consequently, new laws and conventions were established that effectively rebuilt all the racial barriers that had existed prior to the Civil War. Only through a long struggle by engaged citizens to change attitudes through rhetorical advocacy did the attitudes of the general public begin to finally shift. Only when attitude "caught up" with expressed belief did racial equality become a reality in this country.

From this perspective, one of the most common rhetorical situations arises when preestablished attitudes no longer deal sufficiently with new problems. For example, prior to the atomic age, the attitude toward military weapons was that it is always better to have a bigger stick than your opponent. The creation of a weapon capable of ending life as we know it threw this attitude into question. Now civilization had to come to terms with the fact that this attitude may, in fact, lead to our mutual destruction. Citizens like Albert Einstein thus began the hard work of altering this attitude so that we would cease producing nuclear weapons and even begin the process of dismantling our arsenal—an action that prior to World War II would have been considered absurd. Other attitudes throughout history have undergone similar transformations, each occurring after moments of crisis precipitated a collective change in behavior.

Although recognizing that the presence of certain attitudes presents a problem is an important step in changing them, actually changing those attitudes is a difficult process. Societies become so used to following certain routines and behaving certain ways that they find it difficult to stop even when they know it is harmful. Rhetoric seeks to perform the hard work of changing attitude primarily by taking an indirect route through other motivations. The tools of belief, reason, value, feeling, emotion, memory, imagination, and even related attitudes are the means by which we try to motivate people to finally abandon old habits and take up new ones. But as anyone who has tried to change even the smallest bad habit realizes, this effort requires a long-term commitment from oneself as well as the support of others. Rhetoric attempts to generate the positive, collective motivation to alter attitudes in such a way that will bring about a more productive and enriched social life.

The realization that it is our own attitudes that usually stand in the way of instigating progressive social action is always a difficult one. It is far easier to imagine that problems will be solved simply by removing some external menace. Once the tyrant is overthrown, the legitimate king can be reinstated and peace will reign throughout the land. But the reality is much different. Sadly, if people have developed attitudes consistent with a tyranny, they will usually slip back into that form of governance out of habit, at least in the short-term. Usually, then, any real changes require significant alterations of our own attitudes for anything to actually happen. This is the lesson that the Irish rock singer and social activist Bono told to his audience of graduating seniors at the University of Pennsylvania on May 19, 2004. Speaking of his experience as an idealistic teenager, Bono recalls the moment he realized that "revolution" took more than simply going to punk rock shows. He explains:

> I studied rock and roll and I grew up in Dublin in the '70s. Music was an alarm bell for me. It woke me up to the world. I was 17 when I first saw *The Clash*, and it just sounded like revolution. *The Clash* were like, "This is a public service announcement—with guitars." I was the kid in the crowd who took it at face value. Later I learned that a lot of the rebels were in it for the T-shirt. They'd wear the boots but they wouldn't march. They'd smash bottles on their heads but they wouldn't go to something more painful like a town hall meeting. By the way I felt like that myself until recently.[35]

The conflict here is the one between stated beliefs and actual attitudes. His fellow "rebels" expressed beliefs in radical social change and valued "revolution," but their attitudes were limited to spending money for T-shirts and smashing bottles on their heads. His recognition of this contradiction made Bono realize that the larger challenge would actually come in making people's attitudes conform to and support their beliefs. He continues:

> I didn't expect change to come so slow, so agonizingly slow. I didn't realize that the biggest obstacle to political and social progress wasn't the Free Masons, or the Establishment, or the boot heel of whatever you consider "the Man" to be. It was something much more subtle. As the Provost just referred to, a combination of our own indifference and the Kafkaesque labyrinth of "no's" you encounter as people vanish down the corridors of bureaucracy.[36]

The constraints to social change were both internal and external. The largest internal constraint was the attitude of indifference in otherwise caring people that made them unable to commit their energies to any lasting social change. The largest external constraint was the bureaucratic procedures that tended to stand in the way of any significant actions even after people become passionate about an issue. Part of the function of rhetoric, then, is to find a way to motivate people to action and then provide a means through which that action can be channeled. As Bono explains, each individual must find for him- or herself which attitude needs to be challenged and changed within his or her own social context. He thus asks his audience:

> What are the ideas right now worth betraying? What are the lies we tell ourselves now? What are the blind spots of our age? What's worth spending your post-Penn lives trying to do or undo? It might be something simple. It might be something as simple as our deep down refusal to believe that every human life has equal worth. Could that be it? Could that be it?[37]

For Bono in 2004, his own personal issue was the West's attitude toward Africa. He continues:

> Each of you will probably have your own answer, but for me that is it. And for me the proving ground has been Africa. Africa makes a mockery of what we say,

---

[35]Available from The American Rhetoric at americanrhetoric.com (accessed on April 26, 2010).
[36]Ibid.
[37]Ibid.

at least what I say, about equality and questions our pieties and our commitments because there's no way to look at what's happening over there and its effect on all of us and conclude that we actually consider Africans as our equal before God. There is no chance.[38]

At issue here, in other words, is the contradiction between our stated values and our actual attitudes. For Bono, the value that "we are all equal before God" is thus contradicted by our attitudes as expressed in policies regarding AIDS drugs and third world debt. For Bono, it is not enough to feel pity or sympathy for another person; only when those emotions result in productive resolution of a problem through the transformation of an attitude is genuine social change possible.[39]

Discussion: Almost everyone has a collection of bad habits that they wish to break. Discuss a common bad habit of most college students and try to explain why such a habit exists and why it is so resistant to change. If you have to try to convince someone to alter that habit, what other motivations might you appeal to?

CONCEPT REVIEW

CONCEPT	DEFINITION	EXAMPLE
BELIEF	A factual statement regarding the valid or invalid connection between two things.	"Taxes are simply too high."
REASON	The ability to link together beliefs into a coherent system based on evidence.	"When taxes are too high, people don't spend, and when people don't spend, the economy slows. And when the economy slows, people make less money."
VALUE	The general goals that validate our particular actions.	"In the name of independence, freedom, and prosperity, we need to cut our tax rate."
FEELING	The physical sensations we associate with certain things.	"Just think of the weight of cash in your hand. Isn't it more pleasing than a jingle of change in your pocket?"
EMOTION	How we are repelled or attracted to certain things in our environment.	"Shame on politicians who would take money out of our pocket. They are crooks in suits."
IMAGINATION	Our ability to project new possibilities into the past or future based on reorganizing familiar material.	"If we reduced the tax rate to almost zero, we would see an economy that would rival anything ever seen on earth."
ATTITUDE	Our habitual responses to certain things, favorable or unfavorable.	"Every time a politician comes knocking for another tax increase, slam the door on him."

---

[38]Ibid.

[39]For more on Bono's celebrity activism with respect to Africa, see Julie Hollar, "Bono, I Presume?" *Extra!* 20, no. 3 (2007), 21–25.

KEY WORDS

Amplification 100
Attitudes 120
Attracting emotions 115
Beliefs 102
Diminution 100
Dissoi logoi 106
Doubt 103
Emotions 114
End-in-view 110

Ethos 101
Existence 103
Feeling 112
Ideology 102
Imagination 117
Intelligence 106
Logos 101
Manipulation 101
Moods 115

Motive 99
Pathos 101
Reason 106
Repelling emotions 115
Salience 103
(the) Possible 118
Valence 103
Values 109
Weight 103

SUMMARY

The study of motivation is ultimately directed at finding a way to best persuade people to do what you want them to do, usually in the name of some "higher good." Now, if such a "higher good" were obvious and easily attained, rhetoric would probably be unnecessary. One would need only to be pointed in the right direction, and action would follow naturally. This was Plato's early criticism of rhetoric. For him, people naturally pursued the good, meaning that rhetoric could only be useful in persuading them to seek what was, in fact, bad for them. It would be like standing before a clear stream and a muddy puddle. Why would anyone need to be motivated to drink from the clear stream? Only when some manipulative huckster persuaded us that the stream was poisoned would anyone drink from the puddle.

But anyone who has lived in the world knows that what most people consider "good" is usually what is habitual and close at hand. We may know, for instance, that eating fast food every day is probably unhealthy, but the time constraints of our daily life force us to make it a habit to eat it for breakfast, lunch, and dinner. We may also know that smoking might give us cancer, but we enjoy the ritual of stepping outside for a smoke break several times a day to talk with our co-workers outside of the confines of the office. Whenever habits, expressed as attitudes, become part of our daily routine, even bad habits are hard to break—particularly when they require some degree of sacrifice.

The basic starting point for a rhetorical study of motives is therefore to know what mo-

tivates an audience to do what it already does. Often, this step is ignored out of eagerness to start building an argument in favor of one's own position. However, no persuasion can occur without first understanding why people might not wish to follow that position. For example, teenagers who smoke usually do so for social reasons so that they conform to the rituals of their desired social group. Someone trying to convince a teenager to give up smoking by showing them pictures of elderly people breathing out of holes in their throats therefore misses the point. Teenagers for the most part know the long-term health risks, but convince themselves that once they reach a certain age they will simply give up the habit before any harm is done. Consequently, motivations to quit must first directly challenge and overturn the actual motivation they have to keep smoking. It must, in other words, make smoking seem "ugly" or "uncool."

After *diminishing* the motivations, one has to retain his or her previous attitudes (i.e., "You don't need to smoke to be popular"); and after *amplifying* the negative consequences of retaining these attitudes ("In fact, smoking makes you look like a clown"), one must then *amplify* the positive motivations for adopting a new attitude while *diminishing* the negative side-effects. One must study what might motivate someone enough that they expend the necessary energy needed to change behaviors. These motivations can come from any of the concepts we have studied in this chapter.

What attitude needs to be changed?	Smoking with teenage friends
What attitude is desired?	Resistance to smoking, paired with a desire to associate with a different social group
What beliefs need to be removed from or modified with one's belief structure?	Smoking makes me popular / I can quit any time I want / I'm not doing any harm
What beliefs need to be added to one's belief structure?	Smoking isolates you from others / Smoking is addictive / Secondhand smoke harms other people / Smoking prevents you from doing other activities
What kind of reasoning might I employ to alter these beliefs?	The audience has the ability but little motivation to engage in this reasoning / Therefore, one should first rely on emphasizing the severity of the consequences to gain attention and interest
What values resist change?	Popularity, rebellion
What values support change?	Health, independence, self-respect
What positive emotions are attached to the current attitude?	Relaxed, accepting, excited
What negative emotions might be attached to the current attitude?	Guilty, conformist, disgusted
What positive emotions might be associated with altering this attitude?	Free, healthy, proud
What positive feelings are associated with this attitude?	Feel of the cigarette / the heat of the smoke / the effects of nicotine / the physical presence of other smokers
What negative feelings are associated with this attitude?	Bad breath / yellow teeth / stale smell of smoke on clothes / dirty cigarette butts
What positive feelings might be associated with altering this attitude?	Fresh breath / clean air / more energy / more money / freedom from having to smoke at designated times
What memories might support this attitude?	Memories of romantic movies / enjoyable talks with friends or family who smoked / the historical romance with smoking
What memories might challenge this attitude?	The painful death of loved ones who suffered from the effects of smoking / unpleasant experiences with heavy smokers
How might imagination be used to create an unpleasant vision of the future based on the continuation of this attitude?	The teenager as becoming exactly the image in those unpleasant memories
How might imagination create a more attractive vision of future possibility?	The teenager being athletic, attractive, and independent with a larger group of more successful friends

When this persuasive attempt moves beyond the interpersonal to the public, one should readily see how the situational analyses of the previous two chapters become significant. For it is not enough just to appeal to the personal characteristics of a single individual; one must create a rhetorical message capable of speaking to a broader and more diverse audience that nonetheless shares a certain cultural tradition and history. Recent efforts to place restrictions on advertising cigarettes to teenagers and to sue the drug companies in order to channel money into health programs highlights the importance of framing teenage smoking as a "national" exigence that needs co-ordinated public action to resolve.

Let us continue our analysis of Dr. King's speech in Montgomery to show how these motivational concepts functioned in the context of his larger situational analysis. Now that we have studied attitude, we can see how the dominant problem of his speech was how to develop a positive attitude toward nonviolent protest while suppressing the attitudes, already in his audience, that would express frustration through violent means. To repeat King's words: "What could I say to keep them courageous and prepared for positive action and yet devoid of hate and resentment?" This is another way of asking how to develop a nonviolent attitude in the face of emotions that would express themselves in an attitude of violence. One of his primary strategies was to associate a nonviolent attitude with Christian *beliefs,* thereby using a deductive form of *reasoning* which argued that because Christianity is a peaceful religion and that because all the audience members were Christians, they would protest in a peaceful manner. He says:

> I want it to be known throughout Montgomery and throughout this nation that we are Christian people. We believe in the Christian religion. We believe in the teachings of Jesus. The only weapon that we have in our hands this evening is the weapon of protest.[40]

Backing up this belief is his reference to their shared commitment to the *values* of love and justice. For King, the value of justice was the driving force of social change which sought to balance the imbalance of power, while the value of love always kept in mind the idea that the ultimate end sought fellowship between all people. Love kept audience members peaceful while

justice licensed their use of social force to achieve their ends:

> But I want to tell you this evening that it is not enough for us to talk about love, love is one of the pivotal points of the Christian face, faith. There is another side called justice. And justice is really love in calculation. Justice is love correcting that which revolts against love . . . Standing beside love is always justice and we are only using the tools of justice. Not only are we using the tools of persuasion but we've come to see that we've got to use the tools of coercion. Not only is this thing a process of education but it is also a process of legislation.[41]

In addition to setting forth an ideal and a justification for action, King also uses the tools of *emotion* and *feeling* to rally the physical energies of the audience—or in the common way of describing it, to get the audience "fired up." He does so by using the visual power of metaphor to express the pent-up emotions of his audience:

> And you know, my friends, there comes a time when people get tired of being trampled over by the iron feet of oppression. There comes a time, my friends, when people get tired of being plunged across the abyss of humiliation where they experience the bleakness of nagging despair. There comes a time when people get tired of being pushed out of the glittering sunlight of life's July, and left standing amid the piercing chill of an alpine November. There comes a time.[42]

Knowing that part of the *public memory* of being "trampled over by the iron feet of oppression" comes from the actions of the Ku Klux Klan, King also references their activities to bring back into consciousness the horrific nature of their

---

[40]Martin Luther King, Jr., "Address to the First Montgomery Improvement Association (MIA) Mass Meeting" (Montgomery, AL, December 5, 1955). Available from Stanford University's website, http://www.stanford.edu/group/King/publications/autobiography/chp_7.htm (accessed on April 16, 2010).

[41]Ibid.

[42]Ibid.

actions. He uses the memory, however, in an interesting way—not to make his audience angry at them, but to caution his audience that if it engages in violence, it will be following in the same path at the KKK. This memory thus serves as a warning:

> My friends, don't let anybody make us feel that we are to be compared in our actions with the Ku Klux Klan or with the White Citizens Council. There will be no crosses burned at any bus stops in Montgomery. There will be no white persons pulled out of their homes and taken out on some distant road and lynched for not cooperating.[43]

Finally, King channels all those energies toward a future possibility of the *imagination,* employing a metaphor that would reoccur frequently through his speeches in the following years. He announces with confidence:

> And we are determined here in Montgomery to work and fight until justice runs down like water and righteousness like a mighty stream.[44]

The speech that Dr. King gave at Holt Street Baptist Church was one of the shortest of his career as a rhetorical public speaker; yet in that speech he applied a breadth of knowledge about his situation and his audience that demonstrated why he was to become arguably the greatest orator in American history. The tools that King used, however, are nothing magical; they are equally available to anyone who has the commitment to use them. The following chapters on ethos, logos, pathos, and style are some of those tools.

CHAPTER 4 EXERCISES

1. Read closely the text of your rhetorical artifact. Choose three of the categories in this chapter that you feel the speaker appealed to or employed the most in the speech. Give at least two examples for each category.

2. As a class, come up with a rhetorical exigence to which everyone will respond with a short speech. Assign each member of the class a belief, value, or attitude, and have them give an impromptu speech attempting to change either a belief, value, or attitude relating to the exigence. (For example, if the exigence was teenage smoking, a belief would be "smoking can't hurt me"; a value would be "freedom of choice"; and an attitude would be "liking to talk with friends during a smoke break outside.") After the exercise, discuss which speeches were easier to write and which were more persuasive.

3. Using the same exigence, divide the class into three groups labeled Feeling, Emotion, and Reason. Do the same exercise and analyze.

4. Think of a present exigence that is being discussed in the popular media. Find two opposing points of view on this exigence, and analyze the different motivations to which they appeal. How many are the same and which are different?

5. Imagine what life will be like in one hundred years. Which vision seems both plausible and creative?

---

[43]Ibid.
[44]Ibid.

Constructing Artful Rhetoric

The preceding sections have provided the basic rules of public speaking and focused on how to identify situations and topics in which those rules can be applied in a rhetorical manner. This concluding section now focuses on developing the "finer arts" of rhetoric through ethos, pathos, logos, and style. If the rules instruct speakers to establish credibility with an audience, *ethos* tells them how to do it with subtlety; if the rules suggest ending a speech on a positive or negative note, *pathos* explains how to end with dramatic passion; if the rules demand that evidence is given, *logos* details the methods by which the claims can be warranted; and if the rules say to capture attention, *style* shows how to do it with a turn of phrase.

When learning the fine art of rhetoric, you must also keep in mind that you are not simply providing polish to a fully constructed object. Just as the years of fine-tuning a batter's swing is the difference between a ground ball and a home run, attention to the artful qualities of rhetoric distinguish a moment of rare eloquence from a laundry list. Indeed, the more you focus on the finer arts of rhetoric, the more substantial elements such as "style" and "emotion" become. Again, just as major league athletes adopt methods that often violate the principles of little league coaches, rhetorical public speakers who hone their own style often transcend the restrictions of the technical list of rules. The point is not to devalue the rules but to understand that the ultimate goal of any individual rhetor is to develop his or her own style that accomplishes the goal of rhetoric—the inspired motivation of an audience to collective action in the face of shared problems.

Ethos

This chapter discusses how a rhetorical public speaker develops a relationship with an audience. A "relationship" means more than simply letting an audience know a speaker's identity and his or her qualifications. A relationship is something personal that involves an emotional attitude toward another person or group and negotiates their reciprocal identities. This chapter explores the strategies that can be used to develop a relationship between speaker and audience that is most conducive to persuasion. The primary concepts that will de defined are persona, evoked audience, identification, distinction, and polarization.

In Classical Greek, the word for "character" is *ethos*. For the Greeks, to have ethos, one has to possess three things: the *virtues* we hold dear, the *practical wisdom* to make decisions that resolve problematic situations, and the *goodwill* that expresses itself in making sacrifices for the well-being of others. The Classical Greek understanding of character is therefore something very public rather than something private. The modern idea that people don't know the "real me" would make no sense to a Greek in Aristotle's time. The only "me" they knew was the one established on the basis of outward behavior and publicly recognized productive achievements rather than on any knowledge of a private inner self. For the Greeks, people with ethos were those people who earned respect, admiration, and allegiance rather than those who simply possessed a good "soul" that went unseen by others.[1]

The concept of ethos has distinctly rhetorical implications because it deals with aspects of credibility and authority that influence our choice of who to trust when faced with important decisions.[2] In other words, because we often do not have the time or resources to be able to make crucial judgments on our own, we look to those who possess strength of character, or ethos, to help guide our actions. For this reason, Aristotle believed that among the three forms of rhetorical proof (ethos, pathos, and logos), ethos was often the most powerful. Perhaps the greatest evidence of the power of ethos is the constant success of advertising campaigns that transfer the ethos of a celebrity to a product which has nothing to do with that celebrity. Rationally, we don't admit to ourselves that such strategies influence our reasoning, but our buying habits reveal otherwise.

For the purposes of rhetorical public speech, **ethos** is the capacity to influence an audience based on audience's perceptions of the credibility and character of the speaker in relationship

---

[1]For more on the Greek notion of public life, see Chapter 2 of Hannah Arendt, *The Human Condition*, 2nd ed. (Chicago: The University of Chicago Press, 1958).

[2]For excellent essays exploring the concept of *ethos*, see Michael J. Hyde, ed., *The Ethos of Rhetoric* (Columbia: University of South Carolina Press, 2004).

to its own interests and values. It is important that the *audience's perceptions* are at issue in rhetoric, not what the speaker thinks of him- or herself or even the attitudes of other people who are not part of the audience. Ethos in the rhetorical sense is not something absolute and stable that one carries around wherever one goes; it is determined by the relationship one has with an audience. The president of a country may possess great ethos with respect to his or her own constituency and yet be despised by a foreign population. This is because any act can be interpreted differently by different groups. A presidential declaration of war may be seen as a courageous defense of freedom by one side and a brutal act of imperialism by the other. To understand the possible effects of one's rhetoric, then, a person must understand how an audience perceives his or her character.[3]

Establishing ethos is a complex process that involves more than simply offering an audience a list of accomplishments and admirable characteristics. It is an error in public speaking to assume ethos is like a résumé, such that the more one includes on the document, the more attractive he or she looks. Often the result in public speaking is quite the opposite. People get turned off by such strategies because it sounds like bragging. A more subtle and effective approach involves the construction of persona, the evoked audience, and the use of strategies such as identification, polarization, and distinction.

PERSONA

Most people step into any familiar social situation with an **inherited ethos**, which is the actual reputation that a rhetor "carries with them" because of an audience's acquaintance with past behavior. When an inherited ethos is strong, such as the ethos of a mother for her child or that which close friends have with each other; the rhetor rarely has to spend any time establishing their reputation or credibility. It certainly would be strange for a mother to say to her child, "Because I have worked hard these many years learning how to cook healthy meals (good sense), because I care deeply for your future (goodwill), and because I am a just and honorable soul (virtue), please listen to my recommendation to eat your spinach." Having already established her ethos, she simply says "Eat your spinach." Inherited ethos is this kind of unspoken credibility that needs no mention to function.

Ethos becomes a uniquely rhetorical concern of *art* only when rhetors, in some form, create or modify the perception of an audience about them. **Persona** is this rhetorical creation; it represents the constructed ethos that a rhetor creates within the confines of a particular rhetorical text. Persona, in other words, is more a creation of language rather than an inheritance of history. Like the costume that transforms an actor into a new personality on stage, rhetoric can create a "public face" that best suits the immediate needs of a rhetor. Unlike inherited ethos, which is the product of cumulative interactions or exposure over time with an audience, one's persona is always tied to a specific discourse and is completely contained within that discourse. For example, a convict before a parole board enters the hearing with an inherited ethos as a liar and a thief, and he attempts to counter that reputa-

---

[3]For more on speaker credibility, see Chapter 5 of Gary C. Woodward and Robert E. Denton, Jr., *Persuasion and Influence in American Life*, 5th ed. (Long Grove, IL: Waveland, 2004).

tion by describing himself as a "changed man" who has seen the error of his ways. The decision of the board rests on whether the convict's persona of a "changed man" is more convincing than the inherited ethos of a liar and a thief.

Deciding when to construct a persona and when to rely on the strength of one's inherited ethos depends upon the presence and quality of one's reputation within an audience. On the one hand, when a speaker is unknown to an audience, creating a persona is necessary in order to present a favorable "first impression."[4] We are all familiar with those first job interviews when we must define ourselves as an ideal employee. On the other hand, when a speaker enters a situation as a respected leader, there is no need for such self-promotion; indeed, it would be seen as bad taste. Rarely do we enjoy listening to famous and powerful people talking about their fame and power. But most speaking situations usually fall somewhere in between these two extremes. In these cases, one must construct a persona that somehow addresses, modifies, and transcends the limits of one's inherited ethos.[5]

Because the construction of personae deals not just with possession of knowledge or skills, but with notions of character, it relies heavily on personal stories and the form of delivery. **Personal stories** are narrations of one's life experience that provide insight into the speaker's character. Phrases like "The time I was behind enemy lines . . ." or "When I saved my sister's life . . ." or "Growing up in a tough neighborhood . . ." signify to an audience that a person is relating a story that offers a window into his or her deeper self. The **form of delivery** reveals character by using phrases, words, accents, or gestures commonly associated with certain "types" of people. Hence, a president often vacillates between acting "presidential" by speaking in firm, calm, and authoritative terms in formal settings and behaving as an "ordinary American" by doing volunteer work with rolled-up sleeves and telling jokes around a barbeque.

The personae available for a rhetor are literally infinite. However, there are general types of personae that are always familiar and that conform to our social conventions. Take, for instance, just a few popular personae: the country lawyer, the wise sage, the teenage rebel, the religious prophet, the CEO, the father/mother figure, the loyal friend, the iconoclast, the president, the confidant, the drill sergeant, or the door-to-door salesperson. Any person attempting to create his or her own persona, of course, will always individualize his or her character such that no two personae will ever be alike. But these models provide general guides for action.

In their review of the research on the roles typically played by rhetors in rhetorical situations, Roderick Hart and Susanne Daughton identify four recurring personae: the apologist, the agent, the partisan, and the hero. These roles represent fitting responses to situations that also take into account the personality and intentions of the speaker. The role of **apologist** is employed when speakers wish to rebuff attack by appearing the virtuous victim of an unjust accusation. The **agent** speaks on behalf of some institution as a spokesperson of legitimate authority. This allows the rhetor to speak with greater power than he or she would alone, and it

---

[4]An interesting account of an actual scholarly persona is found in James Darsey, "Edwin Black and the First Persona," *Rhetoric & Public Affairs* 10, no. 3 (2007), 501–507.

[5]The relationship between rhetor and audience can be described in terms of the ratio between their level of credibility and the level of agreement. These considerations are explained in detail in Chapter 7 of Woodward and Denton, *Persuasion and Influence in American Life*.

also allows the rhetor to speak "for others," thus allowing him or her to "stand up" to opposition in the name of a community. The **partisan** is one who represents not a group or institution but an ideology or ideal. This individual tends to thrive in heated debates during times of turmoil and upheaval, when people are looking for new directions based on new ideas. Finally, the **hero** is defined by his or her personal character, particularly as it relates courage, commitment to action, and a romantic attachment to a vague but inspiring future. The hero may not have a coherent political vision or workable idea, but he or she makes up for these limitations by boldly striding into the unknown against all obstacles with the optimistic faith that things will work out for them in the end.[6]

One of the most fascinating personae in American history, who was part-partisan and part-hero, was that of former slave and civil rights champion Sojourner Truth. Born Isabella Van Wagenen (a Dutch name given by her Dutch slave owners) in about 1797, Truth endured many years of abuse until finally achieving her freedom in 1827 and changing her name in 1843. Despite growing up illiterate, she was a woman of remarkable intelligence and presence. She was tall for her era—almost six feet—with a low and powerful voice that had a song-like quality to it. Her straight-talking and unsentimental style, combined with her imposing figure, made her a national symbol for strong women, both black and white. Her most famous extemporaneous address, "Ain't I a Woman?" was delivered at the Women's Convention in Akron, Ohio, on May 29, 1851. This type of convention was a major component of the early women's rights movement, which involved the organization of women's conferences to bring together feminists to discuss goals and strategies. However, many of these conferences attracted men (including several ministers) who came largely to heckle the speakers and to argue that women's proper place was one of being both subservient to and cared for by men.

It was the heckling of one of these ministers that inspired Truth to speak. Reacting to a black-robed minister who argued for male superiority based on "superior intellect" and "manhood in Christ," Truth argued that women were in fact more powerful than men and also that black women had been denied even the limited rights given to white women. Her argument constructs a persona that establishes her superior strength, capability, and authority. A firsthand account described how "Sojourner walked to the podium and slowly took off her sunbonnet. Her six-foot frame towered over the audience. She began to speak in her deep, resonant voice."

> Well, children, where there is so much racket there must be something out of kilter. I think that 'twixt the negroes of the South and the women at the North, all talking about rights, the white men will be in a fix pretty soon. But what's all this here talking about?[7]

Interesting about her introduction is her acknowledgement of an exigence that has caused the concern and uncertainty which has brought people together at this

---

[6]Roderick Hart and Susanne Daughton. *Modern Rhetorical Criticism*, 3rd ed. (Boston: Pearson, 2005), 220–221.

[7]Howard Zinn and Anthony Arnove, *Voices of a People's History of the United States* (New York: Seven Stories Press, 2004, 128.

particular occasion. Her question then sets the stage for her to interpret and re-solve the problem:

> That man over there says that women need to be helped into carriages, and lifted over ditches, and to have the best place everywhere. Nobody ever helps me into carriages, or over mud puddles, or gives me any best place! And ain't I a woman?[8]

Her argument here is responding to the chivalrous notion that it is the responsibility of men to provide for women, not for women to provide for themselves. This belief that women should be cared for, however, is clearly at odds with her experience as a woman. Her question, "Ain't I a woman?" is thus meant to clarify the contradiction between the expressed beliefs and actual attitudes. To make her point that women can, indeed, care for themselves without men, she then relies on her own persona. The narrative account of the events records that at this point in the speech, "Sojourner raised herself to her full height" and "bared her right arm and flexed her powerful muscles." She continues:

> Look at me! Look at my arm! I have ploughed and planted, and gathered into barns, and no man could head me! And ain't I a woman? I could work as much and eat as much as a man—when I could get it—and bear the lash as well! And ain't I a woman? I have borne thirteen children, and seen most all sold off to slavery, and when I cried out with my mother's grief, none but Jesus heard me! And ain't I a woman?
>
> Then that little man in black there, he says women can't have as much rights as men, 'cause Christ wasn't a woman! Where did your Christ come from? Where did your Christ come from? From God and a woman! Man had nothing to do with Him. If the first woman God ever made was strong enough to turn the world upside down all alone, these women together ought to be able to turn it back, and get it right-side up again! And now that they is asking to do it, the men better let them.[9]

The entire argument for women's rights is thus grounded in Truth's own persona as an individual of great strength and power. Without her ability to "bear the lash," to "eat as much as a man," to have "ploughed and planted," she would not have been able to convince her audience of her equality with men. But she goes even further, adding that her ability to bear children—like the birth of Christ—makes her even more powerful than men. This explains the not-so-subtle threat with which she concludes her speech.[10]

Discussion: Moving to a new place (either long-term, such as for college or a new career; or short-term, such as an exchange program or summer camp) often creates a new opportunity to create a novel persona that is no longer constrained by one's inherited ethos. When did you consciously try to create a new persona after making such a move? When you returned to your own environment, did you feel constrained by your old inherited ethos? Did you feel you had actually become a new person?

---

[8]Ibid.

[9]Ibid.

[10]The changing narrative surrounding Truth's rhetoric is explored in Roseann M. Mandziuk and Suzzane Pullon Fitch, "The Rhetorical Construction of Sojourner Truth," *Southern Communication Journal* 66, no. 2 (2001), 120–137.

EVOKED AUDIENCE

If the persona is the image that the rhetor constructs of him or herself as a speaker, the **evoked audience** is the attractive image that the rhetor constructs of and for the audience in order to encourage it to act according to that image. If the speaker's constructed self-image can be considered as the "first" persona, then the evoked audience can be considered as the "second" persona. The concept of the second persona was advanced by Edwin Black. For him, an astute rhetorical critic can thus see "in the auditor implied by a discourse a model of what the rhetor would have his real auditor become."[11] The function of the evoked audience, or this "second persona," is to create an attractive image of unity that makes members of an audience desire to be a part of it by acting collectively toward the same end.

In its most general form, we find politicians using evoked audiences whenever they speak of the *American people* as a collective body of people who love liberty, freedom, and democracy. By creating a category of identity that can unify a group of separate individuals, an evoked audience creates the possibility of cooperative action because it contributes to the creation of a sense of unity that may not have existed before the speech. For example, we often take for granted that everyone who is born in the geographic boundary of the United States is an "American," but prior to the revolution, people identified themselves more with their local city or region. For revolutionaries to start using the term *American* thus helped make possible a national identity that stood apart from the British Empire.[12]

Like the concept of persona, the evoked audience is a partly fictional identity that usually overstates the unified character of the people listening to a speech (who in reality are far more diverse). Like persona, the evoked audience often is what a rhetor *wants* an audience to be rather than what it literally *is*. Yet this ideal often brings a new reality into existence. For instance, a collection of teenagers may all be good at a certain sport, but they are usually not yet a team until the coach starts telling them to act like one. The coach's rhetoric creates a sense of commonality by evoking the team spirit within the individual players that may not have been fully present before. The most typical sign that such a team spirit is being attempted by a speaker is the repetitive use of "we" or "you," such that an audience feels it is being grouped together under a single category. One can imagine a parent telling his or her children, "If we are a family, then we will eat together at the dinner table." The implicit choice now placed upon the audience is whether or not to accept that group membership.

Therefore, although there is a fictional quality about an evoked audience, this does not mean that it is an illusion. Clearly, a speaker who speaks to an audience of school children as if it were all members of Congress is not literally accurate. However, motivational teachers *can* speak to them as "future leaders of America" and anticipate an energetic response. In other words, the evoked audience should always select and amplify shared qualities that are already present (or at least potentially present) within an audience. The average audience of college students, for instance, can be referred to

---

[11]Edwin Black, "The Second Persona," *Readings in Rhetorical Criticism,* ed. Carl R. Burgchardt (State College, PA: Strata Publishing Co., 1995), 90.

[12]For more on the "public" as an evoked audience, see Michael McGee, "In Search of the People," *Quarterly Journal of Speech* 71 (1975), 235–249.

as "university students," or "citizens," or "eager young people," or "future leaders," or "party-goers." Each of these designations may be partly true, but each of them only speaks to one portion of that group's identity. Consequently, deciding what identity to evoke in an audience has different consequences for rhetorical persuasion.

Despite what has been said, however, one should not think that the evoked audience is something that the speaker always *does* to the audience. Many times, an audience goes to a speech, as with a "rally," precisely to feel a part of a common identity. In this case, the evoked audience is merely the vehicle through which this desire is actualized. In other words, the audience must be *active,* not *passive,* in generating its sense of common identity. Historically, this desire for community becomes acute during times of tragedy. Such an event occurred on April 19, 1995, when U.S. citizen Timothy McVeigh detonated a truck bomb in front of the Murrah Federal Building in Oklahoma City. The explosion destroyed the entire front side of the building, killing 169 men, women, and children and injuring hundreds of others. After the bombing, on April 23, long-time Christian-Evangelical Preacher Billy Graham participated in a special memorial service for the victims of the disaster. Knowing that his audience included people of many faiths, however, Graham tried to find an evoked audience in which everyone could participate. He began simply with the fact that almost everyone there lived in Oklahoma, thereby constructing an image of the state's citizens as strong and faithful. He said:

> The wounds of this tragedy are deep. But the courage and faith and determination of the people of Oklahoma City are even deeper. A part of my family lives in Oklahoma. My father had a brother, an older brother, a giant of a man, and he came to Oklahoma and he founded a business in Tahlequah, in Muskogee. I came to Oklahoma City and held two or three crusades. The first one was here in these fairgrounds many, many years ago. Some of you might have been little children at that time.
>
> But I've known something of the strength and the courage and the character of people that live in Oklahoma . . . What an example Oklahoma City and the people of Oklahoma have given to the world, because the television has been carrying it as much as any event I can ever remember like this. And the cooperation between officials of every level of government and the community, no matter what religious group we belong to and what political views we may have.[13]

The evoked audience here is clearly a group of caring, courageous, and cooperative citizens, all working together and sacrificing for the common good regardless of differences in religion or politics. Graham even subtly includes himself within that audience when he mentions his own history with the state, thus creating a persona of an Oklahoma native speaking to his fellow citizens.

Discussion: The creation of team spirit on a sports team is often crucial to its success. At the same time, individual players are often praised and criticized in order to create a healthy spirit of competition. In your experience with organized athletics, how did you see the coach navigate the tension between creating a unified, evoked audience on the one hand and distinguishing individual players on the other? Which strategy was more effective in the long run?

---

[13]Available from The American Rhetoric at americanrhetoric.com (accessed on April 28, 2010).

IDENTIFICATION

When Billy Graham connects aspects of his persona with that of the evoked audience, such as when he relates his own connection to Oklahoma, he engaged in the rhetorical strategy of identification. When we "identify" with someone, we see ourselves as sharing some quality or experience with another person or group. Usually this feeling comes after the revelation of a life experience that we see as similar to our own. The process of making friends with people often begins with this process of identification in which two strangers find themselves sharing in some common interest, habit, belief, or feeling. In this sense, the process of identification is how two or more people come to form a bond that generates commonality out of what might seem, at first, to be different perspectives.

In rhetoric, **identification** is the strategy of creating a common bond with an audience by drawing parallels between the characteristics of speaker and audience. For Kenneth Burke, *identification* is a broad term which "ranges from the politician who, addressing an audience of farmers, says, 'I was a farm boy myself,' through the mysteries of social status, to the mystic's devout identification with the source of all being."[14] What each of these examples has in common is a sense that two or more distinct and unique individuals share in some "essence" or "quality" that transcends their individuality (love of farming, class identity, and divine origin, respectively). This sense of commonality thus leads to people uniting in a common purpose. For instance, when Sojourner Truth argues that she also possesses "masculine" qualities, she creates a commonality between men and women that had not previously been present. In short, identification represents the persuasive attempt on the part of the rhetorical agent to say "I am one of you" in order to create a sense of "we." The justification for such a strategy is that we tend to prefer listening to people who feel and think like we do.[15]

As the example taken from Billy Graham demonstrates, identification can be used to solidify a preexisting similarity. However, identification can also be one way in which previously marginalized groups attempt to include themselves as active parts of the general public. For instance, after the American victory in the Revolutionary War, many opponents of slavery—particularly the slaves themselves—hoped it would lead to an end of that oppressive institution. One such person was Benjamin Banneker, a child of a freed slave who taught himself mathematics and astronomy and eventually published several successful almanacs. On August 19, 1791, he sent one of his almanacs to Thomas Jefferson along with a letter that rebuked Jefferson for his proslavery views. He went on to compare black slavery to the British rule over the Colonies. One strategy Banneker used to convince Jefferson of the evils of slavery was identification. However, the power of his identification comes only after beginning with the appearance of difference and division:

> I suppose it is a truth too well attested to you, to need a proof here, that we are a
> race of beings, who have long labored under the abuse and censure of the world;
> that we have long been looked upon with an eye of contempt; and that we have

---

[14]Kenneth Burke, *A Rhetoric of Motives* (Berkeley: The University of California Press, 1969), xiv.

[15]For more on identification, see Gary C. Woodward, *The Idea of Identification* (Albany: State University of New York Press, 2003).

long been considered rather as brutish than human, and scarcely capable of mental endowments.[16]

This appearance then becomes the very problem to be resolved through identification, which establishes commonalities between the two groups of people due to their both being, in effect, "children of God." He goes on:

> Now Sir, if this is founded in truth, I apprehend you will embrace every opportunity, to eradicate that train of absurd and false ideas and opinions, which so generally prevails with respect to us; and that your sentiments are concurrent with mine, which are, that one universal Father hath given being to us all; and that he hath not only made us all of one flesh, but that he hath also, without partiality, afforded us all the same sensations and endowed us all with the same faculties; and that however variable we may be in society or religion, however diversified in situation or color, we are all of the same family, and stand in the same relation to him.[17]

Banneker's persuasive strategy clearly is meant to draw from the very principles of equality that Jefferson had enshrined in the Declaration of Independence. In short, he argues Jefferson's statement that "all men are created equal" clearly includes all human beings, including African-American slaves.

Discussion: Strategies of identification are often at their height during adolescence. As we struggle to "fit in," we try to find ways of bridging what are inevitably superficial differences in order to get along as a group. Do you remember some of your successful and failed strategies of identification during this stressful time of life? And when did a successful strategy of identification actually end up having bad consequences?

DISTINCTION

Identification is a mainstay of rhetorical persuasion, but it is not always sufficient. Especially in times of uncertainty in which we seek good advice rather than loyal friendship, we often look to those people who are very *unlike* us because they possess uncharacteristic excellence in character or special expertise in a very specific subject. In other words, we often want speakers not to "fit in" but to "stand out." In this case, we look not for identification but for **distinction**, which is the attempt to establish credibility by the possession of special knowledge and/or unique experience that are superior to the audience. **Special knowledge** refers to the kind of knowledge one receives by learning technical discourses and procedures, such as the knowledge one receives from attending a university. Whether experts are scientists, theologians, ethicists, economists, or movie critics, they all base their arguments on the knowledge not accessible to the general public. **Unique experience** refers to the kind of expertise one acquires by having "been there" or "gone through that." For example, it is a common dramatic technique used in all war movies that the highly educated new officer always defers to the practical experience of the veteran soldier once combat begins. The officer might be more capable

---

[16]Zinn and Arnove, *Voices of a People's History of the United States,* 58.
[17]Ibid.

to discuss broader military strategy (thus having special knowledge), but the enlisted soldier usually knows better what to do in the heat of battle (thus possessing unique experience). The ideal, of course, is a fusion of both qualities within a single person.

In cases of *distinction*, the persona of the rhetor stands apart from the evoked audience; in cases of *identification*, it is aligned with it. Both represent forms of credibility, but distinction is credibility from *difference* (even if it is just difference in degree), whereas identification is credibility from *likeness*. Frequently, some combination of the two is most useful.[18] To continue the military metaphor, a four-star general cites the possession of superior knowledge and broader experience in order to justify leading a campaign, but he or she usually makes an effort to also establish how he or she is still a common soldier "at heart" in order to command loyalty. Presidential candidates, too, often spend a great deal of time touting their expertise while simultaneously spending most of their days eating hot dogs, going bowling, or kissing babies. They want to appear as ordinary citizens and extraordinary leaders simultaneously.

This balance between humility and expertise is apparent in the speech given by conservative talk-show host Rush Limbaugh before the incoming House GOP "freshmen" who had been elected in 1994. This election was significant insofar as it gave the Republican Party the majority in the House of Representatives for the first time since 1954. During that election, much credit was given to Limbaugh for his energetic and influential advocacy of conservative positions over the radio. Limbaugh, however, wished to moderate such claims, arguing in fact that his direct influence was limited. In his opening remarks, he thus seeks to place himself actually *below* his foreground audience of both Congressional representatives and *within* his background audience of the American public. He says:

> To all of you in this room, the freshmen class of 1994—for me to sit here and actually think I had some serious, profound role in it—you are the ones who took the risks. You are the ones who ran for office. You are the ones who raised the money. You're the ones who took the flak. You're the ones who took the heat.
>
> I'm just a media guy who happens—and this is a key and I think all of you should never forget this because these reporters who were asking me questions about talk radio were all trying to say in a roundabout way, that I took a bunch of brainless people and converted them to mind-numbed robots and every day would send out code in my show that would force them to march to the polls on November the 8th and pull the lever I wanted them to pull. And the fact of the matter is that's not what's happened . . . What happens on talk radio is real simple: We validate what's in people's hearts and minds already.[19]

So far, Limbaugh seeks to create identification with his *radio* audience while actually flattering his *political* audience. Yet he also signals his distinction as a "media guy."

---

[18]The desirability of a mixture of both qualities is exemplified by the notion of "source credibility" as explained by Jack Whitehead in "Factors of Source Credibility," *Quarterly Journal of Speech* 54 (1968), 59–63.

[19]Available from The American Rhetoric at americanrhetoric.com (accessed on April 29, 2010).

This category gives him a special status that actually stands above both audiences. Later, he then makes use of this strategy of distinction in giving advice to the representatives about his area of expertise. He continues:

> I was told to give you some advice about the media. You don't know how small I feel giving you advice. But I'll be glad to anyway since I've been asked to. The first thing I would like to tell you, you're coming into the beltway—inside the beltway—and as we're all human beings, and we all are susceptible to human nature, and we all want to be liked; we all want to be loved; and you all want to live in surroundings which are not hostile. But inside the beltway for people like us this is not possible. And so sometimes to avoid the hostility, we say things and then begin do things designed to gain the approval of those who are hostile toward us. I want to warn you against it. I want to warn you: you will never ever be their friends. They don't want to be your friends.
>
> Some female reporter will come up to one of you and start batting her eyes and ask you to go to lunch. And you'll think, "Wow, I'm only a freshman. Cokie Roberts [award-winning journalist] wants to take me to lunch. I've really made it." Don't—seriously—don't fall for this. This is not the time to get moderate. This is not the time to start trying to be liked. This is not the time to start gaining the approval of the people you've just defeated.[20]

Limbaugh's distinction as a "media guy" allows him to give such advice because he is trusted to know something about how the media influences the public's view of their political representatives. His stature as a popular talk-show host gives his words weight that makes his audience pay attention. The audience gives him authority as a rhetor.[21]

Discussion: Give an example of when, as a child playing with friends, you appealed to your unique experience to guide your friends' behavior and made use of special knowledge to inform their judgments. Were you successful? Did you have an argument about whose experience or knowledge was better?

POLARIZATION

For something to be "polarized" is to have two objects that repel each other from a distance. For instance, the North Pole and the South Pole represent two sides of the earth, but they are not antagonistic toward one another. They are simply far apart. Two magnets of the same polarity, however, will literally repulse each other when brought together. Similarly, two friends separated by thousands of miles are not polarized, but simply distant; two enemies in the same room, however, will probably seek opposite corners. Polarization thus represents a kind of movement that intentionally separates two things. For example, we are often forced to choose between aligning ourselves with one group or another with little room for

---

[20]Available from The American Rhetoric at americanrhetoric.com (accessed on April 29, 2010).

[21]For a Burkean interpretation of Limbaugh's public rhetoric, see Edward Appel, "Rush to Judgment: Burlesque, Tragedy, and Hierarchal Alchemy in the Rhetoric of America's Foremost Political Talk Show Host," *Southern Communication Journal* 68, no. 3 (2003), 217–230.

compromise. Either we are "with them or against them." And those who seek compromise in this situation are thus usually attacked from both sides for being wishy-washy. In a polarized environment, the decision not to choose is also a choice that puts us at risk for being abandoned, rejected, or ignored.

By its nature as an art that thrives in conflict and uncertainty, rhetorical discourse often magnifies these choices and uses the contrast to force a decision. In rhetoric, **polarization** is the strategy of dividing an audience into a positive "us" and a negative "them" in order to create unity through difference. The "them" in this case is usually a **criticized audience** that represents a group antagonistic to the rhetor's interests, like another political party, or simply a demonized audience that is used as a convenient foil, like a group of "traitors" or "evil-doers." The strategy is then to argue that if one does not follow the path preferred by the rhetor (a path that ends in belonging to an evoked audience), then this person will align him- or herself with a group of people who lack ethical or practical judgment. Most children become acquainted with this strategy early on in their lives when they are encouraged to behave during the year so that Santa Claus includes them on his "nice" list rather than his "naughty" list. This same model can be applied effectively in the analysis of contemporary partisan politics.[22]

Including "polarization" within a public speaking textbook may appear to border on the unethical. After all, are we not usually advised to invite as many people as possible to hear our speech? Is it not completely inappropriate in a tolerant age to pick out a group of people (or a type of person) to criticize or condemn? The work of Kenneth Burke is instructive here. Throughout his writings, Burke lamented the tendency for **scapegoating** in public rhetoric, in which all of a public's "sins" are placed upon a largely defenseless group and then run out of town.

At the same time, however, Burke also recognized that "division" is a natural state of human nature, and that "insofar as the individual is involved in conflict with other individuals or groups" then the actions of that individual "fall under the head of Rhetoric." Moreover, rhetorical action cannot avoid the effects of polarization. Burke wrote that "one need not scrutinize the concept of 'identification' very sharply to see, implied in it at every turn, its ironic counterpart: division."[23] For instance, even the statement "we should all love one another" can be used to divide those who love from those who hate. Burke's point is that we must be aware of the implicit acts of polarization that occur in all our identifications, to make them explicit, and to do our best to make our criticisms of others intelligent, precise, just, and sympathetic.

Furthermore, polarization becomes less problematic when it is based more on values or attitudes than on one's belonging to this or that social group. Certainly, parents who ask their children whether they want to be a "doctor" or a "couch potato"

[22]Some examples of the rhetoric of polarization include Andrew King and Floyd Douglas Anderson, "Nixon, Agnew, and the 'Silent Majority': A Case Study in the Rhetoric of Polarization," *Western Speech* 35, no. 4 (1971), 243–255; William D. Harpine, "Bryan's 'A Cross of Gold': The Rhetoric of Polarization at the 1896 Democratic Convention," *Quarterly Journal of Speech* 87, no. 3 (2001), 291–304; David E. Foster, "Bush's Use of the Terrorism and 'Moral Values' Issues in his 2004 Presidential Campaign Rhetoric: An Instance of the Rhetorical Strategy of Polarization," *Ohio Communication Journal* 44 (2006), 33–60.

[23]Burke, *A Rhetoric of Motives*, 23.

are using polarization primarily to inspire them to do their best. In this case, the negative audience is not real but hypothetical—it represents a "type" of behavior we find distasteful. This still involves ethical responsibility, but it often can be used for purposes of genuine encouragement. The responsibility of speakers is thus to identify all possible divisions and to avoid unnecessary or unintentional castigation of other groups, even in the name of the most noble and respectable goal or virtue.

A strategic variation on this "encouraging" strategy of polarization often occurs in court trials when lawyers appeal to the "better angels of our nature" in making a favorable decision. For instance, on May 29, 1924, two wealthy and highly educated university students from Chicago named Nathan Leopold, Jr., and Richard Loeb lured 14-year-old Bobby Franks into a car and subsequently kidnapped and killed him, taking care to cover their tracks by burning the body and pretending the boy had been taken for ransom. In reality, the two students had murdered Franks to test a theory that they were "Nietzschean supermen" who could commit a perfect crime without being caught. Predictably, when the method and motives of their crimes were revealed after their captures, there was widespread public demand for their execution.

In the midst of this turmoil, lawyer Clarence Darrow took the case for their defense. His intention was not to prove their innocence but rather to put capital punishment itself on trial. After convincing his clients to plead guilty, he embarked on a defense that the two young men weren't completely responsible for their actions, but were the products of the environment in which they grew up, an environment that condoned intolerance and cruelty. At the conclusion of his summation, Darrow polarized two competing value systems in an effort to make his audience choose the path of "love" over that of "hatred." The first path he described as the path of execution:

> The easy thing and the popular thing to do is to hang my clients. I know it. Men and women who do not think will applaud. The cruel and the thoughtless will approve.[24]

Certainly, this path does not appear to be an attractive one. It is the "easy" one applauded by people who "do not think" and approved by the "cruel and thoughtless." Worse still, this path has harmful consequences for another group of people. He continues:

> It will be easy today; but in Chicago, and reaching out over the length and breadth of the land, more and more fathers and mothers, the humane, the kind, and the hopeful, who are gaining an understanding and asking questions not only about these poor boys but about their own, these will join in no acclaim at the death of my clients. These would ask that the shedding of blood be stopped, and that the normal feelings of man resume their sway.[25]

According to Darrow, pursuing the easy path of cruelty has long-term negative consequences for "the humane, the kind, and the hopeful" who are struggling to raise their children in a peaceful country. For this virtuous group of people, crime

---

[24]Gregory R. Suriano, *Great American Speeches* (New York: Gramercy Books, 1993), 153–154.
[25]Ibid.

needs to be punished without falling victim to the very forces of cruelty which motivated the criminals. Hence, he effectively polarizes two groups of people—those who would hate and those who would love—and implies that a judge or jury who would condemn murderers to death belong to the same group as the murderers themselves. This argument is made clear in his closing sentences:

> I know the easy way. I know Your Honor stands between the future and the past. I know the future is with me, and what I stand for here; not merely for the lives of these two unfortunate lads, but for all boys and all girls; for all of the young, and as far as possible, for all of the old. I am pleading for life, understanding, charity, kindness, and the infinite mercy that considers all. I am pleading that we overcome cruelty with kindness and hatred with love . . . I am pleading for the future; I am pleading for a time when hatred and cruelty will not control the hearts of men. When we can learn by reason and judgment and understanding and faith that all life is worth saving, and that mercy is the highest attribute of man.[26]

This is certainly not a fair fight by the end. On the one side stands the "easy way" of cruelty and hatred; on the other side stands the "future" of life: understanding, charity, kindness, infinite mercy, love, reason, judgment, and faith! Who would chose to be a party to the first group? Certainly not the judge, who decided to sentence the two boys to life in prison—where they were subsequently murdered by other inmates.[27]

Discussion: What creative types of "encouraging" polarization strategies were used by your parents when you were growing up? What "name" did they give to each group? Did they actually affect your behavior at all?

CONCEPT REVIEW

Concept	Definition	Example
PERSONA	The image of the speaker "created" by the speech itself.	"I've always worked hard to make my own way. I paid for my first car and made all the repairs myself. You know I've been responsible. Don't I now deserve a new car?"
EVOKED AUDIENCE	The image of the audience "created" by the speaker.	"I know you have always taught me to be independent. I couldn't ask for more loving parents who taught me to be my own person."

---

[26]Ibid.

[27]For more on Darrow's courtroom rhetoric, see Martin Maloney, "The Forensic Speaking of Clarence Darrow," *Speech Monographs* 14, no. 1 (1947), 111–126. For more on the trial of Leopold and Loeb, see Charles E. Morris III, "Passing by Proxy: Collusive and Convulsive Silence in the Trial of Leopold and Loeb," *Quarterly Journal of Speech* 91, no. 3 (2005), 264–290.

Concept	Definition	Example
IDENTIFICATION	The establishment of "common ground" between speaker and audience.	"And I think I've become that person. But I also know that Grandpa bought Dad the car he used to drive across country. I have that same desire. But I can't make that drive in that old rusty Chevette."
DISTINCTION	Proving that the speaker has special knowledge or experience that sets them above the audience.	"I know this seems greedy, but I'm just trying to tell you what I've learned. Twenty years ago, a person could go without a good car. But these days, people judge you by your possessions. A good car means a good job. Trust me on this."
POLARIZATION	Separating the evoked audience from a criticized audience.	"My friend Kyle wanted a new car too, but his cold-hearted parents said he didn't need it. But then they used the money to go on a Mexican cruise, and then Kyle lost his job because his car broke down and he couldn't get to work. You don't want to be like them, do you?"

KEY WORDS

Agent   131
Apologist   131
Criticized audience   140
Distinction   137
Ethos   129
Evoked audience   134

Form of delivery   131
Hero   132
Identification   136
Inherited ethos   130
Partisan   132
Persona   130

Personal stories   131
Polarization   140
Scapegoating   140
Special knowledge   137
Unique experience   137

SUMMARY

Even for people who are widely loved and admired (those, that is, with a highly favorable inherited ethos), there is still more rhetorical work to do than just showing up. For example, Martin Luther King, Jr., walked into Holt Street Baptist Church already with a positive inherited ethos. Although King was only twenty-six years old at the time of the speech, he had been pastor of Dexter Avenue Church for over a year and had already earned a reputation for his powerful preaching. Still, he now had to establish himself as a social leader by solidifying his audience into a movement. Because he did not need to "introduce" himself, his *persona* was largely constructed through his manner of speaking rather than any references that would *distinguish* himself from the audience. His strength as a leader was not something to prove through a recitation of credentials, but through a demonstration of courage and vision. For instance, the transcript records that the first "thundering applause" and vigorous audience feedback (given in parentheses in the text of the speech) occurred several paragraphs into his speech when King switched gears from talking about Rosa Parks and the problems at hand to express his own personal emotions and desires in response to these problems:

> And you know, my friends, there comes a time when people get tired of being trampled over by the iron feet of oppression. [*Thundering applause*] There comes a time, my friends, when people get tired of being plunged across the abyss of humiliation where they experience the bleakness of nagging despair. (*Keep talking!*)

There comes a time when people get tired of being pushed out of the glittering sunlight of life's July, and left standing amid the piercing chill of an alpine November. (*That's right!*) [*Applause*] There comes a time.[28]

The repetition of "there comes a time," followed by such language of despair, in effect establishes King's persona better than any résumé. It shows a speaker who has steeled himself to move forward against all obstacles and has committed himself to sacrifice for a higher cause. Instead of a young, 26-year-old man fresh out of getting his Ph.D., we have a resolute warrior for social justice. Most important, he has established this persona without even referring to himself in the first person.

The next major task for King was to create an *evoked audience* that shared a sense of *identification* and purpose against forces that were *polarized* against it. The members of this evoked audience needed to have a very clear sense of who and what they were about so that they could act with confidence as a group, trusting that what one wanted, the others wanted just the same. One general quality they all shared, as King points out early on, is that "We believe in the Christian religion. We believe in the teachings of Jesus." Yet this point of identification is general; it applies to all American Christian churches, black or white, liberal or conservative. It does not do enough to solidify a group identity specific to its rhetorical situation. Knowing this, King ends his speech on a very concrete description of who he wants his audience to be:

As we stand and sit here this evening and as we prepare ourselves for what lies ahead, let us go out with a grim and bold determination that we are going to stick together. [*Applause*] We are going to work together. [*Applause*] Right here in Montgomery, when the history books are written in the future, (*Yes!*) somebody will have to say, "There lived a race of people, (*Well!*) a *black* people, (*Yes sir!*) 'fleecy locks and black complexion,' (*Yes!*) a people who had the moral courage to stand up for their rights. [*Applause*] And thereby they injected a new meaning into the veins of history and of civilization." And we're gonna do that. God grant that we will do it before it is too late. (*Oh yeah!*)[29]

For King, it is not enough simply to attribute to his audience the virtues of bold determination and moral courage. It is not even enough to say it will inject new meanings into the veins of history and civilization. He also makes sure to point out that members of the audience are a *black* people of "fleecy locks and black complexion" that distinguish them from other people. This is a much different kind of rhetoric than the one used in his "I Have a Dream" speech in which he tended to focus more on the brotherhood of all mankind. Here, the immediate issue is not integration. The issue is solidification and motivation. And as a *member* of that community, his strategy also serves to *identify* him with its interests, thereby creating continuity between his persona and the evoked audience. Therefore, the more specific he can be in terms of what unifies his immediate audience, the more unified his movement will be, at least in the short term.

Finally, this strategy of identification is made stronger by polarizing King's audience with an audience made up primarily of white racists. Convenient about this act of polarization is that it not only gives a name to groups that are in political opposition to King's audience; it also associates a certain method—of violence and intimidation—with that polarized audience. Consequently, King simultaneously uses these racist groups to give a name to "evil" and to demonize the method of violence even when put to use in the name of

---

[28]Martin Luther King, Jr., "Address to the First Montgomery Improvement Association (MIA) Mass Meeting" (Montgomery, AL, December 5, 1955). Available from Stanford University's website, http://www.stanford.edu/group/King/publications/autobiography/chp_7.htm (accessed on April 16, 2010).
[29]Ibid.

"good." Hence, King kills two birds with one stone:

> My friends, don't let anybody make us feel that we are to be compared in our actions with the Ku Klux Klan or with the White Citizens Council. [*Applause*] There will be no crosses burned at any bus stops in Montgomery. (*Well, that's right!*) There will be no white persons pulled out of their homes and taken out on some distant road and lynched for not cooperating. [*Applause*] There will be nobody amid, among us who will stand up and defy the Constitution of this nation. [*Applause*] We only assemble here because of our desire to see right exist.[30]

The construction of an audience is not simply a matter of "mere description." The creation of a social movement requires the shared faith that a group of strangers can be counted on to act toward the same goals with the same methods. The only way such a faith can be produced is by constructing a common identity that people voluntarily adopt, even if it is just a temporary one. The rhetorical strategy of ethos involves creating a persona that can be trusted by an audience so that it willingly comes together to pursue a common end. The fact that such "coming togethers" happen so rarely in history demonstrates the difficulty in creating this sense of unity in the long term.

CHAPTER 5 EXERCISES

1. Analyzing your rhetorical artifact, which was the primary strategy to constitute ethos with the audience? Choose one and explain using quotations.
2. Break into groups of two and briefly interview your partner about the accomplishments in their life, drawing on specific examples. Then give impromptu speeches of introduction for the other person, creating for them an exaggerated persona (by using the strategy of distinction) that presents them in a heroic light. Did the speech about yourself sound anything like you?
3. Divide yourselves by class either by year (freshman, sophomore, etc.) or by major. Have each group come up with a speech that argues why its year or major has distinction and then use polarization to show why it is better than the others. Was any element of these speeches persuasive to the other groups?
4. Randomly break into groups of four. For a few minutes, try to find what you have in common. Then create a name for a "club" to which you all belong and give a list of characteristics (which you all possess) that are necessary to be part of that club. (The name of the club should also reflect something about these shared qualities.) Present this to the class. How many other people belong to that club? Which club is the most exclusive and which one was the most inclusive?
5. Come up with some absurd ethical argument (e.g., clothing should be optional when coming to class). Now create an impromptu speech that relies on creating an evoked audience that would naturally favor this argument (e.g., we are all "free spirits" who reject any kind of constraint on our freedom). Which was the most persuasive?

---

[30]Ibid.

Logos

This chapter addresses the forms of reasoning that can be used to persuade an audience based on factual evidence. Of all forms of proof, those from reasoning are the most cognitive (as opposed to "affective" or "emotional"). In rhetoric, reasoning is the capacity to interpret and organize elements of a problematic situation in order to make certain practical judgments seem more prudent than others. Reasoning, however, comes in two primary forms: logical and narrative. Logical reasoning deals with specific relationships among facts described in a "mathematical" sense. Narrative reasoning addresses matters of fact in terms of linear stories that paint a more vivid picture of a scene. The relevant concepts for logical reasoning are the relationships among claims, grounds, and warrants, the list of most common warrants (generalization, sign, causal, principle, authority, analogy), and the list of common fallacies (either/or, slippery slope, bandwagon, ad hominem, false cause, scapegoating, red herring, non sequitur, excessive authority). The relevant concepts for narrative reasoning are narrative probability and narrative fidelity. The goal of this chapter is to show how to develop rational arguments, based on the best available evidence, that are also clear and persuasive.

When citizens of Classical Greece used the word *logos,* they usually used it to mean *words, arguments,* or *reason.* For example, the term *dissoi logoi* (meaning "double arguments") was a common phrase that referred to the Greek belief that there were always two or more arguments opposed on every issue. The Greeks acquired this belief largely because of their reliance on courts of law to decide almost any dispute. Any time two people came into conflict, their instinct was to bring this conflict into court in order to hear both sides and come to a practical judgment. In these sorts of rhetorical contexts, **logos** refers to the use of rational arguments and evidence to persuade an audience of the reasonableness of one's position. It is based on the belief that human beings are rational beings with the potential to make decisions based on logic, principles, and evidence.[1]

This faith in the rationality of human beings is one of the primary justifications for rhetoric. Without the faith that people make better practical judgments when presented with more comprehensive and accurate facts, we would be forced to rely purely on either habit or luck. However, this faith in human rationality should not be interpreted to be somehow in competition with the other rhetorical appeals of ethos and pathos. Reason plays a vital role in human decision-making, but it is rarely, if ever, sufficient to making

---

[1]For the various meanings of *logos,* see George B. Kerferd, *The Sophistical Movement* (Cambridge, UK: Cambridge University Press, 1981), 83.

good decisions. Often, our emotions are necessary to judge right from wrong, effective from ineffective, and pleasure from pain. Likewise, our ability to discern who is a more reliable advisor during times of crisis can rarely be made by logic alone. In fact, our need to trust other people usually arises precisely when logic reaches its practical limit. The very idea of the rhetorical situation supports this conclusion—for if we had all the facts that we needed to make a decision, we would hardly need to be persuaded of anything. Only when we lack sufficient reason do we usually seek out a path based on a more intuitive form of judgment.

Yet lack of sufficient reason still means that we must make the best of what we have. The use of logos in rhetoric effectively requires us to chart a path based on the available evidence at hand. Charting this path requires us to challenge, supplement, or change parts of our belief structure in order to alter the cognitive "maps" we use to understand our environment. For example, when Christopher Columbus sought to reach India by crossing the Atlantic Ocean, he relied on the best maps available. These maps, of course, ignored the huge land mass of North and South America that stood in between Europe and India, and his "discovery" of these continents forced Europeans to significantly modify their maps. The rhetorical use of logos is very much like the maps Columbus relied on before anyone could confirm what he might encounter. It attempts to guide judgment based on the best available evidence, knowing, on the one hand, that what ends up happening probably will require further adaptation but, on the other hand, that no new discovery can be made unless we risk venturing into the unknown.

LOGICAL REASONING

The first kind of reasoning is **logical reasoning**, which is the use of inferences and proofs to establish relationships among propositions which warrant specific conclusions. Whenever we debate with ourselves or with others about why one thing or action is better than another, and use reasons to defend or arrive at our conclusion, we engage in the process of logical reasoning. Thus, a statement of fact or belief on its own, such as "I think it will rain today," only becomes an expression of reasoning when it is defended or justified with a reason, such as "because there are dark clouds on the horizon." By incorporating reasons for our beliefs, we make our thought process more complex and capable of modification. Otherwise, we are stuck simply trading beliefs with one another. Reliance of reasons thus allows us the freedom to change our beliefs by reaching a common ground based on accepted forms of evidence.

Based on the Aristotelian-inspired model developed by Stephen Toulmin, reasoning consists primarily of the relationship between three things: the claim, the grounds, and the warrant. A **claim** is the primary position or conclusion being advanced by a speaker ("We should drink more red wine."). The **grounds** are the supporting evidence for the claim ("Because we want to savor the good life."). The **warrant** is the inferential leap that connects the claim with the ground, usually embodied in a principle, provision, or chain of reasoning ("Wine is a necessary condition for bringing about the good life."). What makes this relationship so complicated in rhetoric is the fact that the warrant is usually left unstated. The assumption is that the audience will "fill it in" for itself by drawing from such resources as social judgment, public opinion, convention, values, beliefs, or attitudes. Because the warrants are, in many ways, obvious, it is thus poor rhetorical form to state the connection that everyone can make for themselves. Take the following examples:

Claim: "We need to outlaw abortion."
Grounds: "Because abortion is murder."
Warrant (unstated): "Anything that is murder must be outlawed." [Principle]

Claim: "Stop smoking."
Grounds: "Because you value your health."
Warrant (unstated): "Cigarette smoking damages your health." [Causal]

Claim: "We are clearly headed toward a recession."
Grounds: "Because job growth has slowed considerably in the last quarter."
Warrant (unstated): "Slow job growth indicates a coming recession." [Sign]

Claim: "We should go on a bike tour through Europe this summer."
Grounds: "Just like they did in that movie."
Warrant (unstated): "Our experience will be as enjoyable as the one in the movie." [Analogy]

Claim: "I'm never buying this make of car again."
Grounds: "Because I had to bring it constantly for repairs."
Warrant (unstated): "All cars of this make will be as prone to breakdown as this one." [Generalization]

Claim: "Don't climb that ladder."
Grounds: "Because my dad told me not to."
Warrant (unstated): "We should always do what my dad tells us." [Authority]

In each of these cases, the warrant acts as a "bridge" between the claim and the grounds and remains unstated because it draws from common knowledge or obvious inferential leaps that would be redundant to make explicit. Yet the relationship between claims, grounds, and warrants can be made even more complicated by the addition of backing, rebuttal, and qualification. **Backing** is a reason used to justify the warrant ("Italians have used wine to bring about the good life for centuries."). **Rebuttal** acknowledges the conditions where the claim might not hold ("Of course, I would never suggest giving wine to an alcoholic."). **Qualification** admits to the degree of certainty or confidence that the speaker has in the claim ("If I am wrong, then let Bacchus strike me down!"). One can thus "map" an argument using the following diagram:

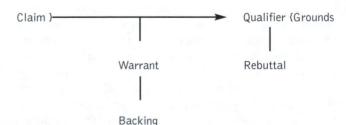

For example:
Let us declare Independence from England now!}

```
                                    ┌──────────► I only know {Because there are warships
                                    │            what I see          in Boston Harbor.
                                    │
                                    │
                                    │
                                    Unless my eyes deceive me
```

Warships in the harbor
are a sign of war/Declaring independence
beforehand will be politically beneficial

The Boston Massacre is also a sign of impending war/
Independence provides us the element of surprise

Although backing, qualifiers, and rebuttals give a speech added sophistication, the most difficult part of persuasive reasoning is the construction of an argument that employs a legitimate warrant to connect the grounds to the claim. In addition to a warrant by authority (which effectively rests on the assumed credibility of a source), there are five primary warrants that can be used to constructs persuasive arguments: generalization, analogy, sign, causation, and principle.[2]

Generalization

Generalization warrants drawing a general conclusion about a class of people, events, objects, or processes based on specific examples drawn from experience. For example, after trying many specific lemons and finding each of them sour, we are warranted in making the general claim "all lemons are sour" based on the grounds that "these lemons are sour." It is also known as argument by "specific example" when various examples are used to support a general claim. For example, I might claim that "I only win when I wear my lucky socks" and then use as grounds the numerous examples of games that I won and lost with or without my socks. The only difference between the example of the lemons and that of the socks is the order in which evidence is presented; in the case of the lemons, the examples about tasting preceded the conclusion. In the case of the socks, the claim was made first and was followed by past examples. But what qualifies as a claim or grounds has nothing to do with the order of presentation.

---

[2]This model is elaborated in Stephen Toulmin, *The Uses of Argument* (Cambridge, UK: Cambridge University Press, 1958). See also Wayne Brockriede and Douglas Ehninger, "Toulmin on Argument: An Interpretation and Application," *Quarterly Journal of Speech* 46 (1960), 44–53.

However, the order in which the argument is constructed does have an effect on how an argument is understood. Presenting grounds first tends to raise the curiosity of an audience ("I have witnessed many bloody wars in my days, so . . ."), whereas presenting evidence afterward more strongly reaffirms a claim of fact (". . . because I have witnessed too many bloody wars."). In both cases, the claim that "There is no such thing as a bloodless war" is warranted on the generalization that all other wars have been bloody. But the style of the presentation does have an effect on how it is emotionally received by an audience.

The legitimacy of a generalization rests on the capacity for the rhetor to prove that these examples are not isolated cases but are numerous and consistent enough to represent a pattern. Often termed as the *inductive leap,* the end of a classical inductive argument ends in a leap from isolated cases to a broader principle that can then be reapplied deductively to future cases. For example, the repeated loss of jobs is used to prove an economic recession, the repeated rejection of minority applicants is used to justify accusations of racism, or the repeated mistakes of a politician is used to prove general incompetence. Once these principles are proved, they can then be used deductively in future arguments. The situations in which warrants from generalization are employed are those in which people do not know which general facts or beliefs are truer than others. The ethical responsibility of one employing inductive reasoning is to make sure the breadth of examples are genuinely representative of a situation and not "cherry-picked" simply to show one side of the story. In other words, one should toss out a whole barrel of "good" apples by a false generalization from one "bad" one.

A standard use of generalization in political speeches is the use of a specific citizen or community to stand in for a whole class of virtuous Americans. In 1992, for example, conservative commentator and author Patrick Buchanan delivered a speech at the Republican National Convention after a failed bid to win a place on the Republican ticket. His responsibility as a convention speaker was to praise the Republican candidate George H.W. Bush and to criticize Democratic candidate Bill Clinton. Central to the theme of his speech was the argument that Democratic policies overlooked the needs of average working Americans who were the foundation of the nation. To make his point, Buchanan spoke about the individual people he met during his campaign:

> There were those workers at the James River Paper Mill, in Northern New Hampshire in a town called Groveton—tough, hearty men. None of them would say a word to me as I came down the line, shaking their hands one by one. They were under a threat of losing their jobs at Christmas. And as I moved down the line, one tough fellow about my age just looked up and said to me, "Save our jobs." Then there was the legal secretary that I met at the Manchester airport on Christmas Day who came running up to me and said, "Mr. Buchanan, I'm going to vote for you." And then she broke down weeping, and she said, "I've lost my job; I don't have any money, and they're going to take away my little girl. What am I going to do?"[3]

So far, these examples lack a claim and hence do not consist of an argument. They are just specific instances waiting for a conclusion to bring them together, a way of

[3]Available from The American Rhetoric at americanrhetoric.com (accessed on April 28, 2010).

ordering the speech that raises tension and curiosity. Buchanan thus proceeds to deliver the claim:

> My friends, these people are our people. They don't read Adam Smith or Edmund Burke, but they come from the same schoolyards and the same playgrounds and towns as we came from. They share our beliefs and our convictions, our hopes and our dreams. These are the conservatives of the heart. They are our people.[4]

Interestingly, Buchanan actually states the warrant explicitly: "These people are our people." This warrant thus connects the claim "These are the conservatives of the heart" to the grounds of the numerous examples of virtuous, hard-working Americans. Consequently, his purpose up until this point is one of identification—of creating commonality between himself and his audience based on shared values and problems. Of course, this identification is then used as a resource for a further claim: "We must take back our cities, and take back our culture, and take back our country." The point is that it is only through generalization that the audience knows what Buchanan means by "we."[5]

Discussion: Think about the many generalizations people make about dogs. How did you develop your ideas about dogs through repeated experiences? How do the generalizations made by dog owners differ from those who never have owned one?

Analogy

Analogy warrants the comparison of two things that might not otherwise go together for the purposes of drawing a conclusion based on their sharing a vital similarity. For example, if a person has never tasted a certain food, we try to draw analogies between other foods, like the old cliché that every strange meat tastes like chicken. Although the two foods are not the same, they can thus fruitfully be compared in order to make a practical judgment based on a more familiar experience. In everyday life, we thus draw analogies whenever we react to another person's experience by saying, "This reminds me of the time when . . ." We know that our own experience is not the same as our friends, but we think it is "close enough" to be helpful in guiding judgment or aiding in understanding.[6]

The constructive purpose of an analogy is to help understand a confused or problematic situation by drawing parallels with another, more familiar, one. This allows us to make more informed judgments in response to some exigence by seeing what worked and what didn't in similar contexts. For example, when the terror attacks of September 11, 2001, occurred, it was such an extraordinary event that people struggled to find an analogy through which to make sense of it. For

---

[4]Ibid.

[5]For an analysis of Buchanan's conservative rhetoric, see Robert C. Rowland, "Entelechial and Reformative Symbolic Trajectories in Contemporary Conservatism: A Case Study of Reagan and Buchanan in Houston and Beyond," *Rhetoric & Public Affairs* 4, no. 1 (2001), 55–84.

[6]For more on argument by analogy, see James R. Wilcox and Henry L. Ewbank, "Analogy for Rhetors," *Philosophy and Rhetoric* 12 (1979), 1–20; James S. Measell, "Classical Bases of the Concept of Analogy," *Argumentation and Advocacy* 10 (1973), 1–10.

some, the closest historical analogy was Pearl Harbor; for others, it was the Oklahoma City bombing; and for many people, it simply was in a class by itself—without analogue. But the struggle to find an analogy shows how judgment of present events can be assisted by reference to other, more familiar, past events. And as new events become understood, they, in turn, become sources for analogy. Undoubtedly, any future terror attack will now be compared to 9/11.

In rhetoric, rhetors use analogical reasoning to warrant claims for or against actions grounded on similar successes or failures in past situations. For example, one of the most frequent analogies used to condemn American military action is that of the Vietnam War, just as the analogy used to support it is World War II. By saying "this is another Vietnam," a rhetor implies we are stuck in a quagmire, while saying "this leader is another Hitler" is to argue against any policy of appeasement. The use and effectiveness of such analogies hinge on whether the comparison is accurate and convincing in the context in which it is made. The ethical responsibility of a rhetor is to make sure that this analogy "holds up" under scrutiny and is not made for short-term gain at the expense of long-term insight.

The choice of analogies that a rhetor uses speaks volumes about his or her attitudes. For example, the civil rights movement in the United States is now largely associated with the nonviolent means of civil disobedience championed by Dr. Martin Luther King, Jr., and his frequent use of biblical metaphors of the "Promised Land." However, support for Dr. King's method of resistance was by no means universal in the black community. The most outspoken critic of the effectiveness of nonviolent methods of social change was Malcolm X. In his speech "Message to the Grass Roots" delivered on November 10, 1963, he uses an analogy to warrant his claim that the only effective revolution is a violent one. First, he establishes the problem to be solved—the definition of the nature of a revolution. He asks:

> What is a revolution? Sometimes I'm inclined to believe that many of our people are using this word "revolution" loosely, without taking careful consideration [of] what this word actually means, and what its historic characteristics are. When you study the historic nature of revolutions, the motive of a revolution, the objective of a revolution, and the result of a revolution, and the methods used in a revolution, you may change words. You may devise another program. You may change your goal and you may change your mind.

Clearly, part of Malcolm X's argument about the nature of a revolution is also going to involve arguments from generalization insofar as he promises to look at a series of revolutions and draw from them general characteristics. He goes on:

> Look at the American Revolution in 1776. That revolution was for what? For land. Why did they want land? Independence. How was it carried out? Bloodshed. Number one, it was based on land, the basis of independence. And the only way they could get it was bloodshed. The French Revolution—what was it based on? The land-less against the landlord. What was it for? Land. How did they get it? Bloodshed . . . The Russian Revolution—what was it based on? Land. The landless against the landlord. How did they bring it about? Bloodshed.

With the generalization now established that a revolution seeks land and employs the means of bloodshed to get it, he then seeks to draw an analogy to the present situation:

> So I cite these various revolutions, brothers and sisters, to show you—you don't have a peaceful revolution. You don't have a turn-the-other-cheek revolution. There's no such thing as a nonviolent revolution . . . A revolution is bloody. Revolution is hostile. Revolution knows no compromise. Revolution overturns and destroys everything that gets in its way. And you, sitting around here like a knot on the wall, saying, "I'm going to love these folks no matter how much they hate me." No, you need a revolution.[7]

The success of this analogy is based on the belief that African-Americans living in 1963 face the same conditions as those revolutionaries in Russia, in France, and in America. If these conditions are not the same, then the analogy does not hold. Also, an audience must also ask whether the revolutions mentioned by Malcolm X actually brought about beneficial consequences for the people.[8]

Discussion: Analogical reasoning is often at the heart of good comedy. We laugh when we see our situation in a new and unfamiliar way that seems absurd. What analogies have you heard that put some current public controversy or personal crisis in a "funny" light? Why did it work? And when did such an effort fail?

Sign

Sign warrants the diagnosis of some underlying condition based on the appearance of external clues or indicators. This warrant is similar to generalization insofar as it draws a general conclusion based on the analysis of particular things. However, generalization attempts to unite many specific things under a general class or "heading," as if the goal was to place items in their right boxes. Sign is more interested in identifying what lies *behind* the examples and which causes them to appear, much as a doctor is not interested in classifying a skin rash so much as determining what kind of infection or condition brought it about. Warrants based on sign are usually called for in situations when people are concerned with identifying the nature of a problem—in attempting to make the "unseen" into something tangible and objective. They are thus strongest when based on thorough historical and scientific research.

In the rhetoric dealing with matters of social justice, argument by sign is often used to warrant claims of the existence of pervasive oppression of some form. For example, on July 18, 1848, a group of women met at the house of Elizabeth Cady Stanton in Seneca Falls, New York, and drafted the document "Declaration of

[7]Howard Zinn and Anthony Arnove, *Voices of a People's History of the United States* (New York: Seven Stories Press, 2004) 400.

[8]For more on Malcolm X's rhetoric, see Finley C. Campbell, "Voices of Thunder, Voices of Rage: A Symbolic Analysis of a Selection from Malcolm X's Speech, 'Message to the Grass Roots'," *Speech Teacher* 19, no. 2 (1970), 101–110; John Louis Lucaites and Celeste Michelle Condit, "Reconstructing 'Equality': Culturetypal and Counter-Cultural Rhetoric in the Martyred Black Vision," *Communication Monographs* 57, no. 1 (1990), 5–24; Robert E. Terrill, "Protest, Prophecy, and Prudence in the Rhetoric of Malcolm X," *Rhetoric & Public Affairs* 4, no. 2 (2001), 25–53.

Sentiments and Resolutions," which launched the women's suffrage movement. Modeling the document on the Declaration of Independence, Stanton asserted that "all men and women are created equal" (an argument of praise for the equal power of women) and then proceeded to use sign to warrant her claim that the "history of mankind is a history of repeated injuries and usurpations on the part of man toward woman, having in direct object the establishment of an absolute tyranny over her." In effect, Stanton is trying to diagnose the reason for the pervasive inequality in the sexes. She offers as grounds these "facts submitted to a candid world":

> He has never permitted her to exercise her inalienable right to the elective franchise.
>
> He has compelled her to submit to law in the formation of which she had no voice.
>
> He has withheld from her rights which are given to the most ignorant and degraded men, both natives and foreigners.
>
> Having deprived her of this first right as a citizen, the elective franchise, thereby leaving her without representation in the halls of legislation, he has oppressed her on all sides.
>
> He has made her, if married, in the eye of the law, civilly dead. He has taken from her all right in property, even to the wages she earns.[9]

Clearly, if any of these facts are themselves found to be at fault, then the validity of her general claim is called into question. This shows the fragility of reasoning by sign. Because it proves a single argument relies on numerous supporting facts, it requires the rhetor to make sure that every single supporting fact is also defensible. If there are any "weak links" in the chain, the whole argument structure falls apart.[10]

Discussion: Human beings are notorious for being hypochondriacs, both about the health of their own body as well as the "social" body. On one hand, when have you "diagnosed" a condition based on only a few instances only to be proven false? On the other hand, what superstitions still exist that attribute seemingly mundane signs to major causal events (like the sign of a black cat indicates the coming of bad luck)?

Causation

Causation warrants a practical conclusion based on the likely effects brought about by some underlying cause. Causal reasoning is embodied in "if–then" statements of the kind: "Put on your coat, because if you go outside without a jacket, then you will get cold." This kind of reasoning is employed wherever we are encouraged to act (or not act) based upon a cause-effects analysis of what might happen in the future based on analysis of the present. In concentrating on matters of causal relation, causation thus is similar to warrant by sign. However, sign concentrates on diagnosing an unknown cause based on effects already present.

---

[9]Zinn and Arnove, *Voices of a People's History of the United States,* 126.

[10]For more on Stanton's rhetoric, see Susanna Kelly Engbers, "With Great Sympathy: Elizabeth Cady Stanton's Innovative Appeals to Emotion," *RSQ: Rhetoric Society Quarterly* 37, no. 3 (2007), 307–332.

Causation focuses more on predicting the future effects based on present causes already known. In rhetoric, rhetors use warrant by causation whenever they advocate for actions because of the pragmatic consequences (e.g., "Tax cuts will revive our economy."), whereas they use sign when they attempt to explain effects due to underlying causes (e.g., "The loss of jobs and the stifling of the economy are clear indications that we are laboring under a tax burden.").

Due to its scientific nature, causal reasoning naturally relies heavily on expert testimony to establish its accuracy. The function of such testimony is twofold: (1) to determine what is likely to occur based on current causal forces if left to operate on its own ("If we do nothing, the economy will continue toward the abyss"), and (2) to evaluate possible courses of action based on their likely effects ("We can either put our heads in the sand or we can radically cut income taxes."). Of course, a rhetor should always be careful to appeal to "expertise" that already has some "weight" with an audience. The warrants of astrology are hardly persuasive to a group of astronomers and vice-versa. The ethical balance is to argue what you believe to be the true causes while citing primarily those sources that already have a favorable ethos with an audience.[11]

A classical example of struggle over the validity of causal warrants is the debate over gun control. The motto "guns don't kill people, people kill people" actually is a way of reorienting the *cause* of violence from the capacity of the agency (the gun) to the moral choices of the agent (the person). But in his February 11, 1997, speech to the National Press Club, actor and then President of the National Rifle Association (NRA) Charlton Heston addressed a second matter of causation dealing with guns, but this one being positive rather than negative—that guns actually bring about and help protect the other freedoms we hold dear. Heston was addressing an audience of journalists, and he felt that they irresponsibly tended to attribute violent crime to the widespread presence of guns in the United States. For members of the audience, the claim that "America is a violent nation" would be connected to the grounds that "We have more guns per capita than any Western nation" with the causal warrant "The presence of guns increases the tendency to use them for violent crime." Before moving to his positive point, then, Heston had to first criticize the validity of this warrant and replace it with another. He argues:

> Think about it—what else must young Americans think when the White House proclaims, as it did, that "a firearm in the hands of youth is a crime or an accident waiting to happen"? No—it is time they learned that firearm ownership is constitutional, not criminal. In fact, few pursuits can teach a young person more about responsibility, safety, conservation, their history and their heritage, all at once. It is time they found out that the politically correct doctrine of today has misled them. And that when they reach legal age, if they do not break our laws, they have a right to choose to own a gun—a handgun, a long gun, a small gun, a large gun, a black gun, a purple gun, a pretty gun, an ugly gun—and to use that gun to defend themselves and their loved ones or to engage in any lawful purpose they desire without apology or explanation to anyone, ever.

---

[11]For a discussion of causal inferences, see David Zarefsky, "The Role of Causal Argument in Policy Controversies," *Argumentation and Advocacy* 13 (1977), 179–191.

This is their first freedom. If you say it's outdated, then you haven't read your own headlines. If you say guns create only carnage, I would answer that you know better. Declining morals, disintegrating families, vacillating political leadership, an eroding criminal justice system and social morals that blur right and wrong are more to blame—certainly more than any legally owned firearm.[12]

In these passages, Heston first employs an argument by principle, stressing twice the warrant that "Gun ownership is a constitutional right." However, knowing that principle is not enough, he substitutes what he sees as a fallacious causal warrant (that "Guns cause violence.") with one he believes is more legitimate (that "Declining morals are the cause of social violence."). Finally, he concludes by constructing an argument in which private gun ownership produces beneficial causes:

Please, go forth and tell the truth. There can be no free speech, no freedom of the press, no freedom to protest, no freedom to worship your god, no freedom to speak your mind, no freedom from fear, no freedom for your children and for theirs, for anybody, anywhere without the Second Amendment freedom to fight for it. If you don't believe me, just turn on the news tonight. Civilization's veneer is wearing thinner all the time.[13]

In a savvy adaptation to his audience of journalists, Heston makes the claim that "We have freedom of speech today" based on the grounds that "We are free to own guns" based on the causal warrant that "Gun ownership allows citizens to protect their rights." In this way, Heston does not merely criticize what he sees as false reasoning, but gives his audience an actual reason to support his own claims based on a shared interest in preserving free speech—and, indeed, civilization itself.

Discussion: One of the most fascinating examples of the human imagination comes in the form of the causal arguments put forth by children. What is the most fantastic causal argument that you put forward as a child or hear another child propose? What do you think was the basis for this argument?

Principle

Principle warrants judging the character of some particular object, event, or process based on a universal belief or definition. A **principle** is defined as a comprehensive and fundamental law, doctrine, or assumption that can account for many particular things. For example, the principle that "All humans are mortal" is a fundamental *law* that guarantees that every particular human being will some day die; "All men and women are created equal" is a *doctrine* that justifies striking down any particular laws that violate equality of opportunity; and "Adult swans are white" is an *assumption* that allows a person to judge, with some confidence, whether or not a certain bird is a swan based on its color. Reasoning by principle does not deal with

[12]Charlton Heston, "On Gun Control," available at http://www.save-now.com/news/archives/Charlton-Heston-Gun-Controle.htm (accessed on May 5, 2010).

[13]Charlton Heston, "On Gun Control," available at http://www.save-now.com/news/archives/Charlton-Heston-Gun-Controle.htm (accessed on May 5, 2010).

causes and effects. It deals with defining something as one thing or another (a "human" or a "god," a "swan" or a "mallard") or as possessing one quality or another ("mortality" or "immortality," "white feathers" or "brown feathers"). It helps us place things in the correct categories based on the relationship between general descriptions and particular things so that we can say, "This is an X."

The strength of warrant by principle hinges on whether or not the principle to which a rhetor appeals (usually a belief or a value) is already deeply held by a particular audience. For example, the belief that "candy is sweet" is one to which most children readily agree, whereas "candy is full of empty calories" is not. Hence, the statement, "Try it, it is candy" will automatically be understood by a child to mean that they should try it because candy is sweet. But they will not understand, "Don't eat it, because it's just candy" if it assumes they will make the connection between the candy and the health effects of eating empty calories. Although both are perfectly reasonable arguments, the latter speaks more directly to the child's experience. The ethical responsibility of the rhetor, then, is to select principles that are both accurate and acknowledged by an audience. Otherwise, one either reaffirms false beliefs or fails to persuade.[14]

One frequent political use of reasoning by principle is to help define the character of a particular nation or society. This problem of self-definition was particularly acute for the Puritans, led by John Winthrop, who left Britain for the shores of North America, where they had to forge a new identity in a strange land. This identity was based on a shared belief that they were servants of God who were on a divine mission to purify the church and combat the forces of the Antichrist. Their duty in New England was to establish a society that embodied all the elements of God's glory and thus function rhetorically to shame and to inspire others to follow their example. In his speech "A Model of Christian Charity" delivered in 1630, Winthrop draws on the preexisting principle that New England society is blessed by God. The first part of his speech merely restates the belief that is already shared by his audience. He begins:

> The Lord will be our God, and delight to dwell among us, as His own people, and will command a blessing upon us in all our ways, so that we shall see much more of His wisdom, power, goodness and truth, than formerly we have been acquainted with. We shall find that the God of Israel is among us, when ten of us shall be able to resist a thousand of our enemies; when He shall make us a praise and glory that men shall say of succeeding plantations, "May the Lord make it like that of New England."[15]

In this introduction, Winthrop makes the claim that "God will dwell among us more in New England" based on the grounds that "His own people have left 'Old' England to found a new society." This is based on the widely held principles that "The Puritans are God's chosen people" and that "God prefers to dwell amongst his chosen people," inferring that in "Old" England, the population was full of

---

[14]For more on argument by principle, see Chapter 4 of Richard M. Weaver, *The Ethics of Rhetoric* (Davis, CA: Hermagoras Press, 1985).

[15]Ronald Reid and James Klumpp, *American Rhetorical Discourse* (Long Grove, IL: Waveland Press, 2005), 24.

non-Puritans who did not follow God's path, thereby making it a place in which God did not wish to dwell. His conclusion follows:

> For we must consider that we shall be as a city upon a hill. The eyes of all people are upon us. So that if we shall deal falsely with our God in this work we have undertaken, and so cause Him to withdraw His present help from us, we shall be made a story and a by-word through the world. We shall open the mouths of enemies to speak evil of the ways of God, and all professors for God's sake. We shall shame the faces of many of God's worthy servants, and cause their prayers to be turned into curses upon us till we be consumed out of the good land whither we are going.[16]

The difference from the introduction is that Winthrop is no longer making claims about the audience's relationship with God; he is now addressing the political relationship between New England and the rest of the world. Thus, Winthrop claims that "We shall be as a city upon a hill" and based on the grounds "The eyes of all people are upon us." These two assertions are connected by the principled warrant that "All people look up with reverence and expectation upon things blessed by God." Of course, this position comes with responsibility. His claim that "They must not deal falsely with our God" based on the grounds that "It will cause Him to withdraw His present help from us" is connected by the principle that "God only helps those who deal truly with Him." As the saying goes, with great power comes great responsibility.[17]

Discussion: When we say that we take a *principled stand* on something, we often mean that we do so from allegiance to a principle that stands in contradiction to some utilitarian causal argument. When have you taken such a stand in your life? Do you regret doing so based on the perceived benefits you might have gotten from using a causal argument?

FALLACIES IN LOGIC

Fallacies represent not only the failure for a warrant to successfully "bridge" the claim and the grounds, but a failure of construction so egregious that the whole argument tumbles into the abyss. That is to say, people can be "wrong" or "unpersuasive" while still holding to the standards of logical reasoning. A fallacy stands for those arguments that should probably never have been made in the form and context they were delivered. Often called "invalid" forms of reasoning, fallacies are described as distorted forms of normal reasoning that rely on exaggeration or misdirection to produce persuasive effects. Rhetoric is usually associated with "fallacious" reasoning for this purpose. To produce immediate effects, political rhetors often rely on fallacies rather than more precise logic for the simple reason that audiences often find fallacies easier to understand, more interesting to hear, and sometimes more persuasive to act upon. In other words, at times we find persuasive in the present moment which on reflection seems patently absurd and offensive. The goal of studying

[16]Ibid.

[17]For more on Puritan rhetoric, see Patricia Roberts-Miller, *Voices in the Wilderness: Public Discourse and the Paradox of Puritan Rhetoric* (Tuscaloosa: University of Alabama Press, 1999).

fallacies is thus to be able to better identify fallacies during their invention and/or reception in order to avoid performing and/or considering poorly constructed arguments that we would be better off rejecting.[18]

It is important to keep in mind, however, that there is no one clear criteria by which to distinguish between a *valid* and *invalid* reasoning. All forms of reasoning must be judged with respect to the context in which they are spoken. Take the example of the statement "Either we fight or we die." If someone were to make such an argument whenever he or she got into any interpersonal conflict with someone, most people would think that individual was insane; it would be the worst form of an either/or fallacy that forces people into extreme positions. However, put that statement in the mouth of a Jewish citizen living in the Warsaw Ghetto during the Nazi occupation of Poland, and it becomes an irrefutable truth. One should be careful, in other words, to judge people's words as fallacies without taking into consideration the situation which gave those words meaning.

The importance of context also forces one to attend to the background assumptions of an audience. The fact is that two different audiences will come to completely different conclusions whether or not something is a fallacy. A typical phenomenon in partisan politics is that one will always find a way to rationalize the mistakes of his or her favored candidate while seeing in the other candidate nothing but flagrant errors in logic. This is simply human nature; but it also shows something about how to approach the use of reason in rhetoric. A rhetor who does not take into account the perspectives of an audience will usually find that much of his or her reasoning is rejected because he or she didn't cite common authorities, employ familiar forms of reasoning, or promote desired conclusions. Because of this, some rhetors will then be tempted simply to "cater" to the biases of an audience regardless of whether or not they believe what they say. The balance, as usual, is between advocating the position one believes to be true while adopting the message so that the audience will still be able to follow willingly along. One must find a way to make an ethical and valid argument effective.

The determination of a fallacy should thus address the following questions: (1) *Understood purely on the level of symbolic relationships, do the assertions contained in warrant, claim, and grounds add up to a coherent whole?* (i.e., the argument "I hate animals, so I'm buying myself a cat" does not make sense in the mathematical sense that $A \neq B$, at least until one includes the intention of trying to overcome one's dislike of animals.); (2) *Understood as a practical tool to address a problematic situation, does the argument address matters relevant to its resolution?* (i.e., the argument "Life is short, so why not?" is reasonable advice for a person planning a trip to France, but it is inappropriate for someone pondering jumping off of a bridge.); (3) *Understood as part of a persuasive message, does the language employed draw from audience beliefs and linguistic conventions such that it conveys the intended meaning?* (i.e., the argument "I love the United States, for it

---

[18]Books which explore fallacies include Alex C. Michalos, *Improving Your Reasoning*, 2nd ed. (Belmont, CA: Prentice Hall, 1986); T. Edward Damer, *Attacking Faulty Reasoning*, 2nd ed. (Belmont, CA: Wadsworth, 1987); Patrick J. Hurley, *A Concise Introduction to Logic* (Belmont, CA: Thomson Learning, 2000). There are also many websites which provide an extensive list of fallacies, such as http://www.don-lindsay-archive.org/skeptic/arguments.html as well as classic propaganda strategies such as http://propagandacritic.com.

is a land of freedom" makes sense spoken by a naturalized citizen to her daughter on the eve of the daughter's college graduation, but it is a fallacy spoken by a slave-owner to his slaves.). The point is that the determination of a fallacy is significantly context-dependent. This does not reduce fallacies to whether or not they persuade an audience in the short term; rather, it takes into account a longer-term perspective on whether a statement will "hold up" over time to an audience of history.

Either/Or

Perhaps the most powerful of the fallacies, **either/or**, presents audiences with a stark choice by presenting two clear but completely opposite and incompatible alternatives based on excessive exaggeration of good and bad qualities. The point of either/or is to remove any possibility of compromise or "middle ground" by eliminating gray area and defining the available options in black and white. Like the strategy of polarization, the intention of either/or is to collectively move people in a single direction by portraying one path of action in a wholly positive light while demonizing the other. These options can be described in terms of cause and effect, such as the argument that "We must either defend liberty or tyranny will reign," or in terms of competing definitional categories, such as the assertion that "You are either a patriot or a traitor." This is interpreted as a fallacy by audiences who seek compromise and middle ground and tend to avoid committing to extremes. It also generally falls flat in times of calm when there is no crisis that demands drastic action.

Discussion: Can you think of a situation you experienced when what might have appeared to be an either/or fallacy was actually an appropriate response?

Slippery Slope

Imagine a person standing on top of an oiled slide that ends in a pit of spikes. If that person takes one last step, down they go. This is the **slippery slope** fallacy, which exaggerates the series of inevitable and terrible consequences that will follow from performing some action. It is a variation of either/or fallacy insofar as it presents a person with a stark choice, but its emphasis is on *prohibiting* an action rather than *encouraging* one. Thus, where an either/or fallacy would say, "We must either *defend liberty* or tyranny will reign," a slippery slope fallacy would say, "We must *not pass this legislation* or tyranny will reign." In terms of being interpreted as a fallacy, the same conditions apply as with either/or. Only in a heightened state of tension marked by fear of the unknown do slippery slope fallacies work. Those able to take a "step back" and reflect usually find that no slope is ever so slippery or straight.

Discussion: Which popular controversies are often phrased in terms of slippery slope arguments? What makes them, more than others, so amenable to this fallacy?

Bandwagon

The name for this fallacy derives from the phrase "to jump on the bandwagon." **Bandwagon** is a form of argument that encourages an audience to do something simply because a majority of other people is doing it. Usually, bandwagon arguments do not appear in such blatant phrases such as "Believe this because everyone else does." For instance, in advertising, bandwagon strategies are employed whenever a product is sold under the assumption that it will make one fashionable and popular. In politics, they are used whenever a principle or position is advocated because it is part of the "American spirit" or reflects the "values of the Heartland" or is reflective of the "will of the people."

The "invalid" aspect of this argument is that popularity does not equal legitimacy. Anyone who does not identify with the selected group, for instance, immediately recognizes this argument as a fallacy. Audiences who *do* identify with the group, by contrast, may also recognize this argument to be invalid, but, because it is also flattering, they may not mind hearing it. The effects of bandwagon fallacies, however, usually result in something of a polarization between "in" and "out" groups. Consequently, bandwagon arguments, even when well-intentioned, often result in indirect forms of exclusion for those who don't jump on board.

Discussion: What are the indirect methods in which popular advertisements employ the bandwagon effect? Can this be accomplished without even showing other people, but rather by showing merely objects or actions associated with a group?

Ad Hominem

Latin for "against the man," an **ad hominem** is an argumentative strategy that undermines an opposing position by attacking the personal character of its advocates rather than the position itself. Ad hominem thus assaults a competitor's ethos, and by doing so makes the arguments of that competitor appear to lack credibility. In political campaigns, most negative advertising takes the form of ad hominem fallacies. For instance, it is an ad hominem to argue that all of an opposing candidate's policy suggestions are suspect because that candidate had an extramarital affair, lied on his or her taxes, or is an alcoholic. What makes such an argument invalid is that the strength and logic of an argument is completely separate from the person who argues; it confuses personal virtue with propositional truth.

One must be careful to distinguish an ad hominem argument from a legitimate questioning of character, however. When a person's character is precisely the issue as it is when a candidate promises to be truthful, wise, and compassionate when in office, questioning that person's character based on past actions is completely justified insofar as past actions are predictors of future ones. It only becomes a fallacy when someone attacks a person's character when it has absolutely nothing to do with the actual issue at hand. Unfortunately, ad hominem attacks are usually successful against people who an audience is already predisposed to doubt. That is why it is so much more important for those speaking from marginal positions to be that much more "pure" of virtue than those speaking from a position of authority.

Discussion: Modern presidential campaigns often seem to be one never-ending series of ad hominem fallacies. Which ad hominem strategies in recent memory stand out as particularly effective? What made them so powerful?

False Cause

The fallacy of **false cause** represents a strategy of attributing causes or effects based on one's immediate desires or fears rather than an objective study of the process. As employed in rhetoric, false causes generally fall into two categories. In the first category, rhetors attribute positive causes or effects to actions or events favorable to the rhetor. For example, leaders of any group will always seek to attribute positive outcomes directly to their wise and steady hand at the helm, even if the leaders may have had nothing to do with the outcomes. By contrast, in the second category, rhetors attribute negative causes or effects to the people, ideas, or objects that the rhetor and his or her audience are already predisposed to dislike. Hence the old adage, "blame it on the weather."

False cause fallacies should be distinguished from arguments that are simply based on limited information. Any rhetorical situation, after all, almost always occurs when all the facts are not in, and when we aren't confident about the entire chain of causes and effects. Certainly, one cannot accuse previous civilizations of false cause fallacies simply because they didn't have the benefit of modern scientific knowledge. False cause becomes a fallacy, then, only when the (a) rhetor knows better but chooses the more politically advantageous cause to benefit his or her self-interest or (b) the rhetor has ready access to better knowledge but has neglected to perform the proper preliminary inquiry before developing an argument. Usually, false cause fallacies based not on intentional manipulation but on the mis-attribution of cause-and-effect come from two sources: (a) *the confusion of correlation with causation,* as when a string of competitive baseball victories coincides with a fan's wearing of a particular pair of socks; and (b) the *confusion of temporal sequence with causal efficacy,* as when the Red Sox's trading of Babe Ruth to the Yankees was said to cause a decade-long "curse" that prevented the team from winning the World Series. In these cases, it is not any intentional deception that is at issue but a failure to examine all the potential causes of victory or defeat.

Discussion: Superstitions of all kinds usually fall into the false cause category. Yet often we follow them even though we know the causal sequence isn't true. What purpose, then, do you think these superstitions hold?

Scapegoating

A more vicious derivative of false cause is the fallacy known as **scapegoating**. This fallacy occurs when the cause of undesired effects is attributed falsely to a marginalized group of people who are generally powerless to defend themselves. The most extreme case of scapegoating, of course, occurred in Nazi-Germany when Jews, homosexuals, atheists, and anyone with a physical or mental handicap was branded as an enemy of the state. By stigmatizing groups, leaders shift the responsibility from themselves to others who are more easily punished. The most frequently referenced example of scapegoating in American history occurred with the Salem witch trials.

However, scapegoating does not happen simply because a person or group is blamed for some undesirable consequence. One can say with some confidence, for instance, that Al-Qaeda and Osama Bin Laden are directly to blame for the 9/11 terror attacks and that drug dealers are rightly blamed for getting children hooked on drugs. Scapegoating occurs only when the group targeted for blame is chosen primarily because they are easy targets and help distract people from the actual causes. Even drug dealers, for instance, become scapegoats when they are used to distract attention from the larger problems of poverty and despair that cause populations to seek out their product.

Discussion: Can you think of a time when you, or someone close to you, were scapegoated in a social situation in order to benefit some other, more popular group? How do you think this situation might have been handled differently in reflection?

Red Herring

Named for the use of a dead fish to throw dogs off a trail, **red herring** is the attempt by a rhetor to distract attention from an issue unpleasant by focusing attention on something unrelated, more sensational, and more beneficial to one's self-interest. This strategy is the rhetorical analogue to shouting "Look over there!" as soon as attention becomes fixed on one's own problems. For example, a speaker might say, "How can we justify wasting taxpayer's money on investigating my financial investments when we are busy fighting a war?" or "My car accident happened because I was so preoccupied with thinking of the terrible state of our roads." Both strategies distract attention away from something damaging to the rhetor (wasting money or driving irresponsibly) and focus attention on something else (war or bad roads). One might also highlight an unrelated but more sympathetic part of oneself to distract attention from the issues, as when one who commits a murder attempts to elicit sympathy based on his or her troubled marriage.

Typically, red herring is most effective when the issue being pointed to also has immediate emotional resonance with an audience. To make someone look "over there" means that there is something interesting over there to look at. The presence of competing objects of interest makes the identification of a red herring a particularly difficult process, however. After all, many times there *are* really more important things to pay attention to than the personal lives of celebrities or politicians. The red herring thus occurs when people who otherwise never talk about certain issues suddenly get passionately concerned when they find themselves in the critical spotlight.

Discussion: The red herring strategy is usually mastered in childhood. Finding a way to distract the critical eye of parents or teachers is part of growing up. Can you remember a time you tried to throw a "dead fish" in the path of an angry authority figure?

Non Sequitur

Latin for "it does not follow," a **non sequitur** is a statement that has no apparent connection with the statements that came before or come after it. Instead of being a logical conclusion or premise, it simply "comes out of nowhere." A person, who in the midst of an argument about economic policy suddenly mentions their love of petunias, commits a non sequitur. There are times, however, when non sequiturs are intended to serve some purpose. For instance, to argue that "television is the enemy of democracy" has no obvious rationale, but perhaps benefits an individual if he or she is arguing for a strict code of media censorship. Other examples might be "I should be President because I love my mother" (especially if one has no other qualifications), or "We shouldn't talk politics on a rainy day" (principally when that discussion is about one's corruption scandal), or "My opponent's affection for cats makes her unqualified for office" (particularly if one has no other advantage over her). Non sequiturs usually occur whenever a rhetor is speaking to a friendly audience and lets his or her guard down. The danger is that unqualified support of an audience sometimes licenses a rhetor to say very silly things.

Discussion: Non sequiturs made by politicians are a never-ending source of entertainment for political comedians. What other famous non sequiturs can you remember being made by figures in the public eye?

NARRATIVE RATIONALITY

As many of the examples used in this book have shown, public speakers rarely restrict themselves to making explicit claims that are grounded in empirical data and warranted by logical reasoning. More often than not, their claims are embedded in stories. These stories may be personal, moral, historical, fictional, or demonstrative, but *as stories* they all share in a common aim—to give meaning to ideas by showing how they function over time in people's lives and in the environment. Thus, the priest who recounts the biblical parable about Noah's Ark to deliver a message about the meaning of redemption, the biologist who explains the development of a giraffe's long neck to demonstrate the meaning of natural selection, and the politician who uses Washington's crossing of the Delaware as an example of American heroism all employ the same rhetorical strategy of making an argument by use of storytelling.

A narrative is thus more than a mere stringing together of events in chronological order. Even the timeline of someone's life, insofar as it has a beginning and an end, is not a narrative. A **narrative** is a dramatic story that creates a desire in an audience and then fulfills that desire by describing the interaction among agent, scene, act, purpose, and agency. This definition of narrative, derived from the work of Kenneth Burke, emphasizes the unique "form" of a narrative that captures and holds the attention of an audience by promising that, through the unfolding of the plot and character, something new and satisfying will be produced at the end. However, this does not mean simply promising some surprise ending. Indeed, the actual conclusion of most great stories is either known already, as in historical narratives, or told ahead of time, like tales that begin by announcing the end, as when a grandparent says, "Let me tell you about the time I helped win the war." Burke explains this effect as:

> the suspense of a rubber band which we see being tautened. We know that it will be snapped—there is thus no ignorance of the outcome; our satisfaction arises from out participation in the process, from the fact that the beginnings of a dialogue lead us to feel the logic of its close.[19]

---

[19]Kenneth Burke, *Counter-Statement* (Chicago, IL: University of Chicago Press, 1931), 145.

The curiosity, then, comes not from a desire to know the conclusion but an interest in seeing how the plot unfolds through the relationship among scene (where), act (what), agent (who), purpose (why), and agency (how). Moreover, we are interested to discover which of these aspects of the plot play the most important role. For instance, we might know that a story ends with the death of the main character, as in a Greek tragedy. But the story is vastly different depending on where we place the blame. If the story deals with war, our character might meet his fate because of where he fought (scene), what he did wrong (act), a flaw in his character (agent), a poorly defined goal (purpose), or the lack of means to achieve that goal (agency). Consequently, part of the joy in hearing different perspectives on the same event is that different people emphasize different parts of a plot, thus creating, in effect, different stories with different moral conclusions.[20]

The rhetorical aspect of narrative becomes clear once we are forced to choose between the validity of competing narratives about the same situation. In our interpersonal life, we are constantly faced with this choice whenever we find ourselves caught in a dispute between mutual friends. Political situations are no different. When faced with competing narratives, an audience must decide which narrative is more "rational" to follow. The two considerations are narrative fidelity and narrative probability. Walter Fisher describes its "rationality" as follows:

> rationality is determined by the nature of persons as narrative beings—their inherent awareness of *narrative probability*, what constitutes a coherent story, and their constant habit of testing *narrative fidelity*, whether the stories they experience ring true with the stories they know to be true in their lives.[21]

In other words, **narrative fidelity** refers to how accurately a narrative represents accepted facts. For example, a chronology of the events of Julius Caesar's life and death has narrative fidelity when they all accord with the facts of the historical record. **Narrative probability** refers to the coherence of the narrative as a story apart from the actual facts. For example, a bare chronology lacks narrative probability because it does not provide a coherent story but only a disconnected series of major events. By contrast, Shakespeare's play *Julius Caesar* has high narrative probability because it provides a dramatic, coherent, and entertaining account of the interactions between characters, despite the fact that it has low narrative fidelity in the most of the interactions were largely invented by the playwright.

The most effective narrative from a rhetorical standpoint should have both high narrative probability *and* high narrative fidelity. By presenting an argument in a form of a story that accurately represents reality in a coherent, engaging, and powerful manner, a speaker invites an audience to vicariously participate in a new vision of reality.

---

[20]These terms are derived from Kenneth Burke's notion of drama, although they leave out the key insight of "dramatistic ratios," which are beyond the scope of this book. For more on drama, see Kenneth Burke, *A Grammar of Motives* (Berkeley: University of California Press, 1962).

[21]Walter Fisher, "Narration as a Human Communication Paradigm: The Case of Public Moral Argument," in *Contemporary Rhetorical Theory: A Reader,* ed. John Louis Lucaites, Celeste Michelle Condit, and Sally Caudill (New York: The Guilford Press, 1999), p. 247. See also Walter Fisher, *Human Communication as Narration: Toward a Philosophy of Reason, Value, and Action* (Columbia: University of South Carolina Press, 1987).

Especially when narratives are broad in scope, these narratives can completely alter an audience's basic worldview. The narratives we tell of our common histories have particular power in structuring our social organizations, our self-conceptions, and our relationships with other groups. Logical rationality plays a crucial role in structuring these things as well, but more often than not they begin and end in narratives.

One way of distinguishing logical reasoning from narrative rationality is to compare ideology with myth. As explained in Chapter 5, an **ideology** is a coherent and interlocking system of beliefs that is used to describe the practical world for the sake of guiding action. The ideology of "democracy," for instance, structures how our government functions (some of its beliefs being a separation of powers, the importance of regular elections, and the centrality of freedom of speech). A **myth**, by contrast, is a timeless story that accounts for the origins, struggles, and destinies of a people through the actions of exceptional people in the past. The myth of the "American Frontier," for instance, provides us a general narrative to understand our present in terms of the past (some of its features being the struggles of valiant pioneers, the heroic resistance of Native Americans, the clash between lawmen and gunslingers, and the eventual coming of civilization). In other words, if democracy, Christianity, and capitalism are ideologies, the American Revolution, the life and death of Christ, and the "American Dream" are myths. Ideology explains present conditions in terms of principles, facts, and consequences; myth explains those conditions in terms of a timeless narrative of the past that continues unendingly into the future.[22]

Narratives play perhaps the most obvious social function in narrating the relationship between our histories and our futures in reference to current problems and questions. For example, following the conclusion of the American Civil War, the United States embarked on the policy of Reconstruction between the years 1863 and 1877 during which Union troops occupied Southern states and enforced federal laws, not the least of which guaranteed civil rights and voting rights for freed men. After the withdrawal of troops, Northern industrialists questioned whether it was safe to invest in an economy still recovering and still possibly "disloyal." To get an answer, the New England Society of New York City, an organization of 300 business and professional men, invited Henry W. Grady, a Southerner and editor and part-owner of *The Atlanta Constitution,* to give a lecture on "The New South" on December 21, 1886. Grady's purpose was to assure investors that the South was ready for Northern investment, and toward that end, he relied on the power of narrative to recast the image of the South as a democratic utopia:

> Under the old regime the Negroes were slaves to the South, the South was a slave to the system. The old plantation, with its simple police regulation and its feudal habit, was the only type possible under slavery. Thus we gathered in the hands of a splendid and chivalric oligarchy the substance that should have been diffused among the people, as the rich blood, under certain artificial conditions, is gathered at the heart, filling that with affluent rapture, but leaving the body chill and colorless.[23]

---

[22]On the distinction between myth and ideology, see Kenneth Burke, "Ideology and Myth," *On Symbols and Society,* ed. Joseph R. Gusfield (Chicago, IL: The University of Chicago Press, 1989), 303–315); Jacques Ellul, *Propaganda: The Formation of Men's Attitudes* (New York: Vintage, 1965), 116–117.

[23]Reid and Klumpp, *American Rhetorical Discourse,* 492.

This narrative develops a desire in the audience by setting forth a desolate picture of the "old regime" in the promise that something "new" is to come. Note also how Grady places blame on the "scene" for the problems of the old regime, specifically the "old plantation." By placing blame on the scene, he is able to make both the slaves and slave-owners (the oligarchy) equally victims of a broken system. The scene of the plantation system thus affects the agents by leaving them "chill and colorless." With the desire to witness a transformation established in his audience, he then moves to the "new":

> The Old South rested everything on slavery and agriculture, unconscious that these could neither give nor maintain healthy growth. The New South presents a perfect democracy, the oligarchs leading in the popular movements social system compact and closely knitted, less splendid on the surface but stronger at the core —a hundred farms for every plantation, fifty homes for every palace, and a diversified industry that meets the complex needs of this complex age.
>
> The New South is enamored of her new work. Her soul is stirred with the breath of a new life. The light of a grander day is falling fair on her face. She is thrilling with the consciousness of growing power and prosperity. As she stands upright, full-statured and equal among the people of the earth, breathing the keen air and looking out upon the expanding horizon, she understands that her emancipation came because in the inscrutable wisdom of God her honest purpose was crossed and her brave armies were beaten.[24]

The major difference in this new narrative is that instead of the scene dominating the agents, the agents (the new democratic oligarchs) now take charge of the scene by dividing up the old plantations into smaller farms. His ironic conclusion is that it is only the defeat of "her brave armies" that finally emancipated the South from the plantation economy and allowed them to emerge victorious and "enamored of her new work." At the end of his speech he received a standing ovation. For his audience, his story seemed to address "hard facts" (thereby achieving narrative fidelity) while at the same time portraying an attractive vision of social progress in which the defeated South actually became *grateful* for its defeat (thereby achieving narrative probability for its Northern audience). Undoubtedly, for a different audience, this narrative would have been received much more skeptically. Grady's strategy of adapting his message to the interests of his audience of Northern industrialists thus shows the ethical dilemma that confronts any rhetor—whether to tell a story the immediate audience wishes to hear, or tell the story that best addresses the long-term problems of the rhetorical background.[25]

Discussion: How do we learn about our nation's history through the recitation of narratives? What are the most common narratives that give meaning to the American experience? By contrast, what are some more marginal narratives that seem to clash with the dominant stories?

---

[24]Ibid.

[25]For more on Grady's speech, see Harold Barrett, "The Lamp of Henry Grady," *Today's Speech* 11, no. 3 (1963), 19–21.

CONCEPT REVIEW

Concept	Definition	Example
PRINCIPLE	Using a shared general principle to define a specific case.	"America supports free speech because free speech is the mark of all great nations."
SIGN	Using external indicators to diagnose or identify an underlying condition.	"The censorship of one newspaper is a sign that we are headed down the path of totalitarianism."
GENERALIZATION	Citing one or more specific cases to prove a general principle.	"Ancient Greece was only the greatest nations in history, and it upheld the doctrine of free speech. Therefore free speech is the mark of a great nation."
CAUSATION	Using a cause-effect analysis to support a claim.	"If we wish to become a great nation, then we will uphold free speech."
ANALOGY	Relying on a comparative examination of a similar situation to inform our judgment about a present situation.	"When Nazi-Germany suspended free speech in the name of national security, it became a tyranny. Let us not follow their example in fear."
EITHER/OR	Framing options in terms of incompatible extremes.	"Either we allow uninhibited free expression, or we choose to align ourselves with the Nazis."
SLIPPERY SLOPE	Warning against an action because it will result in an inevitable slide toward a terrible fate.	"Allow ourselves to restrict just a single protester from speaking his or her mind, and we will begin a trend that ends in everyone being silenced."
BANDWAGON	Advocating a position based on its popularity.	"Don't we want to join the Greeks in the cultural hall of fame as people who championed free expression?"
AD HOMINEM	Attacking an opponent's character in order to undermine his or her position.	"Our state senator says security trumps liberty. But this comes from a man convicted of child abuse."
FALSE CAUSE	Attributing causes or consequences to that which favors you or what is easiest to understand rather than a "scientific" analysis.	"Free speech is responsible for every accomplishment of the nation. By contrast, every time speech is suppressed, our economy lags."
SCAPEGOATING	Blaming a convenient group for all the problems facing a public.	"The security of our nation is not threatened by free speech. It is threatened by lazy people who live off the labor of others."
RED HERRING	Using a more sensational issue to distract attention away from uncomfortable issues.	"There is no real threat from terrorists who advocate violence. Besides, poor building regulations cause more deaths than terrorism. Just the other day, a shoddily-built school collapsed, killing many innocent children."

Concept	Definition	Example
NON SEQUITUR	Making a statement that seems to come "out of the blue" and makes no logical sense.	"I cannot get enough of free speech. Just the other day, after all, I went to the beach."
NARRATIVE RATIONALITY	Making an argument by telling a story that "fits the facts."	"One of the most hard-fought battles over the Constitution was the inclusion of the First Amendment . . ."
NARRATIVE PROBABILITY	Making an argument by telling a story that "fits together."	"George Orwell imaged a world in 1984 in which 'Thought Police' attempted to keep everyone thinking and speaking the same thing . . ."

KEY WORDS

SUMMARY

All of the strategies presented here, both good and bad, represent the effort to use the tools of linkage (and its counterpart, rupture) to piece together (or break apart) a meaningful and ordered representation of a situation on which people can act. To employ rhetorical strategies of *logos* is to engage in the process of creating or deconstructing a "whole" by analyzing the relationships between its parts. In this way, reasoning is much like the art of weaving. On the one hand, a weaver uses all his creative skills to put together certain threads to form a strong, single piece of cloth that provides security and warmth. On the other hand, a weaver also has the critical capacity to identify flaws in the cloth of others and suggest how changes might be made. A rhetor simply substitutes words for thread. Strategies of logos represent the act of taking things apart and putting them back together with words. A person who organizes a bunch of loose threads into a pile is therefore no more a weaver than a person who piles words one on top of another is a wordsmith. What makes a speech reasonable is the same as what makes a cloth strong—it *holds together under pressure*.

In Martin Luther King, Jr.'s speech at Holt Street Baptist Church, one sees logos at work when King feels the need to "make a case" for a claim that might not "hold up" under public criticism. For example, King opens with the following assertions: "My friends, we are certainly very happy to see each of you out this evening. We are here this evening for serious business." But clearly these are not controversial statements that need to be "backed up." These statements do not represent formal acts of *reason*. This does not mean they are not reasonable statements, if one takes *reasonable* to simply mean well-meaning, sympathetic, and generally true. Rather, it means that because he does not support his claims through any form of proof (logical or narrative), his statements do not express a formal act of reason. Consequently, they are not able to be effectively analyzed through the tools of logos.

There are, however, several points in his speech where he takes the time to provide evidence and backing for his assertions. Let us analyze several of them in the order in which they appear:

1. In addressing the issue of the bus boycott, King places recent events within a long history of oppression. Only on this fact could widespread civil disobedience be justified. Otherwise, it would have seemed an overreaction to an isolated event. He explains:

   > For many years now Negroes in Montgomery and so many other areas have been inflicted with the paralysis of crippling fears on buses in our community. On so many occasions, Negroes have been intimidated and humiliated and impressed—oppressed—because of the sheer fact that they were Negroes. I don't have time this evening to go into the history of these numerous cases. Many of them now are lost in the thick fog of oblivion, but at least one stands before us now with glaring dimensions. Just the other day, just last Thursday to be exact, one of the finest citizens in Montgomery—not one of the finest Negro citizens but one of the finest citizens in Montgomery—was taken from a bus and carried to jail and arrested because she refused to get up to give her seat to a white person.[26]

   The reference to "numerous cases" which prove his assertion of years of intimidation, humiliation, and oppression clearly points to the logic of reasoning by sign. Each of these particular, objective incidents reveals an underlying condition of racial intolerance and intimidation in Montgomery.

2. Following on the heels of the arrest of Rosa Parks to prove a claim about social conditions, King takes the time to defend the character of Rosa Parks. Again, he feels the need to mount such a defense in recognition that critics might assert she was a "rabble-rouser" who was arrested not because of her race but because she had caused disruption on public transit. If this counterassertion could be proved, then she would no longer be able to "stand in" for other cases. Hence, King argues as follows:

   > Mrs. Rosa Parks is a fine person. And since it had to happen I'm happy that it happened to a person like Mrs. Parks, for nobody can doubt the boundless outreach of her integrity. Nobody can doubt the height of her character; nobody can doubt the depth of her Christian commitment and devotion to the teachings of Jesus.[27]

   Most of this argument does not represent a form of proof as much as a restatement of the claim that she is a "fine person." The exception comes when King refers to her "Christian commitment and devotion to the teachings of Jesus." This is an example of reasoning by principle. In effect, King makes the claim that "Mrs. Parks is a fine person" based on the grounds that "She is a Christian." The principle warrant is that "All Christians are fine people." As long as we accept that warrant, then the claim holds true—not hard to do in a Christian church!

3. The first two forms of reasoning dealt primarily with proving facts of the matter concerning what was or was not the case at the time. But what about the virtue of their cause and goals? It is one thing to say that there is a problem (racial discrimination) and that people with integrity are attempting

---

[26]Martin Luther King, Jr., "Address to the First Montgomery Improvement Association (MIA) Mass Meeting" (Montgomery, AL, December 5, 1955). Available from Stanford University's website, http://www.stanford.edu/group/King/publications/autobiography/chp_7.htm (accessed on April 16, 2010).
[27]Ibid.

to address the problem (Rosa Parks). It is another thing to say that a particular method of dealing with the problem is right and just. King now has to provide a defense of the burgeoning civil rights movement as a whole. Is it wrong to intentionally violate laws of the city to achieve one's social goal? King responds:

> And we are not wrong, we are not wrong in what we are doing. If we are wrong, the Supreme Court of this nation is wrong. If we are wrong, the Constitution of the United States is wrong. If we are wrong, God Almighty is wrong. If we are wrong, Jesus of Nazareth was merely a utopian dreamer that never came down to Earth.[28]

These examples are carefully chosen to function to as analogical reasoning. By listing the Supreme Court (which gave legal justification for free speech and assembly), the Constitution (which provided the basis for that justification), and God Almighty (who establishes the "just laws" to which all societies are bound), King draws analogies between the principles of his movement and the principles of respected social institutions and worshipped religious deities. Finally, by making reference to Jesus of Nazareth (who appealed to God's laws as rationale for violating the laws of convention), King draws a comparison between the actions of Jesus and the actions of African Americans in Montgomery. Both seek a "higher justice," both adhere to a "higher love," and both are prepared to make physical sacrifices to attain their ideals. To criticize the goals and methods of their movement is thus, by analogy, to criticize the Supreme Court, the Constitution, God, and Jesus.

4. With the situation described and its goals and methods justified, King has only now to describe more fully how its actions are going to bring about the changes they desire. In many ways, King boils this down to one simple mechanism. He says:

> I want to say that in all of our actions we must stick together. Unity is the great need of the hour and if we are united we can get many of the things that we not only desire but which we justly deserve.[29]

The logic here is obvious—as long as its movement attains "unity," then the audience will be able to get what it both desires and deserves. This is a clear case of causal reasoning. "Unity" is warranted not because it has been proven to work through numerous examples (which would be generalization), not because it conforms to Christian beliefs (which would be principle), and not because their situation is like that of Jesus (which would be analogical), but because there is a casual relationship between unity and social action.

Still, an audience might be asking, "How is this all going to play out?" It wants to be able to piece together all of these claims into a big picture that makes sense and appeals to their emotions and imagination. Predictably, King ends on this story that we have already encountered:

> As we stand and sit here this evening and as we prepare ourselves for what lies ahead, let us go out with a grim and bold determination that we are going to stick together. We are going to work together. Right here in Montgomery, when the history books are written in the future, somebody will have to say, "There lived a race of people, a *black* people, 'fleecy locks and black complexion,' a people who had the moral courage to stand up for their rights. And thereby they injected a new meaning into the veins of history

---

[28]Ibid.
[29]Ibid.

and of civilization." And we're gonna do that. God grant that we will do it before it is too late.[30]

Note how this form of narrative rationality is explicitly tied to his earlier causal claim about "unity." King reinforces the causal assertion through a hypothetical narrative of someone looking back from the future at what has been accomplished. Insofar as this story has *narrative probability* (such that the audience members can follow along the plot) and *narrative fidelity* (that this story actually might come to pass in the world through unified action), it functions as a form of "proof" that motivates his audience to action.

For a great speech, all of the pieces of logos just described should "fit together" into a single cloth. An audience member should not leave feeling he or she has just solved ten consecutive logical puzzles that have no relationship to one another. Each step along the way of reasoning should build up upon the step before and predict the step after. This ability to fit the pieces together is one of the most difficult tasks of any speech. It is one thing to collect supporting claims and proofs and pile them on top of one another. It is quite another to create an attractive and persuasive fabric of reason. An expert rhetor must then be both an archivist and an artist; one who digs up material and one who puts that material together into a simple, coherent, and persuasive form.

CHAPTER 6 EXERCISES

1. Analyzing your rhetorical artifact, which was the primary form of logical reasoning used to make a case? Give examples and explain why this form of reasoning was most appropriate to emphasize given the speech topic. Then read the speech to identify any possible fallacies.

2. In response to the question "Why did the chicken cross the road?" give an impromptu speech offering a reason by selecting one of the major forms of logical reasoning. Then try to argue why chickens should be prevented from crossing roads by selecting from one of the fallacies. After each speech, try to identify what form of logos was at work.

3. Find a full-length editorial in a newspaper and identify all the logical reasoning and fallacies it contains.

4. As a class, select a particular argument to make about a current event. Divide yourselves into groups and create an argument using every form of reasoning and two fallacies. Give the speeches and try to identify the forms of reasoning used by other groups. Were they all used correctly?

5. Find an excerpt from a reading you've done in another class by a scientist, historian, philosopher, or other academic scholar. Select a passage that you think employs narrative rationality in what would otherwise be considered a "logical" argument. What functions does it serve?

6. Read the story of Humpty Dumpty. Now briefly write a narrative account of why "All the King's horses and all the King's men" could not piece him back together again. In that account, use at least three forms of logical reasoning. Which account has the most narrative probability and fidelity?

---

[30]Ibid.

Pathos

This chapter explores the ways of constructing appeals to emotion based on charged descriptions of people, objects, events, or actions. Whereas logos persuades based on cognitive beliefs derived from claims of fact, pathos persuades based on affective orientations derived from feelings of like and dislike, desire and fear, and pain and pleasure. The concepts employed thus come in opposite pairs relating to the attractive (+) and repulsive (−) spectrum of emotions, and they are organized according to their relationship to people (saint and sinner), objects (idol and abomination), events (utopia and wasteland), and actions (virtue and vice). The goal of this chapter is to demonstrate how, within certain problematic situations, to attract people to certain things that are beneficial while repelling them from others which are harmful. If logos persuades an audience as to what is the best course of action based on belief, pathos motivates them to actually pursue that course of action out of fear or desire.

In the Greek rhetorical tradition, **pathos** refers to the use of emotional appeals to persuade an audience by putting it in a certain frame of mind that makes it more willing to act in one way instead of another. However, the appeal to emotions does not mean simply arousing irrational expressions of bodily feeling. Emotions represent judgments that we make concerning actual things within our environment—hence, emotions are *objective*. And as a form of intuitive judgment, they also can be surprisingly intelligent. In other words, what we call *intuition* is a kind of emotional judgment that we make about things even when we do not have clear logical reasons for doing so. These intuitions warn us against what is harmful and reveal to us what may be beneficial. Especially when dealing with other people, emotions can sometimes be even more accurate than the conclusions of our logical analysis.

Pathos works in rhetoric, as in good literature, by *showing* and not simply *telling*. Anyone can stand before an audience and suggest that they be angry at one thing and passionate about another. But emotions cannot simply be called forth on command. Because they are generated in reaction to things people can tangibly experience or imagine, emotions are called forth only by rhetoric that offers rich descriptions of great and terrible things which we desire or fear. Instead of telling people to "be horrified at the brutality of the enemy," one can say "the enemy will tear out your eyes and murder your children." Instead of telling people to "feel hope for the future," one can say "we will struggle to the mountaintops to breathe in the crisp air of freedom." Poor uses of pathos will simply name emotions; effective uses of pathos will call them forth without needing a name. Rhetoric uses graphic examples to inspire emotions that make an audience turn away from one thing and towards another.

In other words, the essence of pathos is description, not exposition. Whenever one gives formal reasons, detailed accounts, or logical analysis, one is using logos; the appeal is to one's cognitive belief structure based in propositions and facts. Pathos, by contrast, gives "life" to those beliefs. For example, a speaker can use logos to give a formal cost-benefit analysis for why addressing poverty helps people's lives at the same time that it improves the economy and cuts crime. But one can also describe the squalor of living in a slum, the diseased skin of a hungry child, the lost potential of dying addicts, and the success story of a person who escaped the ghetto through the help of a teacher. Pathos thus incorporates elements of narrative and style to sculpt powerful images that live in people's imaginations and makes them *feel* ideas which logic can only *explain*.

Emotions therefore do not simply name *inner* states of mind and/or body that exist purely inside a person. Emotions are *relational* affairs that deal with things in our environment (real or imagined). For example, John Dewey argues that emotions are the primary means of connecting us to our environment. For Dewey, emotions do not simply arise from some mysterious inner depth; "emotions are attached to events and objects in their movement... toward an issue that is desired or disliked."[1] Emotions arise in the midst of objective situations that relate to our interests. He goes on:

> The rhythm of loss of integration with environment and recovery of union not only persists in man but becomes conscious with him; its conditions are material out of which he forms purposes. Emotion is the conscious sign of a break, actual or impending. The discord is the occasion that induces reflection. Desire for restoration of the union converts mere emotion into interest in objects as conditions of realization of harmony.[2]

Put another way, emotions are intelligent insofar as they inform us of ruptures in our environment and signal their possible restoration. Of course, emotions are also limited; they tend to overemphasize things close at hand and diminish the significance of those things (possibly more important) that do not immediately touch our lives. It is thus the ethical function of rhetoric to try to direct emotions toward the significant and away from the trivial in order to attain a greater and more widely shared harmony.

Despite their incredible variety, all emotions can be characterized by two things—orientation and salience. An **orientation** represents how we stand in relationship to a thing, whether we are attracted (+) or repulsed (−) by it. A *neutral* orientation in which we have no stance thus represents the absence of emotion. For instance, I might have a positive orientation toward my family, a negative orientation to the fire ants in my back yard, and a neutral orientation to my neighbor's mailbox. **Salience** represents how strongly this emotion is felt within a particular situation. When I go on a long business trip I might miss my family terribly (+), when ants bite my child I might desire to destroy the colony (−),

---

[1] John Dewey, *Art as Experience* (New York: Perigree Books, 1934), 20.

[2] Dewey, *Art as Experience*, 41.

and if vandals smash my neighbor's mailbox I may both feel sorry for it (+) and angry at the vandals (−).[3]

Of course, there is a great range of emotions one can feel, and Aristotle goes to great length to detail them in the *Rhetoric*. But for the purpose of simplification, emotions related to rhetoric can be formed into attractive and repulsive orientations to four categories of things—**people**, which represents both individuals and groups (George Washington, the American people, the human race); **actions**, which refer to conscious behavioral choices made by people (eating fast food, declaring war, philosophizing); **events**, which stand for time-bound situations that have a beginning and an end (a car accident, the Middle Ages, the Apocalypse); and **objects**, which represent coherent and durable entities that tend to resist change and have consequences on an environment (the Coliseum, the Roman Empire, Dante's *Inferno*). The concepts of pathos are thus related to each of these four categories in the following way:

Emotional Reference	Positive Orientation (+)	Negative Orientation (+)
People	Saint	Sinner
Actions	Virtue	Vice
Events	Utopia	Wasteland
Objects	Idol	Abomination

To make us feel something strongly, a rhetor must make it stand out from our general environment and endow it with particular qualities that make it worthy of our attention and concern. That is why pathos is necessary in rhetoric. Out of the infinite aspects of our environment, a rhetor must select those things which are vital to address in any effort at a successful resolution. One must necessarily *amplify* and *exaggerate* these things in order for them to stand out and attain salience.

Of course, any time one exaggerates anything; it comes with a significant risk of *over* exaggeration whereby the rhetor blows something so out of proportion that it distorts the actual environment beyond recognition. This can only lead to disappointment or misjudgment. Moreover, the temptation for giving in to excess is one of the primary reasons that rhetoric often has a bad reputation. A rhetor must be careful, then, to always temper the use of pathos with a more reasonable logical analysis. There is nothing wrong with exaggeration when it is done for the purposes of getting an audience engaged and enthusiastic about an issue that it may have otherwise thought important. One must simply supplement this enthusiasm with the kind of practical judgment that can be produced only through long and careful forethought and analysis.[4]

---

[3]For an exploration of the situational characteristic of emotional response, see Phoebe C. Ellsworth, "Some Reasons to Expect Universal Antecedents of Emotion," *The Nature of Emotion: Fundamental Questions,* ed. Paul Ekman and Richard J. Davidson (Oxford, UK: Oxford University Press, 1994), 150–154.

[4]For the relationship between reason and emotion, see John M. Cooper, *Reason and Emotion: Essays on Ancient Moral Psychology and Ethical Theory* (Princeton, NJ: Princeton University Press, 1999).

Also, one must take care to put things back into proportion once the situation is resolved. Exaggeration that is ethical in times of crisis (e.g., amplifying the actual state of a backroom fire in order to get people out of a crowded theater) becomes unethical after actions have been taken to deal with the problem (e.g., persisting in calling the structure a firetrap after safety measures have been instituted). As with all rhetorical acts, one must always attend to the contingencies of a situation, both in the short-term and the long-term, whenever making emotional appeals.[5]

UTOPIA

A utopia is a vision of a perfect event. This event can be personal and momentary, such as the moment parents witness the birth of their first child; it can be shared and historical, such as one's memories of a Golden Age; and it can be shared and futuristic, such as one's visions of the Promised Land. In all cases, the event is portrayed as the culmination of hopes and desires that we yearn to recapture in memory or in actuality. To employ **utopia** is to use the power of an ideal to reveal the limitations of one's actual situation and inspire hope that future "perfect" events will occur. Ronald Reagan, for instance, was famous for referring to the United States in such utopian terms, referring to it as a "Shining City on a Hill." Whenever rhetors engage in this form of exaggeration in which they outline some noble dream for the future or nostalgia for the past, they are engaging in utopia.

This is not to say that utopia is always employed for noble sentiments. Some of the worst crimes in history have been perpetrated by those who use the power of utopia to justify acts of terror and oppression. Yet to abuse a tool does not condemn the tool. The speeches of the most adored and humane leaders of the 20th century, like Ghandi, Martin Luther King, Jr., or Nelson Mandela, equally make use of utopia to liberate and empower. By creating a sense of dissatisfaction with one's present state of affairs and inspiring hope for the future, utopia is one of the most powerful manifestations of pathos.

Ironically, utopia has the most impact for audiences that confront the direst of situations. When people feel they have nowhere to go but up, utopia inspires in them the hope that they can finally lift themselves up out of their conditions. Similarly, as Aristotle pointed out, utopia tends to be more effective with younger audiences that have not had the life experience that typically provides the healthy skepticism which comes with age. Utopia can be powerful, but when employed in the wrong context, it can also make one look very naïve. A coach can employ utopia at the beginning of the season to inspire a team; but when they haven't won a game halfway through the season, talking about winning the national championship might not be the best approach. In this case, a more likely strategy is to use the utopia known as nostalgia for victories in the past.

---

[5]The model of pathos elaborated here owes much to the work of Kenneth Burke, for whom emotion was often an effect of the search for perfection and its consequent need for victimization (either of the self or the other). Burke's struggle, which he shared with all rhetoricians, was to find a way to move toward a better life without the need for scapegoating. His essays collected in Kenneth Burke, *On Symbols and Society,* provide an excellent resource for exploring Burke's nuanced approach to motivation.

The quest for a utopian future has driven almost every social movement in history. In the late 19th century, for instance, small farmers were losing their land to large corporate interests as the high costs of mechanization brought them deeper into debt. The Populist movement responded to this problem by trying to organize small farmers into a collective political force. One of its leaders was Mary Elizabeth Lease, who offered her audience a utopian vision of the future in this speech given at the Women's Christian Temperance Union in 1890. She begins by connecting Populism with the great movements of the past in order to connect it with the social knowledge of her audience:

> Let no one for a moment believe that this uprising and federation of the people is but a passing episode in politics. It is a religious as well as a political movement, for we seek to put into practical operation the teachings and precepts of Jesus of Nazareth. We seek to enact justice and equity between man and man. We seek to bring the nation back to the constitutional liberties guaranteed us by our forefathers. The voice that is coming up today from the mystic chords of the American heart is the same voice that Lincoln heard blending with the guns of Fort Sumter and the Wilderness, and it is breaking into a clarion cry today that will be heard around the world.[6]

Once the basis for the movement has been established, she then launches into utopia in order to motivate her audience:

> Crowns will fall, thrones will tremble, kingdoms will disappear, the divine right of kings and the divine right of capital will fade away like the mists of the morning when the Angel of Liberty shall kindle the fires of justice in the hearts of men. "Exact justice to all, special privileges to none." No more millionaires, and no more paupers; no more gold kings, silver kings and oil kings, and no more little waifs of humanity starving for a crust of bread. No more gaunt-faced, hollow-eyed girls in the factories, and no more little boys reared in poverty and crime for the penitentiaries and the gallows. But we shall have the golden age of which Isaiah sang and the prophets have so long foretold; when the farmers shall be prosperous and happy, dwelling under their own vine and fig tree; when the laborer shall have that for which he toils; when occupancy and use shall be the only title to land, and every one shall obey the divine injunction, "In the sweat of thy face shalt thou eat bread."[7]

Part of what makes this utopia powerful is that in the midst of it appears a repulsive image of greedy kings and wasted children. Not only is her audience headed toward a "golden age," but they are leaving behind an age of toil. This description of the terrible state in which they currently live represents the strategy of wasteland.

Discussion: What past experience in your life do you tend to use as a practical basis for utopia? What methods have you developed to bring that utopian event back to life?

---

[6]Howard Zinn and Anthony Arnove, *Voices of a People's History of the United States* (New York: Seven Stories Press, 2004), 226.
[7]Ibid.

WASTELAND

The opposite of utopia is wasteland. Instead of playing on hope, it draws its power from disgust and fear. Specifically, **wasteland** portrays a horrific event that repels an audience from current or future social conditions. There are two general situations in which wasteland is employed. First, as Lease demonstrates, wasteland can be used to motivate to action by portraying one's current situation as so terrible as to be intolerable. To live in a wasteland is by necessity to seek utopia. Second, wasteland can be used to inhibit a path of action much as the slippery slope fallacy functions in logic. By picturing a horrible fate should one adopt the wrong path, wasteland warns against certain routes of action that will result in destruction. Consequently, this second form of argument is most effective in the opposite situations of the first. In these cases, wasteland most appeals to audiences that either are content with the current situation or are wary of making the wrong decisions because they have much to lose.

The images of wasteland find perhaps their most literal use in the rhetoric of environmentalism. But this was largely a modern development. Before 1962, *environmentalism* was still largely synonymous with the preservationist ideal of protecting natural lands from development (and hence appealed to preserving utopia). After 1962, the environmental movement took on a much broader agenda of regulating human behavior so as to prevent large-scale ecological disaster. The key to this shift was Rachel Carson's book, *Silent Spring,* which specifically warned against the dangers of using chemical pesticides and more generally argued for a wholesale shift in how we conceptualize our relationship to the natural environment. Her primary rhetorical strategy, as indicated by the title, was to predict the wasteland that would come about should we not alter our current practices. This is an excerpt from Chapter 1 of her book, *A Fable for Tomorrow:*

> There was once a town in the heart of America where all life seemed to live in harmony with its surroundings. The town lay in the midst of a checkerboard of prosperous farms, with fields of grain and hillsides of orchards where, in spring, white clouds of bloom drifted above the green fields . . . Then a strange blight crept over the area and everything began to change. Some evil spell had settled on the community: mysterious maladies swept the flocks of chickens; the cattle and sheep sickened and died. Everywhere was a shadow of death . . . There was a strange stillness. The birds, for example where had they gone? Many people spoke of them, puzzled and disturbed. The feeding stations in the backyards were deserted. The few birds seen anywhere were moribund; they trembled violently and could not fly. It was a spring without voices . . . The roadsides, once so attractive, were now lined with browned and withered vegetation as though swept by fire. These, too, were silent, deserted by all living things. Even the streams were now lifeless. Anglers no longer visited them, for all the fish had died.[8]

The beginning of the fable makes it appear as if it were something which occurred in the past, the type of terrible event that begins any gripping horror story. The audience at this point might be interested to know what has happened and

---

[8]Joy Ritchie and Kate Ronald, *Available Means: An Anthology of Women's Rhetoric(s).* (Pittsburgh: University of Pittsburgh Press, 2001), 260.

how the situation was solved. But then Carson shows her hand—this is a vision of wasteland in the future:

> This town does not actually exist, but it might easily have a thousand counterparts in America or elsewhere in the world. I know of no community that has experienced all the misfortunes I describe. Yet every one of these disasters has actually happened somewhere, and many real communities have already suffered a substantial number of them. A grim specter has crept upon us almost unnoticed, and this imagined tragedy may easily become a stark reality we all shall know.[9]

Carson has seduced her audience with a horror story only to tell members of the audience that *they* are the characters within this story, and that the story is real and ongoing. Her hope is that our recognition of our role in this narrative will encourage our action (as any good dramatic hero would do) to save us from a terrible fate.[10]

Discussion: Parents are notorious for employing the strategy of wasteland as a warning to their children against going down certain life paths. Do you recall some of the more graphic wasteland arguments used on you by your parents? Were they successful?

VIRTUE

Whereas utopia tempts our imaginations with tales of a perfect event, **virtue** attracts us to certain concrete actions by investing them with moral and practical value. In other words, to make an audience passionate about virtuous actions is to make them believe that concrete acts of moral purity, not just abstract visions of an ideal world, are the building blocks of social change and/or self-realization. The focus of virtue thus tends to be the individual (or collective entities, like nations, described as if they were individuals) and their specific choices in particular situations. To generate emotional reaction, virtue isolates the action and demonstrates both its great difficulty and its great worth, such that audiences feel that virtue is an effort that is handsomely rewarded. After hearing such a description, people often feel that even actions they had been habitually doing anyway take on a greater significance, meaning they consciously begin to start doing them more often and with greater conscious effort.

Virtue is most effective in rhetorical situations that call for an audience to engage in specific and repetitive actions in order to produce the desired change over the long-term. Rarely is virtue practically effective in cases where people do not have the time to slowly generate momentum in a larger community. In cases in which people must react quickly to crisis situations or adapt frequently to changing conditions, virtue loses its influence because it has no stable behavior on which to fix its attention. However, arguments from virtue have a lasting long-term effect when employed over years or decades in the hope of changing a community or even a society as a whole.

---

[9]Ibid.

[10]For more on Carson's book, see Craig Waddell, ed., *And No Birds Sing. Rhetorical Analyses of Rachel Carson's Silent Spring* (Carbondale, IL: University Press, 2000).

The long-distance vision of virtue is evidenced in this speech by Louis Pasteur, a 19th century French chemist largely responsible for our knowledge of germs. Before Pasteur, nobody knew how contagious diseases were transmitted. Doctors often operated without sterile instruments, and many times successful operations would result in death by infection. Pasteur, however, discovered that contagious diseases are transmitted by germs, thus giving birth to the science of microbiology. To honor his success, France opened the Pasteur Institute in Paris in 1888, and he was invited on November 14 to give an address. In his speech, he praised not his own personal accomplishments but the virtue which he felt contributed to his discoveries. One of those virtues was the spirit of criticism, or the ability to look critically at one's own ideas for the sake of making them better:

> Worship the spirit of criticism. If reduced to itself, it is not an awakener of ideas or a stimulant to great things, but, without it, everything is fallible; it always has the last word. What I am now asking you, and you will ask of your pupils later on, is what is most difficult to an inventor.
>
> It is indeed a hard task, when you believe you have found an important scientific fact and are feverishly anxious to publish it, to constrain yourself for days, weeks, years sometimes, to fight with yourself, to try and ruin your own experiments and only to proclaim your discovery after having exhausted all contrary hypotheses.
>
> But when, after so many efforts, you have at last arrived at a certainty, your joy is one of the greatest, which can be felt by a human soul, and the thought that you will have contributed to the honor of your country renders that joy still deeper.[11]

Pasteur picks out the virtue of criticism for special praise, but the way he praises this virtue signals something about the overall rhetorical strategy of virtue itself. As Pasteur points out, upholding a virtue in only one or two instances may not produce any lasting benefit. It is only after a long and consistent commitment to a virtue that results in a better future—perhaps even a utopia.

Discussion: We often hear praise of big virtues such as honesty, thrift, courage, responsibility, and the like. What are some smaller virtues that people might do every day that you think deserve more acclaim?

VICE

The opposite of virtue is **vice**, a strategy which repels us from certain concrete actions by making them morally offensive and/or practically harmful. Every child and every parent who has ever lived is intimately familiar with the rhetorical strategy of vice. By attaching a stigma to certain types of actions, parents hope they can help their children avoid the temptations that often culminate in self-destructive and socially condemned behaviors. Without such a consensus about vices (alongside necessary virtues), no society could hold together for very long. The rhetorical challenge is to make certain types of actions so abhorrent and distasteful that nobody would ever risk performing them.

---

[11]Safire, William, *Lend Me Your Ears: Great Speeches in History* (New York: Norton, 2004), 535.

Of course, vice can be easily abused as a rhetorical strategy when it is used purely as a means of social control. Especially in highly controlled, centralized, and closed societies, the horrific descriptions of vice produce in people fear of doing anything outside the boundaries of acceptable behavior. However, vice has no less transformative potential than virtue. After all, one of the most revolutionary acts of any historical rhetor is to turn a vice into a virtue and a virtue into a vice. It was a vice for women to think they should play an active role in politics until Susan B. Anthony made it a virtue. And it was once a virtue for slave owners to employ a strict discipline with their slaves until Abolitionists made slavery itself a vice.

Social movements based on virtues and vices were rampant during the early 19th century. One of the earliest reform movements in the United States, in fact, was the temperance movement which sought primarily to ban the recreational use of alcohol. Blamed for causing such social ills as poverty, crime, and unemployment (not to mention a host of mental and physical health problems), alcohol become an abomination and inebriation a vice. Lyman Beecher, a Presbyterian preacher from Connecticut, was one of the leaders of this movement, and in his 1826 speech "The Evils of Intemperance," he laid out the devastating consequences of partaking in this vice:

> The duration of human life, and the relative amount of health or disease, will manifestly vary according to the amount of ardent spirits consumed in the land. Even now, no small proportion of the deaths which annually make up our national bills of mortality, are cases of those who have been brought to an untimely end, and who have, directly or indirectly, fallen victims to the deleterious influence of ardent spirits; fulfilling with fearful accuracy the prediction, the wicked "shall not live out half their days." As the jackal follows the lion to prey upon the slain, so do disease and death wait on the footsteps of inebriation. The free and universal use of intoxicating liquors for a few centuries, cannot fail to bring down our race from the majestic, athletic forms of our fathers to the similitude of a despicable and puny race of men."[12]

Hard to miss is how the continuation of vice leads inevitably to wasteland. The only alternative to this disaster, then, is to change our everyday attitudes with regard to alcohol. This strategy is not so different today from the way we talk about addiction to drugs. Alcohol itself, however, has managed to make itself something of an idol.

Discussion: What common behavior do you wish we could successfully turn into a vice? How would the world look better as a result?

SAINT

Whereas virtue and vice relates to our attitudes, the strategy of saint and sinner addresses issues of *ethos*. In this case, however, the ethos in question does not belong to the speaker but to some other individual or group. In effect, **saint** portrays particular

---

[12]Ronald Reid and James Klumpp, *American Rhetorical Discourse*. (Long Grove, IL: Waveland Press, 2005), 278.

individuals or groups in a positive light in order to make them role models for other people to follow. The successful use of saint largely rests on inspiring emotions like admiration, respect, loyalty, and love by portraying an individual (or group) as standing apart from the crowd and deserving our recognition. Usually, this admiration comes about by hearing stories about this person that represent some value an audience holds dear, like the old fables of George Washington cutting down the cherry tree. A dry list of noble qualities rarely is inspiring for an audience. They want to hear good stories that show and don't tell.

Sometimes a saint doesn't even have to be a real person to work. We can *imagine* a saint or construct a hypothetical image of a type of person we want people to be. This was the strategy of William Graham Sumner, an academic who believed in *laissez-faire* economic policies that celebrated entrepreneurship and hard work. Sumner lived in the late 19th century, when the rise of industrialism sparked calls for the governments to actively address issues of economic inequality through policies that regulated business practices and subsidized programs for the poor. For Sumner, however, these calls were little more than an effort by people to get something for nothing. In his 1883 lecture "The Forgotten Man," he makes the ethical argument that social welfare policies punish and take advantage of hardworking laborers who must then give their hard-earned money to others. For Sumner, the tragedy was that nobody ever heard a word of complaint from these hard workers, precisely because they were too virtuous and independent to be interested in exciting public sentiments. Portraying the honest laborer as a saint, Sumner contrasts him with those who seek government handouts:

> Now who is the Forgotten Man? He is the simple, honest laborer, ready to earn his living by productive work. We pass him by because he is independent, self-supporting, and asks no favors. He does not appeal to the emotions or excite the sentiments. He only wants to make a contract and fulfill it, with respect on both sides and favor on neither side. He must get his living out of the capital of the country. The larger the capital is, the better living he can get. Every particle of capital which is wasted on the vicious, the idle, and the shiftless is so much taken from the capital available to reward the independent and productive laborer. But we stand with our backs to the independent and productive laborer all the time. We do not remember him because he makes no clamor; but I appeal to you whether he is not the man who ought to be remembered first of all, and whether, on any sound social theory, we ought not to protect him against the burdens of the good-for-nothing.[13]

From Sumner's account, the Forgotten Man is simple, honest, productive, independent, self-supporting, fair, quiet, and polite. This saintliness is contrasted with the character of those who are vicious, idle, and shiftless. Employing the either/or logic of polarization, Sumner splits workers into one of two categories in the hope of rewarding one and punishing the other. This *other* represents the sinner.

Discussion: What people in the public eye have generally attained an almost universal quality of a saint? What practical effect does the sainthood of this person have on certain audiences? And what happens to such saints when they fall from grace?

[13]William Safire, *Lend Me Your Ears: Great Speeches in History* (New York: Norton, 2004), 298.

SINNER

The counterpart of saint is sinner. In **sinner**, another person or group is portrayed in a negative light in order to make them repellent to an audience. In the era of negative advertising, hardly anything more needs to be said about sinner than this—associate all that is debased, impractical, and unjust with one's opponents in order to make oneself, at the very least, the lesser of two evils. But this is easier said than done. Sinner cannot simply be reduced to an exercise in name-calling. A rhetor has to use concrete examples and narratives to prove another's sinfulness. In this act lies the rhetorical challenge.

When done poorly, sinner culminates in ad hominem attacks that have little to do with matters of practical judgment. However, sinner performs two legitimate functions—one moral, and one legal. First, it assists in the teaching of virtue by using actual and/or fictional examples of who *not* to be and who *not* to follow. Certainly, the long-term value of figures like Judas Iscariot or Adolf Hitler is that they establish character types that tell us clearly what kinds of attitudes and values to avoid. At the very least, the strategy of sinner makes us aware that not everyone should be taken at face value. Second, sinner provides a concrete picture of a type of person to legally guard against in the development of law. Legal restrictions, after all, are intended not to restrict saints but to protect saints from sinners. Just as the best criminal investigators are often former criminals, the best laws are often written with an insight into the mind of people who would break those laws.

Similar to saint, sinner can also talk abstractly about a certain *type* of person that has negative social effects. For historian Daniel J. Boorstin, one type of sinner was the dissenter. Boorstin had been awarded the Pulitzer Prize for *The Americans: The Democratic Experience,* a book that describes America as the ability for different cultures to collaborate in an effort to progress into the future. In that book, Boorstin tended to praise our human capacity to create consensus out of disagreement and difference through civil discourse rather than revolution or protest. This issue took on particular resonance in the 1960s, when the spirit of dissent, sometimes violent dissent, was spreading through the culture. In his speech before the Associated Press in 1967, Boorstin levels criticism on the *dissenter* as a person who seeks validation of their own viewpoint at the expense of others. Because they make for good sound bites, these people are often covered by the press; but Boorstin argues that they are the biggest threat to honest democratic deliberation because they threaten to break society into incommunicable sects. He begins, however, with the strategy of virtue and vice:

> People who disagree have an argument, but people who dissent have a quarrel. People may disagree but may count themselves in the majority, but a person who dissents is by definition in a minority. A liberal society thrives on disagreement but is killed by dissension. Disagreement is the lifeblood of democracy; dissension is its cancer.[14]

With *disagreement* considered a virtue and *dissent* considered a vice, it is a natural step to consider those who engage in intellectual arguments a saint and those who actively dissent a sinner. He explains:

> Professional dissenters do not and cannot seek to assimilate their program or ideals into American culture. Their main object is to preserve their separate identity as a dissenting minority. They're not interested in the freedom of anybody

---

[14]Safire, *Lend Me Your Ears: Great Speeches in History,* 797.

else. The motto of this group might be an emendation of the old maxim of Voltaire which I'm sure you've all heard. But nowadays people would say, "I do not agree with a word you say. And I will defend to the death *my* right to say so."

Once upon a time our intellectuals competed for their claim to be spokesmen of the community. Now the time has almost arrived when the easiest way to insult an intellectual is to tell him that you or most other people *agree* with him. The way to menace him is to put him in the majority, for the majority must run things and must have a program, and dissent needs no program.

Dissent, then, has tended to become the conformity of our most educated classes. In many circles to be an outspoken conformist, that is, to say that the prevailing ways of the community are *not* "evil," requires more courage than to run with the dissenting pack.[15]

The image of the sinner in Boorstin is a person who is selfish, self-centered, arrogant, offensive, conformist, and aimless. Note, too, how the familiar hint of wasteland creeps into Boorstin's rhetoric, with dissent being a "cancer" that would eat away at the health of democracy. Hence, wasteland, vice, and sinner all work in concert to repel us from certain habits while attracting us to others.

Discussion: What are some common shorthand terms that we frequently hear in political discourse, across the political spectrum, to refer to a sinner? What *type* of person is often assumed not to be a good thing? Is this a fair description?

IDOL

When we think of idols, we think of golden statues that hold some mystical power that can be harnessed and used by the ones who possess them. An idol is an object of worship, a *thing* that we set apart as more powerful and important than anything else. The rhetorical strategy that goes by the same idol effectively is that which makes us feel this worshipful attitude toward objects. **Idol** is the attempt to invest an object with such attractive qualities that an audience seeks to possess or preserve them. Perhaps the most ubiquitous example of idol is modern advertising, which leads us to believe that a car will make us sexy, computers will make us powerful, energy drinks will make us athletic, and cell phones will make us worldly. Any time the primary goal is to make audience purchase a commodity, one will find the use of idol.

However, idol can also be used in more rhetorical contexts. In the first case, idol is effective in rhetorical situations that revolve around issues of preservation or tradition. Idol invests an object with enough *intrinsic* value that people will seek to protect it, thereby making it a crucial strategy both for historical buildings (like the Empire State Building) and artistic artifacts (like Michelangelo's "David") as well as features of our natural environment (like the Grand Canyon). Much of wildlife conservation comes from making idols out of such things as tigers, polar bears, and rainforests, which invest them with a special value that makes them worth respecting.

In the second case, idol can be effectively used in rhetorical situations that require a choice of objects that can be used as practical tools to achieve success. For

[15]Ibid.

example, debates over modern military strategy often come down to rhetorical battles over competing idols. Should we rely on *smart bombs, air power,* or *boots on the ground*? In politics, the Constitution often functions as an idol, as do institutions, political parties, and even bureaucratic procedures. Any time a *thing* (including laws and processes) is held up as a solution to some specific practical problem due to its instrumental value, one is employing idol to make a case.

Perhaps one of the most frequently praised idols is one of the most familiar—that of books. The rhetoric of William Lyon Phelps, English professor at Yale from 1901 to 1933, expressed our natural affection for books of all types. On his retirement, he shared this love of books on an April 6, 1933, broadcast. This may not seem a controversial position today, but in 1933 the world was preparing to enter a period in which the owning of certain books could get one imprisoned or even killed. Just a few weeks later, on May 10, Nazis gathered in Berlin to burn books considered "un-German," thus setting the stage for the suppression of free thought across Europe for the next decade. Phelps's attempt to make idols of books represented for him the struggle to preserve the best of the human spirit in the midst of barbarism. He begins:

> The habit of reading is one of the greatest resources of mankind; and we enjoy reading books that belong to us much more than if they are borrowed. A borrowed book is like a guest in the house; it must be treated with punctiliousness, with a certain considerate formality. You must see that it sustains no damage; it must not suffer while under your roof. You cannot leave it carelessly, you cannot mark it, you cannot turn down the pages, you cannot use it familiarly. And then, some day, although this is seldom done, you really ought to return it.[16]

Like Boorstin, Phelps actually begins by employing the strategy of virtue. Praising the attitude of reading and caring for books, Phelps seeks to put us in an active relationship with books before praising the objects themselves. He continues:

> There are of course no friends like living, breathing, corporeal men and women; my devotion to reading has never made me a recluse. How could it? Books are of the people, by the people, for the people. Literature is the immortal part of history; it is the best and most enduring part of personality. But book friends have this advantage over living friends; you can enjoy the most truly aristocratic society in the world whenever you want it. The great dead are beyond our physical reach, and the great living are usually almost as inaccessible; as for our personal friends and acquaintances, we cannot always see them. Perchance they are asleep, or away on a journey. But in a private library, you can at any moment converse with Socrates or Shakespeare or Carlyle or Dumas or Dickens or Shaw or Barrie or Galsworthy. And there is no doubt that in these books you see these men at their best. They wrote for you.[17]

The key to the strategy of idol is showing what an object represents and embodies—its intrinsic qualities that make it something worthy of admiration. Books, for Phelps, are objects which absorb the best and most intimate thoughts and feelings

---

[16]Safire, *Lend Me Your Ears: Great Speeches in History,* 611.
[17]Ibid.

of great individuals in world history. Like magical portals, they are vehicles we use to transport ourselves to new universes of human experience. Not surprisingly, then, Phelps implies they help bring about the utopia of a free, sympathetic, and democratic society. No wonder, then, that the Nazis decided to burn them as abominations.

Discussion: What are the popular idols of today, in terms of objects that people use? Why do people praise these things? And how are they praised?

ABOMINATION

The opposite of idol is **abomination**, which is the attempt make an object seem so repellent that an audience ignores, shuns, discards, or destroys it. Dealing as it does with objects, this strategy is common in all advertising that seeks to establish a competitor's product as something ugly or impractical. In this case, one needs only to show a picture that makes the thing look unpleasant. As a rhetorical strategy, however, it gets more complicated when people try to show something to be an abomination because of its corrupting cultural influence. For example, critics of popular culture often see in objects like music, video games, pornography, fast food, or fashion the potential for great harm to the general public. Likewise, critics of political culture use abomination to categorize laws, governing bodies, corporations, political parties, or even symbols as things which impede human progress. In this case, abomination represents an object that is not only unpleasant to look at, but which actually has negative effects on us.

Much effort has been spent debating whether it is fair to blame objects for human behavior. Does popular music encourage sex and drug use? Do guns cause people to kill people? Does television lead to laziness? When phrased in terms of abomination, the natural tendency is to consider ourselves immune to such influence. Otherwise we seem almost weak-willed. But invert the question to idol and we are more sympathetic to objects having influence. Do books make us more intelligent? Does the telephone help us keep in touch with our family? Do cars give us more freedom? Does a cross make us more faithful? We are generally more apt to answer more favorably to the latter questions than to the former. But the fact is that we cannot have it both ways. If we can be positively influenced by the objects of our environment, we can just as easily be negatively influenced.

Rarely, however, is any categorical praise or blame usually justified, as any object can be good or bad depending on the context of its use. As with all uses of pathos, one must balance the tendency toward exaggeration with the spirit of good sense and tools of practical judgment. This last example shows all four of the strategies of pathos at work. The issue here involves the fear of what kind of monstrosities that modern technology will produce. Represented most graphically in the novel *Frankenstein,* we have long feared that our own inventions represent the greatest threat to our basic sense of humanity. This fear has become only more acute with the possibility that we may soon have the power to clone human beings. The abomination that was Frankenstein now has the potential to actually exist— or so argues physician, biochemist, and bioethicist Leon Kass. Appointed by George W. Bush to the President's Council on Bioethics in 2001, he gave an address at the University of Chicago on May 17 of that year to warn against the "Brave

New World" that cloning represents—a world in which life has become merely a means to an end:

> Cloning, if permitted, could become more than a marginal practice simply on the basis of free reproductive choice. What to think about this prospect? Nothing good. Indeed, most people are repelled by nearly all aspects of human cloning: the possibility of mass production of human beings, with large clones of look-alikes, compromised in their individuality; the idea of father-son or mother-daughter twins; the bizarre prospect of a woman bearing and rearing a genetic copy of herself, her spouse, or even her deceased father or mother; the grotesque-ness of conceiving a child as an exact replacement for another who has died; the utilitarian creation of embryonic duplicates of oneself, to be frozen away or cre-ate when needed to provide homologous tissues or organs for transplantation; the narcissism of those who would close themselves and the arrogance of others who think they know who deserves to be cloned; the Frankensteinian hubris to create human life and increasingly control its destiny; men playing at being God.[18]

In Kass's argument, we find several strategies of pathos at work. First, cloning as an actual process represents a vice, an expression of arrogance and narcissism largely on the part of the scientists who wish to play God. Second, the people who wish to take advantage of cloning to fulfill their personal needs are sinners insofar as they treat other human beings as instruments to satisfy their own personal de-sires. Third, clones themselves are abominations, grotesque creations on par with Frankenstein who, while worthy of our sympathy, are nonetheless the embodiment of the vices of sinners. Fourth, the entire vision of the future represents a wasteland of walking monsters in which the very soul of the human spirit has been warped by the cold hand of technical reason. He concludes:

> Revulsion is not an argument; and some of yesterday's repugnancies are today calmly accepted—though, one must add, not always for the better. In crucial cases, however, repugnance is the emotional expression of deep wisdom, beyond reason's power fully to articulate it. Can anyone really give an argument fully ad-equate to the horror which is father-daughter incest (even with consent), or hav-ing sex with animals, or mutilating a corpse, or eating human flesh, or raping or murdering another human being?[19]

Kass ironically concludes his lengthy and graphic argument from pathos with the claim that pathos is not an argument. Yet his caveat that "repugnance is the emo-tional expression of deep wisdom, beyond reason's power fully to articulate it" is the very foundation of emotional rationality. As he rightly asks, how else, besides graphic portrayal, can one express the genuine sentiment of horror? The same question might be asked of hope, of inspiration, and of virtue.

Discussion: One of the most influential technologies in the past decade has been the rise of the cell phone and other handheld communication technologies. In terms of its overall use in society, for whom does this technology represent an idol or an abomination?

---

[18]Safire, *Lend Me Your Ears: Great Speeches in History,* 646.
[19]Ibid.

CONCEPT REVIEW

Concept	Definition	Example
UTOPIA	Projecting a "perfect" world to promote a way of life.	"The green society of the next century will see hydrogen cars, clear rivers, and blue sky."
WASTELAND	Projecting a "terrible" world to condemn a way of life.	"Today, however, we inhale the dirty fumes of diesel engines, swim in needle-infested waters, and gaze upon a brown horizon."
VIRTUE	Praising a certain habit of action as beneficial.	"Every time we recycle, we allow another tree to live free from the lumber mill."
VICE	Condemning a certain habit of action as detrimental.	"We never think twice about watering our lawn. But every time we turn on that hose, we drain that much more water from our rivers."
SAINT	Praising an individual or group as an ideal model.	"Our national parks exist only because Theodore Roosevelt had a love of nature and a passion for preserving our world."
SINNER	Condemning an individual or group as representing all that one should avoid.	"Corporate polluters who would carelessly drain their waste into public lands might as well be using your back yard as a landfill."
IDOL	Praising some object as being worthy of respect and use.	"Modern green technology is the way of the future. Although laws and regulations have a role to play, it is technology that will save us."
ABOMINATION	Condemning some objects as meriting rejection or destruction.	"The internal combustion engine, while a marvel of invention, nonetheless has done more to harm our world than all the weapons of war combined."

KEY WORDS

SUMMARY

People often look at emotional arguments as "masking" a hidden message. However, interpreting the *logical meaning* of an argument by pathos is something of an oxymoron. Pathos functions in rhetoric precisely because it isn't a form of logos. The reason it is so powerful is because it does not require or inspire such interpretation. Its *meaning* is its unreflective emotional effect on an audience that makes the audience instinctively *move toward* or *pull away* from something, whatever that thing might be. The categories of interpretation in this chapter are simply useful in clarifying what thing is at issue and which direction we are being moved.

If we turn to King's Holt Street Baptist Church speech, we can readily find several examples of pathos. Unlike the logos examples from King's speech explored in Chapter 7, then, the pathos examples will simply be identified and left to speak for themselves.

Utopia   We are here also because of our love for democracy, because of our deep-seated belief that democracy transformed from thin paper to thick action is the greatest form of government on earth.

Wasteland   For many years now Negroes in Montgomery and so many other areas have been inflicted with the paralysis of crippling fears on buses in our community. On so many occasions, Negroes have been intimidated and humiliated and impressed—oppressed—because of the sheer fact that they were Negroes.

Saint   Just the other day, just last Thursday to be exact, one of the finest citizens in Montgomery—not one of the finest Negro citizens but one of the finest citizens in Montgomery—was taken from a bus and carried to jail and arrested because she refused to get up to give her seat to a white person.

Wasteland   And you know, my friends, there comes a time when people get tired of being trampled over by the iron feet of oppression. There comes a time, my friends, when people get tired of being plunged across the abyss of humiliation where they experience the bleakness of nagging despair. There comes a time when people get tired of being pushed out of the glittering sunlight of life's July, and left standing amid the piercing chill of an alpine November. There comes a time.

Sinner   My friends, don't let anybody make us feel that we are to be compared in our actions with the Ku Klux Klan or with the White Citizens Council.

Vice   There will be no crosses burned at any bus stops in Montgomery. There will be no white persons pulled out of their homes and taken out on some distant road and lynched for not cooperating.

Virtue   I want to say that in all of our actions we must stick together. Unity is the great need of the hour and if we are united we can get many of the things that we not only desire but which we justly deserve.

Idol/Saint   If we are wrong, the Supreme Court of this nation is wrong. If we are wrong, the Constitution of the United States is wrong. If we are wrong, God Almighty is wrong. If we are wrong, Jesus of Nazareth was merely a utopian dreamer that never came down to earth. If we are wrong, justice is a lie.

Clearly, some of the examples of pathos just noted were parts of the same examples used for logos. Consequently, it is important to point out that a single passage need not be classified strictly as one thing or the other. Words often perform many functions simultaneously. One must simply know how each of these qualities might *function* and which aspects are more important than others in particular contexts. For example, King's analogies to the Supreme Court, the Constitution, God, and Jesus function as an argument from logos insofar as one takes the time to analyze the relationship between the parts and determine the underlying principles at work. However, as an argument from pathos, it might simply make a person feel inspired by being associated with such idols and saints.

In other words, whether an argument functions as pathos or as logos is partly determined by how an audience *responds* to that argument. On first hearing King's speech, for instance, one might only be more affected by emotional connotations of these associations. This means the initial reaction was largely one of pathos. On reflection, however, a more complex rational meaning might emerge, culminating in an interpretation weighted toward logos. But these two interpretations do not *negate* each other. One can be both inspired and enlightened by the same set of words. Indeed, finding a way to unify both reason and passion is the goal of any great rhetorical style.

CHAPTER 7 EXERCISES

1. Analyzing your rhetorical artifact, what forms of pathos were employed? Select specific language choices that were made to generate emotional feeling, and then describe the action that you believe was encouraged as a result.
2. As a class, choose a contemporary controversy familiar with everyone. Then select one *attractive* method of pathos and one *repelling* method that is not the pair of the first. Deliver an impromptu speech employing both methods.
3. Using the same controversy, choose one method of pathos and use it in conjunction with one form of logical reasoning. How does the argument change over the previous exercise?
4. Find a print ad that uses a striking visual image to convey pathos. Interpret this image using the concepts.
5. Using one form of pathos, locate a historical person, event, object, or action that fits their category. Give an impromptu commemorative speech describing why the category applies.

Style

This chapter examines the techniques for giving a speech style, or a sense of aesthetic wholeness, that carries with it a clear and powerful meaning. It approaches style not as a series of superficial decorations that one can add to a speech, but as one category of artistic form that gives body to otherwise disconnected parts. This "formal style" is broken down into three components—form, symbol, and poetic category—each of which includes its own specific subcomponents. The goal is to provide a perspective on these techniques of style that give them greater significance (cognitively, emotionally, and practically) than just external bedecking. Style is to be taken seriously as a way of giving qualitative unity to a speech so that an audience is left with a shared experience that endures into the future.

The mastery of formal style is the culmination of the art of rhetoric. This fact is often obscured by the narrow interpretation of style as including only specific tropes and figures like metaphor, simile, or alliteration. In this interpretation, style is merely *decorative*—something superficial added to a more solid base of reasoning in order to make it more palatable (or, more negatively, to hide the lack of substance). Even Aristotle gives style only grudging recognition and notes that stylish delivery, while possessing power to persuade, is due primarily to the "corruption of the audience," for (as demonstrated by the fact that "nobody teaches geometry this way") "all these things are forms of outward show and intended to affect the audience."[1] Yet after dismissing style as being of only minor importance, he then proceeds to dedicate almost a third of his rhetorical treatise on matters of style. Furthermore, on beginning his discussion, he defines the virtue of style not as pleasure but as clarity. For him, *style* means "to be clear" insofar as "speech is a kind of sign, so if it does not make [itself] clear it will not perform its function."[2] A stronger case for the centrality of style could hardly be made. Even for Aristotle, a speech may be as rational and logical as it pleases, but if it fails the test of clarity, it fails in its power to move, to please, and to teach.

To have style, in short, is to possess form. But *form* means something other than mere conventional organization. As John Dewey defines it, **form** is the "sense of qualitative unity" that comes about when one arranges "events and objects with reference to the demands of complete and unified perception."[3] By *qualitative unity,* Dewey means the

---

[1]Aristotle, *On Rhetoric: A Theory of Civic Discourse,* trans. George Kennedy (Oxford: Oxford University Press, 2007), 1404a.

[2]Aristotle, *Rhetoric,* 1404b.

[3]John Dewey, *Art as Experience* (New York: Perigree Books, 1934), 142.

feeling that one can sum up that entire arc of experience within a single term, as when one associates *exhilarating* with climbing a mountain, *tragic* with the death of a loved one, *joyous* with the family reunion at a holiday, or *inspiring* at the conclusion of a passionate speech. Aristotle argued that a dramatic play should possess this kind of form to be perfect. For Aristotle, "a beautiful whole [is] made up of parts," meaning that a drama, "as an imitation of action, must represent one action, a complete whole, with its several incidents so closely connected that the transposal or withdrawal of any one of them will disjoin and dislocate the whole."[4] Similarly, a speech to move an audience cannot simply be a jangling arrangement of disconnected parts, with each part wanting to go in a different direction. All of the parts must work together to support a whole message that is greater than the sum of its parts.

Formal style is therefore present when all of a speech's parts form together into a concrete whole in such a way that is fitting with the occasion and which carries an audience from expectation to fulfillment during the course of the delivery. The parts of formal style thus consist of **figurative style**, which is what Kenneth Burke calls "minor forms" that possess enough "episodic distinctness to bear consideration apart from their context."[5] For instance, although there are many memorable metaphors and images in Dr. King's "I Have a Dream" speech, its formal style is more than the sum of its tropes and figures. The nature of its "qualitative unity" is described by Juan Williams: "King, the most popular of all the civil rights leaders, delivered a speech that would be heard on television stations across the land. It was a speech of *hope* and *determination,* epitomizing the day's message of *racial harmony, love, unity,* and a belief that blacks and whites could live together in *peace.*"[6] Each of the italicized terms represents components of the qualitative unity that makes "I Have a Dream" consistently placed as one of the greatest orations of all time.

Mastering the arts of style is therefore probably the most difficult and most important of all of the components of rhetorical public speech—but only when taken seriously as something more than just frosting on a cake. One must get beyond the idea that logos provides the rational *substance* on which style then provides the candy-coating. This does not mean that the distinction between substance and style is meaningless. But it is more helpful to think of substance *less* as a "core" that embodies the essence of a speech and *more* as a "summary" that extracts the main points for easy comprehension. Substance is like the crib notes for a novel that convey the general movements of the plot without pretending to take the place of the novel itself. Style, meanwhile, represents the total impression one gets after reading the whole book.

Drawing from the work of Kenneth Burke, this chapter will explore three components of formal style—the types of form, the function of symbols, and the nature of poetic categories. Along with the use of figurative styles outlined in

---

[4]Aristotle, *Poetics,* in *The Rhetoric and Poetics of Aristotle,* trans. W. Rhys Roberts (New York: Modern Library, 1984), 1451a3, 30.

[5]Kenneth Burke, *Counter-Statement* (Chicago: University of Chicago Press, 1931), 127.

[6]Juan Williams, *Eyes on the Prize: America's Civil Rights Years 1954–1965* (New York: Penguin Books, 1987), 201.

Chapter 1, these aspects of formal style will contribute to the creation of speech, which is more than just a sequence of reasons and emotional appeals occasionally made attractive through the use of decoration. It will culminate in a whole that is more than the sum of its parts, thus attaining the qualitative unity that is necessary to unite an audience in a common aim.

TYPES OF FORM

When we think of form, the first thing that usually comes to mind is an empty shape waiting to be filled with content. It is something of a hollow outline that lacks the power of movement. According to Kenneth Burke, this idea of form has nothing to do with how form actually occurs in acts of human communication. Like Dewey, Burke defines form as something produced in cooperation among a speaker, a work of art, and an audience as it occurs through interaction over time. In literature, **form** is "an arousing and fulfillment of desires," and a "work has form insofar as one part of it leads a reader to anticipate another part, to be gratified by the sequence."[7] Burke gives a very simple example: "If, in a work of art, the poet says something, let us say, about a meeting, writes in such a way that we desire to observe that meeting, and then, if he places that meeting before us—that is form."[8]

In rhetoric, form is thus achieved when the end of the speech satisfies the desire that is introduced at its beginning, thereby making the whole dramatic presentation a disclosure of what is already anticipated by the audience. Therefore, when Dr. King announces that he has a dream, makes us desire to observe the meaning of that dream, and then places that dream before us—that is form. Within this overall definition, Burke then specifies four particular types of form, each of which may occur and overlap within the same speech.

Conventional Form

Conventional form is present when an audience possesses a *categorical expectancy* of what they are going to hear based on the traditional conventions of a speech genre.[9] For instance, conventional form trains an audience to expect something different from a lawyer's opening statement than from a family member's eulogy of a loved one. Each convention possesses its own rules of sequence and order that lets an audience know what to expect. Violating these expectations is still possible, but it risks alienating an audience by making it more difficult for it to anticipate what will follow. In rhetoric, conventional form is thus usually something to use to one's advantage, adhering to the pattern of speech expected by the audience in order to more effectively convey one's message.

Take, for example, the eulogy by Robert Green Ingersoll, who was one of America's most popular 19th century orators and leading proponents of secular

[7]Burke, *Counter-Statement*, 124.
[8]Burke, *Counter-Statement*, 31.
[9]Burke, *Counter-Statement*, 126.

humanism. When his brother Clark died in 1879, Ingersoll delivered an emotional eulogy beside his grave that, consistent with his views, praised his brother's character in life without mention of an afterlife. Typical of the "grand style" of eulogies, Ingersoll adheres to the conventional form that encourages poetic language that would be less effective in political oratory:

> The loved and loving brother, husband, father, friend, died where manhood's morning almost touches noon, and while the shadows still were falling toward the west . . . Yet, after all, it may be best, just in the happiest, sunniest hour of all the voyage, while eager winds are kissing every sail, to dash against the unseen rock, and in an instant hear the billows roar above a sunken ship. For, whether in mid-sea or 'mong the breakers of the farther shore, a wreck at last must mark the end of each and all. And every life, no matter if its every hour is rich with love and every moment jeweled with a joy, will, at its close, become a tragedy as sad and deep and dark as can be woven of the warp and woof of mystery and death.
>
> This brave and tender man in every storm of life was oak and rock, but in the sunshine he was vine and flower. He was the friend of all heroic souls. He climbed the heights and left all superstitions far below, while on his forehead fell the golden dawning of the grander day.[10]

Note, too, the use of the figurative style of alliteration to help give the form of the speech its powerful unity. These rhythmic emphases help give the eulogy a musical feel that cannot help but evoke an emotional response characteristic of the eulogy genre.

Discussion: Although conventional form is often thought to be a "constraint," more often it is a source of invention. For instance, the haiku or limerick form provides a unique rhythm and structure for words that challenges one to be creative. Can you think of other conventional forms that you have used for creative purposes?

Syllogistic Form

Syllogistic form is "the form of a perfectly conducted argument, advancing step-by-step." Often associated with legal and scientific reasoning, syllogistic form is produced when a conclusion (E) is asserted in the introduction and then followed by a clear sequence of stages that "go from A to E through stages B, C, and D." In syllogistic form, the pleasure comes from mapping out a trail from beginning to end that gets an audience to a destination. It thus tends to have a linear quality, such that the "arrows of our desires are turned in a certain direction, and the plot follows the direction of the arrows."[11] Burke gives the example of a mystery story in which everything falls together in the final speech by the keen investigator. In rhetoric, syllogistic form is thus highlighted whenever the processes of reasoning play an explicit and central role.

A master of bringing syllogistic form into narrative was Russell Conwell, famous for his lecture "Acres of Diamonds." Between 1870 and 1924, Conwell

---

[10]William Safire, *Lend Me Your Ears: Great Speeches in History* (New York: Norton, 2004), 201.

[11]Burke, *Counter-Statement,* 124.

delivered this speech more than 6,000 times until it became the gospel of the American entrepreneur. Conwell was a preacher and academic who saw the solution to the problems of industrialization in the ability of individuals to rise out of poverty through the power of creative thinking and marketing. His example is meant to convey a certain method that the American entrepreneur can use to create and sell products:

> There was a poor man out of work living in Hingham, Massachusetts. He lounged around the house until one day his wife told him to get out and work, and, as he lived in Massachusetts, he obeyed his wife. He went out and sat down on the shore of the bay, and whittled a soaked shingle into a wooden chain. His children that evening quarreled over it, and he whittled a second one to keep peace. While he was whittling the second one a neighbor came in and said: "Why don't you whittle toys and sell them? You could make money at that." "Oh," he said, "I would not know what to make." "Why don't you ask your own children right here in your own house what to make?" "What is the use of trying that?" said the carpenter. "My children are different from other people's children." (I used to see people like that when I taught school.) But he acted upon the hint, and the next morning when Mary came down the stairway, he asked, "What do you want for a toy?" She began to tell him she would like a doll's bed, a doll's washstand, a doll's carriage, a little doll's umbrella, and went on with a list of things that would take him a lifetime to supply. So, consulting his own children, in his own house, he took the firewood, for he had no money to buy lumber, and whittled those strong, unpainted Hingham toys that were for so many years known all over the world. That man began to make those toys for his own children, and then made copies and sold them through the boot-and-shoe store next door. He began to make a little money, and then a little more, and Mr. Lawson, in his *Frenzied Finance* says that man is the richest man in old Massachusetts, and I think it is the truth. And that man is worth a hundred millions of dollars today, and has been only thirty-four years making it on that one principle—that one must judge that what his own children like at home other people's children would like in their homes, too; to judge the human heart by oneself, by one's wife or by one's children. It is the royal road to success in manufacturing.[12]

The use of the example helps make what might otherwise be a dry, analytical process into lively and engaged creative activity. It would have been easy for Conwell simply to have told people that he once knew a man who earned a million dollars by selling the toys that he made for his children. Instead, he told the example in all its detail, including actual dialogue between the man and his neighbors, in such a way that the method can easily be recalled to memory.[13]

Discussion: As Conwell indicates, syllogistic form need not take on the dry and boring appearance of an instruction manual. Syllogistic form not only can provide the foundations for dramatic and documentary narratives, they also can make for

---

[12]Available from The American Rhetoric at americanrhetoric.com (accessed on April 28, 2010).

[13]For more on Conwell's speech, see A. Cheree Carlson, "Narrative as the Philosopher's Stone: How Russell H. Conwell Changed Lead into Diamonds," *Western Journal of Speech Communication* 53 (1989), 342–355.

enjoyable puzzles when one intentionally leaves out important steps for the audience to solve. Can you think of a popular movie that was based on filling in the missing pieces to syllogistic form? What was the most dramatic part of that movie?

Repetitive Form

Repetitive form is the "restatement of the same thing in different ways" in order to consistently represent "a principle under new guises."[14] Repetitive form is thus different than the figurative style of repetition (by which the same word or phrase begins a series of sentences). In repetitive form, it is not the *words* or *phrases* that are repeated, but rather the *idea* or *principle*. Indeed, it is important in repetitive form *not* to repeat the same words or phrases. Repetitive form uses various examples to reinforce the same theme, as when a parade of desperate stories about the poor and suffering convey the same principle that poverty is a systemic social problem. Unlike syllogistic form, which moves in logical sequence to different stages, repetitive form finds it more effective to repeat the same theme using a diverse repertoire of emotional and vivid examples.

A fine use of repetition to convey a principle appears in the rhetoric of César Estrada Chávez, a Mexican-American born in Arizona to a poor family. Moving frequently with his father to find work and eventually becoming a migrant worker to support himself, he experienced firsthand the difficult conditions that migrant workers faced to survive. Eventually he became a labor leader and civil rights activist, co-founding the National Farm Workers Association, which later became the United Farm Workers. Part of his goal as a speaker was to make public audiences aware of the difficult lives these workers led. In his address to the Commonwealth Club of California on November 9, 1984, Chávez uses a series of vivid descriptions to repeat the basic idea that migrant words face horrible conditions of desolation and despair:

> Twenty-one years ago last September, on a lonely stretch of railroad track paralleling U.S. Highway 101 near Salinas, 32 Bracero farm workers lost their lives in a tragic accident. The Braceros had been imported from Mexico to work on California farms. They died when their bus, which was converted from a flatbed truck, drove in front of a freight train. Conversion of the bus had not been approved by any government agency. The driver had "tunnel" vision. Most of the bodies lay unidentified for days. No one, including the grower who employed the workers, even knew their names.
>
> Today, thousands of farm workers live under savage conditions—beneath trees and amid garbage and human excrement—near tomato fields in San Diego County, tomato fields which use the most modern farm technology. Vicious rats gnaw on them as they sleep. They walk miles to buy food at inflated prices. And they carry in water from irrigation pumps.

Note the use of concrete words in these examples. In the first paragraph, we have lonely stretch of railroad track, Braceros, flatbed truck, freight train, tunnel vision,

---

[14]Burke, *Counter-Statement*, 125.

and bodies. In the second paragraph, we have garbage and human excrement, tomato fields, vicious rats gnawing men, and people carrying water for miles. All of this is meant to repeat a common theme: that thousands of farm workers live under savage conditions.[15]

Discussion: The most common use of repetitive form is in popular advertisements for particular brands of products. Think of a few brand names associated with fashion or technology. How many different images or phrases can you think of that repeat the same basic idea or principle associated with that brand?

Qualitative Form

Qualitative form occurs when "the presence of one quality prepares us for the introduction of another" that is emotionally satisfying. Like syllogistic form, qualitative form moves in a progressive sequence. Unlike syllogistic form, however, this sequence is not explicit, mathematical, logical, or predictable; it tends to be based more on the buildup of an emotional tension that seeks its adequate release. We are "put into a state of mind which another state of mind can appropriately follow."[16] For instance, crowded, high-energy action scenes that introduce movies are often immediately followed by calm settings in which only a few character are talking leisurely about an everyday subject. This has no clear logical order, but it provides an important resting place for the audience. The high energy of the first scene is dissipated in the calmness of the second.

Similarly, speeches which begin with descriptions of tragic events and destitute conditions prepare the audience for visions of hope and redemption—much as we think that the day should follow the night. Take the speech given by Southern novelist William Faulkner in 1949 on receiving the Nobel Prize in Literature. Often criticized for his cynical portrayals of human beings that focused on their weaknesses and limitations, he used the speech as an opportunity to state his underlying faith in the possibilities of human nature if people could be released from the bonds of fear by the power of the creative artist:

> I decline to accept the end of man. It is easy enough to say that man is immortal simply because he will endure: that when the last ding-dong of doom has clanged and faded from the last worthless rock hanging tide-less in the last red and dying evening, that even then there will still be one more sound: that of his puny inexhaustible voice, still talking. I refuse to accept this. I believe that man will not merely endure: he will prevail. He is immortal, not because he alone among creatures has an inexhaustible voice, but because he has a soul, a spirit capable of compassion and sacrifice and endurance.
>
> The poet's and the writer's duty is to write about these things. It is his privilege to help man endure by lifting his heart, by reminding him of the courage and honor and hope and pride and compassion and pity and sacrifice which have

---

[15]For more on Chavez's rhetoric, see Joseph Zompetti, "César Chávez's Rhetorical Use of Religious Symbols," *Journal of Communication & Religion* 29, no. 2 (2006), 262–284.
[16]Burke, *Counter-Statement*, 125.

been the glory of his past. The poet's voice need not merely be the record of man, it can be one of the props, the pillars to help him endure and prevail.[17]

Employing the figurative style of rhythm, Faulkner creates a feeling of despair, in which "the last ding-dong of doom" is followed by man's "puny inexhaustible voice, still talking," only to be proceeded by his prophesy of the ultimate heroic triumph of humankind in which they will both "endure and prevail." From the sounds of doom emerges the voice of courage and honor and hope and pride.

Discussion: Think of three different movies that belong to different genres such as the romance, the thriller, the action blockbuster, or the romantic comedy. Now think of the major qualitative transitions in the movies that were particularly satisfying. How many were predictable and which were a surprise?

SYMBOL

At its most *general* level, a **symbol** is anything whose meaning encompasses more than its literal existence. A rock on which one stubs a toe does not function symbolically; but a rock which is thrown through a window does. At this level, all words operate as symbols insofar as they mean more than their sound or their marking. However, at the level of *poetic* form, a symbol possesses a higher degree of significance and uniqueness. It is the difference between the word "nation" and the American flag, the word "love" and the Greek goddess Aphrodite, and the word "freedom" and the history of the Underground Railroad. A poetic symbol thus has a magnitude, depth, and function that exceed even traditional metaphorical usage. To say that "life is but a dream" is certainly to exploit the symbolic character of language; but for Dr. King to build an entire section of a speech around the symbol of his "Dream" is of an entirely different order.

For Burke, a symbol is not a particular reference but a *formula*. As a formula, it encompasses a whole series of relations and adjustments to environmental conditions. For instance, Burke gives the example of the symbol, "The King and the Peasant" (like Prince John and Robin Hood) which is "about a king who has but the trappings of kingliness and a peasant who is, in the true sense, a king."[18] Employing this symbol thus embodies a certain formula for action, such that one seeks to disrobe illegitimate authority while granting moral authority to currently marginalized individuals or groups. Not surprisingly, then, the various symbols of "The King and the Peasant" are frequently employed in rhetoric whenever people out of power challenge the established order. When Dr. King uses the symbol of the "Promised Land," for instance, he does so with explicit reference to the biblical story of Pharaoh and Moses, the former a king who rules unjustly, and the latter a slave who became a kind of king.

Put another way, a symbol combines the functions of the myth and the icon. For Marshall McLuhan, a **myth** is a powerful narrative "vision of a complex process that ordinarily extends over a long period," whereas an **icon** is an "inclusive

---

[17]Available from The American Rhetoric at americanrhetoric.com (accessed on April 28, 2010).
[18]Burke, *Counter-Statement*, 153.

image" that condenses that process into a visual form.[19] For instance, the myth of George Washington crossing the Delaware in the cold of winter to surprise British troops presents a complicated history of the American Revolution in the simplified narration of a courageous, strategic maneuver led by the future president of the nation. The famous painting of George Washington standing up in the boat on his way across the Delaware is the iconic representation of that myth.

In rhetoric, the symbol acts as a **verbal icon** that calls into the imagination an image that stands for a mythic narrative. Thus, some verbal icons employed in American rhetoric include Pilgrims, Pocahontas, New Frontier, the Mississippi, Boston Massacre, Revolution, Founding Fathers, liberty, Walt Whitman, Sitting Bull, Custer's Last Stand, buffalo, God, slavery, Harriett Tubman, Civil War, Emancipation Proclamation, Abraham Lincoln, freedom, reconstruction, railroad, the West, Gold Rush, Alamo, Prohibition, Susan B. Anthony, Great Depression, Jim Crow, Rosa Parks, vote, Pearl Harbor, World War II, Holocaust, New Deal, Beat Generation, Cold War, civil rights movement, space race, Grand Canyon, Vietnam War, Ronald Reagan, the eighties, the fall of the Berlin Wall, grunge music, Bill Gates, and the Web. Although each of these icons may possess a different meaning for different audiences, they each embody a certain coherent system of values, actions, situations, and tendencies that can be used by speakers to summarize a complex situation by reference to these narratives and images that are embedded in public memory. In addition, they establish a precedent for what it means to be an effective icon should a speaker wish to create one anew—just as Russell Conwell tries to do with his toymaker from Massachusetts or César Chávez attempts to accomplish with his Braceros.

The most effective use of a symbol is to use only a few and to make frequent reference to them throughout the whole speech. Unlike figurative style, which often uses brief images and examples to make a specific point, the use of a symbol as a component of formal style should function as a common thread that binds together the speech into a whole, much as Dr. King used the symbols of the Emancipation Proclamation and his "Dream" in his speech after the March on Washington. To understand how a symbol works, however, it is important to identify its six possible functions as defined by Kenneth Burke. Sometimes a symbol may have one primary function, while other times they may have multiple functions operating simultaneously. Being a complex form, a symbol naturally will be able to express itself in different ways at different times depending on the situational context. Indeed, one of the characteristics of a symbol is precisely its adaptability, which gives it a breadth of possible application that exceeds ordinary language. The six functions of a symbol are as follows:

1. *To produce "artistic" effects:* An **artistic symbol** engages an audience with its sheer value as a work of creative invention. Burke notes that often symbols are valued as "a nimble running of scales; they display the poet's farthest reaches of virtuosity."[20] This explains how critics who disagree with a speaker's message may often applaud the way the speech was composed and delivered. An audi-

---

[19]Marshall McLuhan, *Understanding Media: The Extensions of Man* (Boston: MIT Press, 1994), 25, 321.

[20]Burke, *Counter-Statement*, 156.

ence may reject a speaker's description of nonsmoking regulations as the return of Prohibition, but the symbol nonetheless livens up the speech.

Discussion: One can usually identify a particular artistic symbol by the fact that people of completely opposing viewpoints still use it. What common symbol do you recall being employed by two opposing political parties for different purposes?

2. *To interpret a situation:* In a rhetorical situation marked by confusion and uncertainty, an **interpretive symbol** can function to give it order and meaning. Burke writes that it can, "by its function as name and definition, give simplicity and order to an otherwise unclarified complexity."[21] The important thing to keep in mind is that an *interpretation* is not simply a novel description. It must act to create order out of disorder—otherwise it only fulfills the artistic function of imaginative play. Thus, after the terror attacks of 9/11, it was common to try to make sense of that uncertainty by comparing it to Pearl Harbor, thus bringing clarity and direction to a situation marked by confusion and anxiety.

Discussion: When can you recall your family or friends using a symbol to bring clarity to an uncertain situation you experienced personally? Did it turn out to be correct?

3. *To favor acceptance of a situation:* This function can only occur when there is a *preexisting* undesirable or threatening aspect of a situation that many have refused to acknowledge in the hope that it will just go away. According to Burke, a symbol "can enable us to admit, for instance, the existence of a certain danger which we had emotionally denied."[22] A **symbol of acceptance** thus acts to establish a relationship between the audience and that danger which it has ignored, usually by giving the audience a feeling of power it had not previously experienced. For instance, one might encourage a friend to face up to his or her alcoholism by making it seem a noble battle ("You are David to this Goliath"), or by humorously mocking the threat ("Your name is not Jack Daniel"). Either way, the effect of the symbol is to make him or her face up to reality.

Discussion: Symbols of acceptance are frequently used interpersonally to encourage a close relation to come to terms with some character flaw and help them overcome it. Think of a popular movie about "redemption" in which a character accepted such a flaw in order to achieve something. What symbol was used to help the character overcome his or her fears, and in what interpersonal context was it presented to the individual?

4. *To offer a corrective to a situation:* After interpreting or accepting a problematic situation, an audience naturally wants to be offered a destination that will get it out of that situation. A **corrective symbol** offers a vision of possibility that helps correct the imbalances of the present. For example, Burke notes that "life in the city arouses a compensatory interest in life on a farm, with the result

[21]Burke, *Counter-Statement*, 154.
[22]Burke, *Counter-Statement*, 154.

that symbols of farm life become appealing."[23] The symbol as a corrective speaks to the utopian qualities of our imagination, offering a vision of that might become real if we only strive for that goal. "Hollywood" is thus a corrective symbol for aspiring actors, "peace" is a corrective symbol for nations torn by war, and "the Green Economy" is a corrective symbol that unites the aspirations of environmentalists and economists.

Discussion: What corrective symbols are often used by students in order to help them overcome challenges and direct their aspirations? How many of these correctives do you think are pure fantasy, and which are realistic goals?

5. *To express "submerged" emotions:*   An **emotional symbol** allows people to express powerful emotions that they would otherwise suppress. Burke writes that symbols often have the power to "stir remote depths," either as symbols of cruelty and horror or as symbols of hope and love.[24] When used in contexts of heightened tensions, symbols like Satan, Hitler, slavery, genocide, or nuclear war give license for an audience to tap into otherwise suppressed aggression and give it a voice. Yet the opposite is also true. Symbols like God, Ghandi, freedom, patriot, and peace allow people to express their highest ideals without feeling embarrassed.

Discussion: Think of a time you went to a movie and actually heard members of the audience shout back at the screen. What symbol used in the movie elicited this response? Did you feel the desire to do the same?

6. *To emancipate repressed action:*   Lastly, an **emancipatory symbol** have the unique power to invert our moral codes, thus making the better into the worse and the worse into the better. By using symbols, behavior otherwise thought "wicked, absurd, low-caste, [and] wasteful" can be turned "virtuous, discerning, refined, [and] accurate," and vice-versa.[25] Reminiscent of the symbol of "The King and the Peasant," symbols which emancipate action show the hypocrisy and shallowness of what is thought "high" while valorizing that which was once thought "low." For instance, the symbol "sex worker" turns behavior which was once thought immoral and criminal into a normal business enterprise, and the symbol "activist" translates otherwise obnoxious social behavior into the highest expression of a democratic citizen.

Discussion: Think of your past friends or acquaintances who may have intentionally tried to violate social norms and take on the role of an iconoclast or outsider. What symbols did they use to justify their actions which many may have taken to be offensive?

Of American orators, one of the most conscious of the power of symbols was Transcendentalist poet and philosopher Ralph Waldo Emerson. Not only was he a

---

[23]Burke, *Counter-Statement*, 155.

[24]Burke, *Counter-Statement*, 155.

[25]Burke, *Counter-Statement*, 156.

nationally known lecturer on issues ranging from ethics to politics to religion, but he also was a theorist of language. Here, in his essay on "Eloquence," he describes the power of imagery that supports Burke's notion of the symbol:

> The orator must be, to a certain extent, a poet. We are such imaginative creatures that nothing so works on the human mind, barbarous or civil, as a trope. Condense some daily experience into a glowing symbol, and an audience is electrified. They feel as if they already possessed some new right and power over a fact which they can detach, and so completely master in thought. It is a wonderful aid to the memory, which carries away the image and never loses it . . . Put the argument into a concrete shape, into an image—some hard phrase, round and solid as a ball, which they can see and handle and carry home with them—and the cause is half-won.[26]

Emerson then puts his own advice into practice in his address, "The American Scholar," to Harvard's annual Phi Beta Kappa Society in 1837. Indeed, the title of the oration is itself a symbol. Speaking in the first half of the 19th century, Emerson is reacting to what he perceives to be America's intellectual dependence on European thought, much as a child depends on a parent. As his audience was supposed to represent the best of American intellectuals, Emerson uses the occasion to challenge the status quo and establish a new ideal liberated from the traditions of the past. In "The American Scholar," Emerson wishes to create a symbol that condenses a complex ideal into a "concrete shape" that the audience can carry home with it in memory and use to guide future practice:

> The Scholar is that man who must take up into himself all the ability of the time, all the contributions of the past, all the hopes of the future. He must be a university of knowledges. If there be one lesson more than another, which should pierce his ear, it is, The World is nothing, the Man is all; in yourself is the law of all nature, and you know not yet how a globule of sap ascends; in yourself slumbers the whole of Reason; it is for you to know all, it is for you to dare all. Mr. President and Gentlemen, this confidence in the unsearched might of man belongs, by all motives, by all prophecy, by all preparation, to the American Scholar. We have listened too long to the courtly muses of Europe. The spirit of the American freeman is already suspected to be timid, imitative, tame. Public and private avarice make the air we breathe thick and fat. The scholar is decent, indolent, complacent. See already the tragic consequence. The mind of this country, taught to aim at low objects, eats upon itself. There is no work for any but the decorous and the complacent . . . What is the remedy? . . . We will walk on our own feet; we will work with our own hands; we will speak our own minds. The study of letters shall be no longer a name for pity, for doubt, and for sensual indulgence. The dread of man and the love of man shall be a wall of defense and a wreath of joy around all. A nation of men will for the first time exist, because each believes himself inspired by the Divine Soul which also inspires all men.[27]

---

[26]Available from RWE Institute at http://www.rwe.org/complete-works/vii—society-and-solitude/chapter-iv-eloquence (accessed on May 7, 2010).

[27]Available from RWE Institute at http://www.rwe.org/works/Nature_addresses_1_The_American_Scholar.htm (accessed on May 7, 2010).

In this section of the oration we clearly have an example of qualitative form in which an audience is moved from aspiration to disgust to prophesy. Within this form we also have several symbols working in concert. Emerson uses the symbol of the "indolent" scholar hushed to complacency by the "courtly muses of Europe" to force *acceptance* of an undesirable situation upon his audience. However, his *interpretation* of this situation is one of unfulfilled promise, where in each individual "slumbers the whole of Reason." The ideal of the "American Scholar" thus acts as a *corrective*, inspiring his audience to new experiments and ambitions. This ideal also *emancipates* young scholars from obsequious deference to tradition that would otherwise be thought insolent while allowing *submerged emotions* of both resentment and daring to come to the surface. Lastly, the whole structure creates eloquent *artistic effects* that are pleasurable to the ear, the eye, and the mind—thus allowing the members of his audience to take the symbol of the "American Scholar" home with them to reflect upon in conversation and in solitude.[28]

Discussion: Think of the symbol "American Dream." How might it perform each of the six functions in different contexts?

POETIC CATEGORIES

Although rhetoric is not the same as poetry, an advanced public speaker is able to make use of poetic categories in order to more powerfully deliver a message. For Burke, a **poetic category** "stresses its own peculiar way of building the mental equipment (meanings, attitudes, character) by which one handles the significant factors of his time."[29] In other words, a rhetorician uses poetic categories (such as tragedy, comedy, elegy, satire, burlesque, the grotesque, and the didactic) as ways of defining one's place within a situation by giving it dramatic form. In an **epic**, for instance, one reacts to the challenges and necessities of a primitive existence by celebrating the role of the warlike hero (like the valorous knight or the gunslinger in the white hat), whose actions allow even humble peasants of pioneering settlers to endure harsh conditions. Although the epic has limited rhetorical value in a complex industrial and democratic society, other poetic categories still play a dominant role in how we frame political and social action.

The first three of these categories—tragedy, comedy, and the didactic—are characterized by a positive spirit of acceptance. Although not shy of using criticism, they ultimately seek to affirm some underlying order and to seek common ends by deliberate consideration of practical means. The second three of these categories—elegy, burlesque, and the grotesque—are characterized by a critical spirit

---

[28]For more on Emerson, see Roberta K. Ray, "The Role of the Orator in the Philosophy of Ralph Waldo Emerson." *Speech Monographs* 41 (1974), 215–225; John H. Sloan, " 'The Miraculous Uplifting': Emerson's Relationship with His Audience," *Quarterly Journal of Speech* 52, no. 1 (1966), 10–15; Nathan Crick, "The Rhetorical Singularity," *Rhetoric Review* 28, no. 4 (2009), 370–387.

[29]Kenneth Burke, *Attitudes Toward History* (Berkeley: University of California Press, 1968), 34.

of rejection. Although open to subsequent suggestions for change, their purpose is primarily to highlight what is wrong, intolerable, and absurd about a situation. However, a speaker need not choose absolutely between these options. Consistent with all tools of formal style, poetic categories are not mutually exclusive. Often, speeches combine multiple categories that overlap and reinforce one another. Like the uses of form, the goal is to blend them together into a dramatic whole in which the audience feels it has been moved from beginning to end.

Tragedy

Of all poetic categories, **tragedy** plays the most central role in rhetorical speeches that urge citizens to engage in a struggle to better some part of their environment. In its origin as a dramatic form in Classical Greece, tragedy often portrayed great kings and heroes who strove for great and virtuous ends but were brought low by the flaw of **hubris,** or egotistical overreaching, which brought upon them the workings of fate. Yet even in the death of tragic heroes (and this is the important part), there is the tragic dignity of their death which reaffirms something noble in the human spirit and something magnificent in the structure of the universe. Burke says that tragedy thus relies on "a sense of man's intimate participation in processes beyond himself," like the destiny of the nation, the will of God, or the path of justice.[30] Furthermore, the actions of the tragic hero, by participating in those processes, often bring about an experiential form of knowledge that arises from having suffered, endured, and prevailed. Thus, in tragedy, "one learns by experience" such that "the suffered is the learned."[31]

Tragedy is thus not synonymous with words like *horrific, violent,* or *sad,* despite its frequent usage. The unforeseen or accidental death of a loved one may be traumatic for those still living, but that does not make it tragic. A tragic death is one that comes in the midst of—and because of—a struggle toward some grand overarching goal and produces wisdom in the audience who witnesses that struggle. This means that, according to Burke, tragedy as a rhetorical device is "a means of dignifications" which argues "for a cause by depicting a serious person who is willing to sacrifice himself in its behalf."[32] A tragic form in rhetoric thus tends to appear when the following characteristics are present in a rhetorical situation:

- Aspiration toward a grand, poetic goal that is shared by the audience
- Great obstacles that stand in the way of that goal
- The necessity for suffering and struggle by those who pursue that goal
- An embrace of suffering as a form of virtue and wisdom
- A hero, or group of heroes, who exemplify courage and sacrifice
- The likelihood that partial successes will only come gradually and that perfect success may either exceed one's life or may never actually be attained

---

[30]Burke, *Counter-Statement,* 200.

[31]Kenneth Burke, *A Grammar of Motives* (Berkeley: University of California Press, 1969), 39.

[32]Kenneth Burke, *Essays Toward a Symbolic of Motives: 1950–1955* (Lafayette, IN: Parlor Press, 2007), 28.

Given these characteristics, almost all speeches of advocacy and most of the speeches of commemoration contain elements of tragedy. Let us return to the rhetoric of Elizabeth Cady Stanton—in this case, her "Solitude of Self" address to the Congressional Judiciary Committee on January 18, 1892. The political function of the address was to argue for the necessity of education in outfitting modern women to find their own unique roles in a contemporary industrial democracy, an education that would succeed in "giving woman all the opportunities for higher education, for the full development of her faculties, forces of mind and body; for giving her the most enlarged freedom of thought and action; [and] a complete emancipation from all forms of bondage, of custom, dependence, superstition."[33] To make her case, she did not seek to make education merely a gift from the state to make life easier for women. Quite the opposite, Stanton argued that education might actually make life harder by forcing women to confront the solitude of self that comes with independence and self-discipline. Yet she asks for no pity. As the cause is great, so must be the sacrifices one endures. She says:

> We ask no sympathy from others in the anxiety and agony of a broken friendship or shattered love. When death sunders our nearest ties, alone we sit in the shadows of our affliction. Alike mid the greatest triumphs and darkest tragedies of life we walk alone. On the divine heights of human attainments, eulogized and worshiped as a hero or saint, we stand alone. In ignorance, poverty, and vice, as a pauper or criminal, alone we starve or steal; alone we suffer the sneers and rebuffs of our fellows; alone we are hunted and hounded thro dark courts and alleys, in by-ways and highways; alone we stand in the judgment seat; alone in the prison cell we lament our crimes and misfortunes; alone we expiate them on the gallows. In hours like these we realize the awful solitude of individual life, its pains, its penalties, its responsibilities; hours in which the youngest and most helpless are thrown on their own resources for guidance and consolation. Seeing then that life must ever be a march and a battle, that each soldier must be equipped for his own protection, it is the height of cruelty to rob the individual of a single natural right.[34]

Fitting of the tragic vision, however, the cause that redeems this suffering is worthwhile. Continually inspiring women is the ideal which has drawn all great artists, scientists, and leaders in history. She continues:

> Women are already the equals of men in the whole of dream of thought, in art, science, literature, and government. With telescope vision they explore the starry firmament, and bring back the history of the planetary world . . . The poetry and novels of the century are theirs, and they have touched the keynote of reform in religion, politics, and social life. They fill the editor's and professor's chair, and plead at the bar of justice, walk the wards of the hospital, and speak from the pulpit and the platform; such is the type of womanhood that an enlightened public sentiment welcomes today, and such the triumph of the facts of life over the false theories of the past.[35]

---

[33]Available from the Public Broadcasting Service (PBS), http://www.pbs.org/stantonanthony/resources/index.html?body=solitude_self.html (accessed on May 7, 2010).

[34]Ibid.

[35]Ibid.

As a poetic category, tragedy appears whenever people rally themselves to suffer greatly for a great cause. By seeking to attain the potential given to human nature by dedicated struggle against constraints toward an ideal end, Stanton's speech thus does not break new ground in poetic form; it simply channels the power of Greek tragedy within the setting of late 19th century America.

Discussion: Which popular new stories do you recall that were told through a tragic framing of heroic struggle? List all that come to mind. On closer inspection, how many of them were actually tragic, and how many were simply "bad news"?

Comedy

The other major poetic category that derives from Classical Greece is comedy. What most distinguishes a comedy from a tragedy is that comedy tends to focus on the *details of human relationships* while tragedy focuses our attention to *superhuman ideals* and the forces that surround them. If tragedy makes us look past our immediate suffering toward some distant end, comedy tends to refocus attention to the subtleties of our actions, intentions, and environment. The essence of comedy is therefore not the "joke" but the "observation." Whereas **humor** brings about a burst of laughter through the momentary violation of expectations and the absurd juxtaposition of incongruous things (such as a small child wearing big shoes), comedy creates a more enduring lightness of attitude by disclosing previous unnoticed details, relationships, intentions, or interpretations that bring about the pleasurable feeling of learning (like that produced by reading children's fables). Consequently, a tragedy can often effectively use humor without being a tragedy while comedies can endure long stretches where nobody laughs.

As indicated by most of Shakespeare's comedies, the plot of a comedy usually revolves around an initial misunderstanding or deception that is progressively worked out by the characters until a desirable reconciliation between parties is achieved. Even in Aristotle's time, in comedy, "the bitterest enemies in the piece . . . walk off good friends at the end, with no slaying of any one by any one."[36] Burke thus says of comedy that "its emphasis shifts from *crime* [in tragedy] to *stupidity*," thereby "picturing people not as *vicious* but as *mistaken*."[37] In comedy, the end does not come with the triumph of the hero over the villain (as in an epic) or with the noble death of the hero in his struggle for greatness (as in a tragedy). It comes with the resolution of misunderstandings.

In rhetoric, comedy is often used as a way of resolving disputes, easing tensions, and giving people broader perspective on issues through a combination of witty observations and enlightened interpretations. In comedy, one does not laugh *at* others but *with* them, often concerning foibles for which he or she is responsible. Rhetorically, it thus "provides the *charitable* attitude towards people that is required for purposes of persuasion and co-operation."[38] Consequently, comedy is

---

[36]Aristotle, *Poetics*, 1453a35.
[37]Burke, *Attitudes Toward History*, 41.
[38]Burke, *Attitudes Toward History*, 166.

often used in speeches of introduction, identification, enrichment, and administration in which the goal is a feeling of voluntary participation in a shared experience. Rather than seeking to magnify the glory of the end and the virtue of suffering, as with tragedy, comedy puts ends within reach and views suffering largely as the unnecessary consequence of ignorance. A speech that uses comedy thus generally appears in a situation that has the following characteristics:

- An audience predisposed to believing that most people have good intentions
- A problem which is clearly the result of misunderstanding and lack of effort
- The resources to clarify those misunderstandings and give an enlightened perspective on a situation
- A speaker with the wit to unmask error in a way that brings laughter and goodwill rather than ridicule and rancor
- A desired end that requires cooperation by currently antagonistic parties

Perhaps the paradigmatic rhetorical situation that calls for a comic approach is when the speaker's immediate audience is one that is the target of constructive criticism and of progressive reform. For instance, when chairman of the Federal Communications Commission, Newton Minnow, spoke before the National Association of Broadcasters on May 9, 1961, he came with an inherited ethos as an outspoken critic of the airwaves; yet his intent was not simply to ridicule and shame his audience. It was to ask for its assistance and appeal to its better nature. Therefore, although the speech became famous for his description of the state of television as a "vast wasteland," the overall tenor of the speech was comical and respectful. The comical tone was set by his introduction, which poked fun at his reputation and preceded his speech—a reputation in part gained by his association with John F. Kennedy's ideal of leading America ambitiously into the "New Frontier":

> As you know, this is my first public address since I took over my new job. When the New Frontiersmen rode into town, I locked myself in my office to do my homework and get my feet wet. But apparently I haven't managed yet to stay out of hot water. I seem to have detected a very nervous apprehension about what I might say or do when I emerged from that locked office for this, my maiden station break.
>
> So first let me begin by dispelling a rumor. I was not picked for this job because I regard myself as the fastest draw on the New Frontier . . . It may also come as a surprise to some of you, but I want you to know that you have my admiration and my respect. Yours is a most honorable profession . . . I can think of easier ways to make a living. But I cannot think of more satisfying ways.[39]

Notably, Minnow intentionally dismisses the "tragic" reading of his persona as an idealistic gunslinger. Instead, he is a respectful friend. With Minnow's goodwill established, he creates a space for himself to offer criticism of the state of broadcasting, a state of which he feels is the responsibility of the executives in the audience:

> When television is good, nothing—not the theater, not the magazines or newspapers—nothing is better. But when television is bad, nothing is worse. I invite each

---

[39]Available from The American Rhetoric at http://www.americanrhetoric.com/speeches/newtonminnow.htm (accessed on April 28, 2010).

of you to sit down in front of your television set when your station goes on the air and stay there, for a day, without a book, without a magazine, without a newspaper, without a profit and loss sheet or a rating book to distract you. Keep your eyes glued to that set until the station signs off. I can assure you that what you will observe is a vast wasteland.[40]

With the problem now established, Minnow offers reforms grounded in both a faith in people and in the assumption that broadcast executives are acting under false assumptions that they have not taken the effort to faithfully investigate, the most prominent of these being that broadcasting simply caters to the public taste:

> I do not accept the idea that the present over-all programming is aimed accurately at the public taste. The ratings tell us only that some people have their television sets turned on and of that number, so many are tuned to one channel and so many to another. They don't tell us what the public might watch if they were offered half-a-dozen additional choices . . . I believe in the people's good sense and good taste, and I am not convinced that the people's taste is as low as some of you as-sume . . . If parents, teachers, and ministers conducted their responsibilities by fol-lowing the ratings, children would have a steady diet of ice cream, school holidays, and no Sunday school. What about your responsibilities? Is there no room on tele-vision to teach, to inform, to uplift, to stretch, to enlarge the capacities of our chil-dren? . . . Search your consciences and see if you cannot offer more to your young beneficiaries whose future you guide so many hours each and every day.[41]

Consistent with the comical attitude, Minnow diagnoses the problem as a combi-nation of laziness and misunderstanding. He believes in the goodwill of broadcast-ing executives and the capacities of the broadcast audience. The problem is not the people in charge of the industry; it is simply their lack of sufficient contentiousness and ambition. His hope is thus to reform them as one reforms the bad habits of a friend—by firm but sympathetic cajoling, advising, and support.

Discussion: It is not infrequent that what are felt to be tragic situations by those directly involved are interpreted comically by those observing from a distance. Indeed, one of our great habits is to look back at past personal trauma and make light of it (now that we are observers rather than participants). Can you think of a past experience you now reflect on comically, but which was experienced quite dif-ferently in the moment?

Didactic

The word *didactic* comes from the Greek *didaskein,* which means "to teach." The **didactic** speaker thus has the ethos of the educator who wishes to draw on the re-sources of reason, narrative, and emotion to enlighten an audience. However, like speeches of enrichment, a didactic speech is not simply the dry telling of facts. Quite the opposite, didactic speakers are often passionately committed to their

---

[40]Ibid.
[41]Ibid.

ideals and beliefs. They include not only professors and scientists but religious leaders, political propagandists, self-help gurus, utopian reformers, and prophetic poets. In the didactic, one is promised not just knowledge but transcendence, or the movement from a lower plane of existence to a higher one that comes with the possession of knowledge about the nature of things. In other words, the didactic poet helps one to "see the light."

For Burke, the essence of the didactic form is what he calls the "coaching of an attitude" by means of verbal persuasion.[42] The metaphor of coaching is very apt. To coach someone is more than just to tell him or her what to know and what to do; it is to motivate the individual toward a goal by providing the tools for achievement. In Burke's words, coaching thus "involves 'character building' in that one shapes his attitudes, the logic of his life, by the co-ordinates he chooses, and one shapes his actions with reference to the judgments that follow from the co-ordinates."[43] In other words, if a community chooses the coordinates of establishing God's Kingdom on Earth, as did the Puritans in America, then leaders will emerge as the coach of that community by providing them the moral, political, and religious guidance to attain their ends.

The didactic shares qualities with both the tragic and the comic. On the one hand, this striving for a goal makes the didactic close company with the tragic, but it differs by emphasizing *knowledge* as a means to attaining one's desire rather than *struggle* and *sacrifice*. It thus tends to favor a more peaceful, communal, and cooperative context in which an audience seeks self-improvement rather than one marked by conflict. On the other hand, in its reformist ideals, the didactic is very close to the comic, but it lacks the critical wit and tends to favor a more utopian ideal. In comedy, one tries to bring about humility and goodwill by diminishing our petty complaints and trivial pleasures in light of the big picture; in the didactic, one brings about enlightenment by showing how, through knowledge, we can attain a better life. In sum, situations that invite a didactic speech have the following qualities:

- A problem or tension that seems caused by lack of knowledge or wisdom
- An audience desirous to improve itself and others
- The presence of respected authorities whom the audience looks to for guidance
- Supplementary, written text that supports and reinforces the claims of the speaker
- Relative political autonomy of the audience that allows knowledge to be put into practice without fear of oppression or stigma

Not surprisingly, modern democracy, which relies so heavily on the resources of science and technology, frequently places scientists in the role of the didactic speaker. However, such speakers rarely restrict themselves in public to talking only of scientific matters. Instead, they use their ethos as teachers to expand their expertise in the political, moral, and social realms. For example, Margaret Mead was not only curator of the American Museum of Natural History in New York and an

---

[42]Burke, *Attitudes Toward History*, 322.

[43]Burke, *Attitudes Toward History*, 326.

anthropology professor at Columbia University; she was also an advocate for reforming how human beings use the resources of their environment to achieve sustainable development that benefits all rather than just a few. In her speech, "The Planetary Crisis and the Challenge to Scientists" at the American Museum of Natural History on December 6, 1973, Mead tries to coach the public into an attitude of universal cooperation toward environmental sustainability and political harmony. Characteristic of the didactic form, she promises that knowledge will bring transcendence and a more peaceful and just world:

> This is the first time in history that the American people have been asked to defend themselves and everything that we hold dear in cooperation with all the other inhabitants of this planet, who share with us the same endangered air and the same endangered oceans. This time there is no enemy. There is only a common need to reassess our present course, to change that course and to devise new methods through which the whole world can survive. This is a priceless opportunity.
>
> To grasp it, we need a widespread understanding of the nature of the crisis confronting us—and the world—a crisis that is no passing inconvenience, no byproduct of the ambitions of the oil-producing countries, no figment of environmentalists' fears, no byproduct of any present system of government—whether free enterprise, socialist, or communist, or any mixture thereof. What we face is the outcome of the inventions of the last four hundred years. What we need is a transformed life-style which will be as different from our present wasteful, short-sighted, reckless use of the earth's treasures as the present twentieth-century world is from the agrarian world of the past. This new life-style can flow directly from the efforts of science and the capabilities of technology, but its acceptance depends on an overriding citizen commitment to a higher quality of life for the world's children and future generations on our planet.[44]

We have here all the elements of a didactic speech—a crisis, a respected authority, resources for knowledge, the opportunity for action, the promise of rational cooperation, and most of all, the ideal of transcendence—the "new lifestyle" which flows directly from science and technology. The didactic thus reveals to us the potential that lies before us if we only seek the right path which knowledge illuminates.

Discussion: In the cartoon representations of conscience, the angels and devil on our shoulders are competing didactic speakers vying for our allegiance. Can you recall people who works of art in your life that played the role of angel and devil in this regard? Which was more persuasive at the time?

Elegy

The **elegy** is a fitting transition from the poetic categories that emphasize acceptance to those that focus on rejection. In poetry, the elegy is a mournful, melancholy, or plaintive poem, often presented as a funeral song or a lament for the dead. Like tragedy, elegy often focuses on the magnitude of human suffering; yet unlike tragedy, it turns sufferers into undeserved victims rather than noble heroes.

---

[44]Gregory R. Suriano, *Great American Speeches* (New York: Gramercy Books, 1993), 279–280.

The embodiment of the elegy is what Burke calls the perfected technique of complaint; it is a "wailing wall" that invites people to express their suffering in public in such a way that emphasizes "the disproportion between the weakness of the self and the magnitude of the situation."[45] The goal of the elegy, in other words, is to condemn the magnitude of injustice in the world and appeal to some higher moral law to help the helpless and give strength to the powerless. In rhetoric, the elegy is often employed by individuals or groups who feel they have been unjustly oppressed by an illegitimate power. The rhetorical situation that gives rise to an elegy usually has the following qualities:

- The existence of a clearly-defined group that feels it is being oppressed
- An identifiable source of authority and power that can be blamed for that oppression
- Graphic examples of unjust and unnecessary suffering
- An audience of third-party observers capable of influencing the situation based on empathetic understanding

Perhaps the historical event which gave rise to the most powerful elegies in America was that of slavery—the institution that represents the purest form of unjust exploitation of one group by another. For instance, during his address to the Rochester Ladies' Anti-Slavery Society on July 6, 1852, the former slave turned writer and abolitionist, Frederick Douglass, used the opportunity to indict America in the strongest language possible. In this section of "The Meaning of July Fourth for the Negro," Douglass uses the form of the elegy to bring the suffering of slaves into the public alongside the unequalled barbarity of America's peculiar institution:

> What, to the American slave, is your Fourth of July? I answer: a day that reveals to him, more than all other days in the year, the gross injustice and cruelty to which he is the constant victim. To him, your celebration is a sham; your boasted liberty, an unholy license; your national greatness, swelling vanity; your sounds of rejoicing are empty and heartless; your denunciation of tyrants, brass-fronted impudence; your shouts of liberty and equality, hollow mockery; your prayers and hymns, your sermons and thanksgivings, with all your religious parade and solemnity, are, to Him, mere bombast, fraud, deception, impiety, and hypocrisy— a thin veil to cover up crimes which would disgrace a nation of savages . . . Go where you may, search where you will, roam through all the monarchies and despotisms of the Old World, travel through South America, search out every abuse, and when you have found the last, lay your facts by the side of the everyday practices of this nation, and you will say with me that, for revolting barbarity and shameless hypocrisy, America reigns without a rival.[46]

As exemplified in Douglass's speech, the desired effect of the elegy is for the audience to ask itself, "How can we allow this to happen?" In the face of such details, it is made to feel that such indiscriminate, unjustified suffering cannot be tolerated. As Stephen Browne cautions, however, the elegiac form often leads simply to "sentimentalism" rather than action. As evidenced by the proliferation of graphic

---

[45]Burke, *Attitudes Toward History*, 44.
[46]Suriano, *Great American Speeches*, 56.

accounts of slavery during the 19th century, audiences often atone for complicity merely by seeking to "punish themselves with its representations."[47] Consequently, the elegy rarely succeeds as a *pure* rhetorical form; usually it acts as an introduction that is eventually incorporated within a tragic or comic category.

Discussion: In popular terminology, a "pity party" is a kind of elegy that one performs for oneself in order to solicit expression of sympathy and pity from others, whereas a "diatribe" is an elegy directed toward the unjust abuse of power by another person. Although both are elegies, the latter is often looked upon with greater respect than the former. Think of movie representations of pity parties and diatribes. Are they presented complimentary to or critical of the speaker delivering them?

Burlesque

If the elegy is tragedy without redemption, burlesque is comedy without charity. In comedy, one uses good humor to offer criticism meant to enlighten and reform one's friends. In **burlesque**, one uses the language of absurdity to ridicule and belittle one's opponents. The writer of burlesque, writes Burke, "makes no attempt to get inside the psyche of his victim. Instead, he is content to select the externals of behavior, driving them to a 'logical conclusion' that becomes their 'reduction to absurdity.' "[48] Consequently, the method of burlesque tends to be used as a weapon to reduce certain individuals, ideas, and practices to the level of farce and thus invite their rejection and condemnation. Thus, whereas comedy seeks to show the limitations of an attitude by placing it within a much more complex environment, burlesque does the opposite; by exaggerating certain qualities while neglecting others, it creates caricatures that stand out from their environment because of their lack of proportion. A situation that invites burlesque contains the following characteristics:

- A target group, individual, or object with widely known and readily identifiable qualities
- A polarized political environment in which there are clear divisions of interest
- Need to accept or reject certain people or proposals in the near future based on perceived likes or dislikes
- Access to media that allows rapid dissemination of short, entertaining segments

One of the most prominent acts of burlesque in recent memory was the performance by comedian Stephen Colbert at the 2006 White House Correspondents Dinner. Typically, this dinner is a forum not for burlesque but for **satire**, which is a more sympathetic form of caricature whose purpose is not to ridicule but to cause laughter. The sitting president hosts the media correspondents to a dinner and invites a comedian to poke fun at the administration, much in the form of the court

---

[47]Stephen Browne, "'Like Gory Spectres': Representing Evil in Theodore Weld's *American Slavery as It Is*," *Quarterly Journal of Speech*, 80, no. 3 (1994), 277–292.
[48]Burke, *Attitudes Toward History*, 54.

jester. Colbert, however, went beyond satire to burlesque. As a political comedian whose humor is based on assuming a mock persona of a self-obsessed, ill-informed television pundit, Colbert took the unprecedented step of aligning himself with then President George W. Bush and proceeding to burlesque both him and his administration. Here is his introduction:

> Mark Smith, ladies and gentlemen of the press corps, Madame First Lady, Mr. President, my name is Stephen Colbert, and tonight it is my privilege to celebrate this president, 'cause we're not so different, he and I. We both get it. Guys like us, we're not some brainiacs on the nerd patrol. We're not members of the Factinista. We go straight from the gut. Right, sir?
>
> That's where the truth lies, right down here in the gut. Do you know you have more nerve endings in your gut than you have in your head? You can look it up. Now, I know some of you are going to say, "I did look it up, and that's not true." That's 'cause you looked it up in a book. Next time, look it up in your gut. I did. My gut tells me that's how our nervous system works . . .
>
> I'm a simple man with a simple mind. I hold a simple set of beliefs that I live by. Number one, I believe in America. I believe it exists. My gut tells me I live there. I feel that it extends from the Atlantic to the Pacific, and I strongly believe it has 50 states, and I cannot wait to see how *The Washington Post* spins that one tomorrow. . . .
>
> Most of all, I believe in this president. Now, I know there are some polls out there saying that this man has a 32% approval rating. But guys like us, we don't pay attention to the polls. We know that polls are just a collection of statistics that reflect what people are thinking in "reality." And reality has a well-known liberal bias . . . Sir, pay no attention to the people who say the glass is half-empty, because 32% means it is two-thirds empty. There's still some liquid in that glass is my point, but I wouldn't drink it. The last third is usually backwash.[49]

As evidenced by the awkward silence that pervaded most of the speech and the immediate criticism that followed it, Colbert violated the sense of decorum and charity that defines polite satire. It thus shows the risks of using burlesque in rhetoric, as it often comes across as cruel, unfair, and a kind of bullying. As a situated speech act, one might have reason to characterize the speech as a failure; however, the speech was immediately replayed on the Internet and drew a wider and more sympathetic audience online that made it a major topic of discussion. This demonstrates how burlesque is often more successful after the event, once parts of it are rebroadcast through electronic forms of communication, than it is during the speech act itself.

Discussion: Burlesque is an old and venerable category of political criticism dating back to the earliest days of the nation. Political cartoons, in particular, make constant use of burlesque. Can you think of a political cartoon in a major newspaper that was particularly striking? Was it also effective?

---

[49]Available from About.com at http://politicalhumor.about.com/od/stephencolbert/a/colbertbush.htm (accessed on May 7, 2010).

Grotesque

Something that is grotesque is more than simply ugly or terrifying; a **grotesque** form is the combination of clashing characteristics in the same object that produces discomfort rather than laughter. For instance, Burke identifies a gargoyle—a human head on an animal's body—as a classic example of the grotesque. Thus, for him, the grotesque is a kind of "planned incongruity" (a forced juxtaposition of opposites) which occurs when "the perception of discordances is cultivated without smile or laughter."[50] For example, the experience of the grotesque might come about by images of great wealth beside great destitution (as in Charles Dickens's *A Tale of Two Cities*) or of children suffering and enduring hardships meant for adults (as in Charles Dickens's *David Copperfield*). As indicated by the work of Dickens, who wrote during a wave of industrialism in England that completely altered the old agrarian landscape, the grotesque as a poetic form tended to come about when there was a clashing of old traditions with new practices. The feeling of two incompatible forms of life side-by-side naturally expresses itself in forms of art that embodies this tension.

Rhetorically, the grotesque functions to highlight conflicts and tensions within one's social environment. Like the elegy and burlesque, the grotesque does not necessarily suggest any course of action or propose any new policy. It functions largely to bring to public consciousness an exigence that remains ignored or contested. By placing opposites in close juxtaposition, it implies that the situation is unsustainable and that a more balanced solution is needed—even though it may not say what it is. A situation that calls for the grotesque has the following characteristics:

- A social and political environment that is enduring through major changes
- A palpable tension between older traditions and new practices
- Events, people, or processes that vividly demonstrate these tensions and changes
- Pervasive feelings of uncertainty, discontent, and disgust at the present condition
- An audience that desires to vent frustration and consider new possibilities

Similar to the conditions that inspired the books of Charles Dickens, the atmosphere of late-nineteenth-century and early-twentieth-century America saw rapid industrialization of a traditionally agricultural economy. In this situation, many Americans, young and old, left home and family to find work in the mills and mines that sprung up across the national landscape. Soon, however, images of the soot-stained faces of children began to appear in the press, leading to calls for labor protections in the new industrial economy. One of the most extraordinary leaders of the movement was Mary Harris, who went by the name "Mother Jones." Used as the model for Upton Sinclair's novel, *The Coal War*, Mother Jones organized mine workers in West Virginia and Colorado despite being in her eighties. The clash of her grandmotherly persona with her aggressive oratorical style made her a grotesque figure in her own right, drawing people to her speeches just to bear witness to the spectacle. In this excerpt from her speech "Agitation—The

---

[50]Kenneth Burke, *Permanence and Change: An Anatomy of Purpose* (Berkeley: University of California Press, 1954), 112.

Greatest Factor for Progress" given in March 24, 1903, she subsequently attacks the "society" men and women who had come to hear her speech for entertainment:

> I see a lot of society women in this audience, attracted here out of a mere curiosity to see "that old Mother Jones." I know you better than you do yourselves. I can walk down the aisle and pick every one of you out. You probably think I am crazy but I know you. And you society dudes—poor creatures. You wear high collars to support your jaw and keep your befuddled brains from oozing out of your mouths. While this commercial cannibalism is reaching into the cradle; pulling girls into the factory to be ruined; pulling children into the factory to be destroyed; you, who are doing all in the name of Christianity, you are at home nursing your poodle dogs. It's high time you got out and worked for humanity. Christianity will take care of itself. I started in a factory. I have traveled through miles and miles of factories and there is not an inch of ground under that flag that is not stained with the blood of children.[51]

The mention of the "blood of children" is important for Jones's rhetorical purpose. Her audience here is partly "society women" who explicitly value motherhood. Consequently, the idea that their commercialism actually supports the abuse of children (who at the time had no labor protections) reveals the depth of their hypocrisy and the height of the grotesque situation in which they all live—where children suffer and die in the mines while good Christian society women warm their poodle dogs by the coal fire.[52]

Discussion: Think of famous photographs that are often used to represent the history of the 20th century. Which of them are intentionally grotesque? What was the historical situation that made such an image representative of its era?

CONCEPT REVIEW

Formal Style	Definition	Example
CONVENTIONAL FORM	A traditional way of arranging certain types of speeches based on organizational structure rather than content	(State of the Union Address) "Madame Speaker, Mr. Vice President, Members of Congress, and the American People: I've come here tonight to address the crises facing our nation and the paths forward we might follow."
SYLLOGISTIC FORM	A formal unity created by arranging parts in a causal or logical sequence	"To fight terror, we must first boost our homeland defenses, then gain intelligence about terrorist groups, and finally disrupt and destroy their organization."

---

[51]Howard Zinn and Anthony Arnove, *Voices of a People's History of the United States* (New York: Seven Stories Press, 2004), 258.

[52]For more on Mother Jones's rhetoric, see Mari Boor Tonn and Mark S. Kuhn, "Co-constructed Oratory: Speaker–Audience Interaction in the Labor Union Rhetoric of Mary Harris 'Mother' Jones," *Text & Performance Quarterly* 13, no. 4 (1993), 313–330.

Formal Style	Definition	Example
REPETITIVE FORM	The repetition of the same idea or principle worded different ways with different examples	"Terrorists know no bounds. They kill innocent children. They blow up schools. They murder their own citizens."
QUALITATIVE FORM	The buildup of an emotional tension or expectation that finds appropriate satisfaction in subsequent parts of the speech	"When terrorists struck our homeland, we felt a rush of fear and uncertainty. Why us? What should we do? But the answer soon came: we must resolve to fight this battle with all the strength we possess."
ARTISTIC SYMBOL	A symbol that is intrinsically interesting to the imagination and draws in an audience because of its aesthetic value	"The Twin Towers, once striving toward the sky, came crashing down on that September day—but standing on Ground Zero one can still feel their presence."
INTERPRETIVE SYMBOL	A symbol that gives clarity and order to a confused and disordered situation	"Make no mistake. We were not struck by criminals. We are fighting a new kind of enemy. We now are engaged in a War on Terror that will last for years."
CORRECTIVE SYMBOL	A symbol that offers a vision of ideal possibility which "corrects" the current problematic situation	"Victory in the War on Terror will give way to a new Age of Peace, where all humankind will treat others with the love and respect due our fellow human beings."
ACCEPTANCE SYMBOL	A symbol that forces an audience to admit an undesirable condition that it had previously denied	"Often people think they can have their vices and be left alone. But they do not understand that illegal trafficking supports the terrorist infrastructure. The Drug User is also the Terrorist Enabler."
EMOTIONAL SYMBOL	A symbol that allows an audience to express powerful feelings it had previously felt necessary to keep hidden	"In this war, we do not wish to feed the unhealthy nationalism that is a natural human response. Let us praise not the State but the Citizen Heroes who embody the highest ideals of our country in action."
EMANCIPATORY SYMBOL	A symbol that turns behaviors previously thought inappropriate or questionable into acts of virtue and excellence	"In this struggle, no individual is free from obligation. Nobody should treat the friends with disrespect, but Justice and Love demands that we come forward with any evidence of terrorist activity to save the lives of innocents."
TRAGEDY	The necessity of suffering and struggle as one strives for ultimate aims which may surpass one's lifespan	"The Age of Peace may be impossible. It may require us to bring our struggle to every part of the earth and require the sacrifice of lives in the process. But the striving toward that goal is worth the sacrifice."
COMEDY	The need for all parties in a conflict to find humility and perspective by placing their actions within a larger and more complex picture	"To all those people who may wonder if they should fear us, I say that too often nations are divided by misunderstanding rather than rancor. Perhaps we need to put each of our nations on Facebook. So let us fight this war not just by hunting enemies but by becoming friends."

Formal Style	Definition	Example
DIDACTIC	The effort to coach an audience to accept a certain attitude to a situation by teaching it the facts and theories which support a particular orientation	"I know that many nations see democracy simply as a mask for economic exploitation by the West. But this is not the essence of democracy. Its spirit derived from the people themselves and their desire for self-determination. Nobody can give democracy away or force it upon others. It is something one can do only for oneself."
ELEGY	The perfected complaint which condemns something (a person, nation, spirit, or force) for causing the unneeded suffering of a people	"But I admit, when I think of the people in the planes that hit the towers, and the innocents who were in the building, I cannot help wishing to cry out, 'How can this have happened? What have we done to deserve this?' And I have yet to find an answer."
BURLESQUE	The mockery of an opposing person or position by exaggerating one element and holding it up to ridicule	"But really, what should be fear from terrorists? The Taliban were such cowards that they feared a pair of lifeless Buddha statues that had existed for over a thousand years. What can one fear of a person who is scared to death of . . . rocks?"
GROTESQUE	The pairing of opposites in such a way that brings about feelings of disgust and the rejection of the situation that makes such comparison possible	"Even now, after the Taliban were removed from power in Afghanistan, their presence remains. The soccer stadium, where they once held public executions, is back in use as an athletic field. But they had to put a new layer of dirt on the field so that players would not be stepping on the blood of so many people."

KEY WORDS

SUMMARY

To have communicative *style* is to have a consistent way of doing and saying things that carry with it a sense of qualitative unity. To borrow from Marshall McLuhan, a person with a "hot" style makes every message into a special delivery that is eagerly opened as fast as it is discarded, whereas a person with a "cool" style merely lays a message out to be mulled over and considered at one's leisure.[53] What matters in style, then, is not the literal content of the message but the manner of its presentation. Any marriage proposal has the same request, but there is a significant difference between the hot presentation of a question broadcast on the JumboTron during a baseball game and the cool presentation of a question posed during a quiet walk in the park. And this difference is not just about the nature of the "decoration." The choice of style in a proposal shows something about the person proposing, and therefore has a content of its own. Ironically, then, we often learn more about the real meaning of a message by the style of its delivery than by the interpretation of the words in isolation.

In this spirit, let us have a final look at Martin Luther King, Jr.'s speech at Holt Baptist Church in its entirety. Certainly, one might be able to select certain figurative styles that King employs throughout the speech—a metaphor here, a parallelism there, and the like—and gain some understanding of their persuasive function. However, formal style can only be understood in the context of the speech in its entirety, in how it flows from one stage to another and culminates (or not) in the parts forming a unified whole. For the sake of clarity, the speech will be analyzed in three distinct parts, each of which seems to have its own coherent form. In addition, the audience's reactions will be included in parentheses in order to give a sense of how King is reacting to feedback. We begin with the first section of the speech, where King addresses the topic of the occasion:

> My friends, we are certainly very happy to see each of you out this evening. We are here this evening for serious business. (*Yes!*) We are here in a general sense because first and foremost we are American citizens, (*That's right!*) and we are determined to apply our citizenship to the fullness of its meaning. (*Yeah. That's right!*) We are here also because of our love for democracy (*Yes!*) and because of our deep-seated belief that democracy transformed from thin paper to thick action (*Yes!*)

is the greatest form of government on Earth. (*That's right!*)

> But we are here in a specific sense because of the bus situation in Montgomery. (*Yes!*) We are here because we are determined to get the situation corrected. This situation is not at all new. The problem has existed over endless years. (*That's right!*) For many years now, Negroes in Montgomery and so many other areas have been inflicted with the paralysis of crippling fears (*Yes!*) on buses in our community. (*That's right!*) On so many occasions, Negroes have been intimidated and humiliated and oppressed because of the sheer fact that they were Negroes. (*That's right!*) I don't have time this evening to go into the history of these numerous cases. Many of them now are lost in the thick fog of oblivion, (*Yes!*) but at least one stands before us now with glaring dimensions. (*All right!*)

> Just the other day, just last Thursday to be exact, one of the finest citizens in Montgomery (*Amen!*)—not one of the finest Negro citizens, (*That's right!*) but one of the finest citizens in Montgomery—was taken from a bus (*Yes!*) and carried to jail and arrested (*Yes!*) because she refused to get up to give her seat to a white person. (*Well. That's right!*) Now the press would have us believe that she refused to leave a reserved section for Negroes, (*Yes!*) but I want you to know this evening that there is no reserved section. (*All right!*) The law has never been clarified at that point. (*Hell, no!*) Now I think I speak with legal authority—not that I have any legal authority, but I think I speak with legal authority behind me (*All right!*)—that the law, the ordinance, the city ordinance has never been totally clarified. (*That's right!*)

> Mrs. Rosa Parks is a fine person. (*Well. Well said!*) And since it had to happen I'm happy that it happened to a person like Mrs. Parks, (*Yes!*) for nobody can doubt the boundless outreach of her integrity. (*Sure enough!*) Nobody can doubt the height of her character. (*Yes!*) Nobody can doubt the depth of her Christian commitment and devotion to the

---

[53]Marshall McLuhan, *Understanding Media: The Extensions of Man* (Cambridge: MIT Press, 1994), 23.

teachings of Jesus. (*All right!*) And I'm happy, since it had to happen, it happened to a person that nobody can call a disturbing factor in the community. (*All right!*) Mrs. Parks is a fine Christian person, unassuming, and yet there is integrity and character there. And just because she refused to get up, she was arrested.[54]

King opens strong with a statement of *identification* ("we are American citizens") and a *statement of purpose* ("we are determined to apply our citizenship to the fullness of its meaning"). This reaffirms for the members of the audience who they are and why they are gathered there together. King then proceeds to review the *uncontested exigence* with which they are all familiar ("This situation is not at all new"). A distinct change in tone then occurs, as King's opening confidence drifts into an *elegy* that focuses largely on the audience as a historical victim of injustice ("humiliated and oppressed" and "inflicted with the paralysis of crippling fears"). This elegiac tone continues through his discussion of Rosa Parks, whom he portrays as a fine person who was "taken from a bus and carried to jail and arrested." That such a thing could happen to such a fine person King portrays as a cause for *complaint*—a complaint made all the more serious by the fact that the law concerning bus segregation has "never been totally clarified." This point of clarification, which stands out awkwardly in the transcript, thus finds its justification as being consistent with the elegiac tenor that King is employing at this early point in the speech.

The other major stylistic element is the use of Rosa Parks as a *symbol*. As a representative of "one of the finest citizens in Montgomery," Parks performs multiple functions. For the reading public watching from a distance, her arrest *interprets* the situation of racial segregation for those unfamiliar with its absurdity. For King's immediate audience, Parks as a symbol is more multifaceted. For those few African-Americans who still might

have believed that such a thing couldn't happen to them because of their class status, she forces *acceptance* of the situation—which in turn *releases* pent-up emotions and frustrations. Her courageous action in refusing to change seats then acts as a *corrective* to the situation that exemplifies a new method of resistance—which in turn *emancipates* actions which are technically against the law. Finally, the story of Rosa Parks is simply *artistically* engaging, allowing it to be narrated in a way that channels the mythic power of stories.

The courage of Rosa Parks, and her symbolic function as a corrective, thus signals that King does not wish to rely heavily on the elegy form to merely solicit pity. The sharp change in style following his discussion of Parks thus abandons the form of the elegy in favor of a different poetic category. He continues:

> You know, my friends, there comes a time when people get tired of being trampled over by the iron feet of oppression. [*Sustained applause*] There comes a time, my friends, when people get tired of being plunged across the abyss of humiliation, where they'd experienced the bleakness of nagging despair. (*Keep talking!*) There comes a time when people get tired of being pushed out of the glittering sunlight of life's July and left standing amid the piercing chill of an alpine November. [*Applause*] There comes a time. [*Applause continues*] (*Yes, sir. Speak!*)
>
> And we are here, we are here this evening because we are tired now. (*Yes!*) [*Applause*] And I want to say that we are not here advocating violence. (*No*) We have never done that. (*Repeat that. Repeat that!*) [*Applause*] I want it to be known throughout Montgomery and throughout this nation (*Well!*) that we are Christian people. (*Yes!*) [*Applause*] We believe in the Christian religion. (*Yes!*) We believe in the teachings of Jesus. (*Well!*) The only weapon that we have in our hands this evening is the weapon of protest. (*Yes!*) [*Applause*] That's all.

---

[54]Martin Luther King, Jr., "Address to the First Montgomery Improvement Association (MIA) Mass Meeting" (Montgomery, AL, December 5, 1955). Available from Stanford University's website, http://www.stanford.edu/group/King/publications/autobiography/chp_7.htm (accessed on April 16, 2010).

And certainly, certainly, this is the glory of America, with all of its faults. (*Yeah!*) This is the glory of our democracy. If we were incarcerated behind the iron curtains of a Communistic nation, we couldn't do this. (*Well. All right!*) If we were dropped in the dungeon of a totalitarian regime, we couldn't do this. (*All right!*) But the great glory of American democracy is the right to protest for right. (*That's right!*) [*Applause*]

My friends, don't let anybody make us feel that we are to be compared in our actions with the Ku Klux Klan or with the White Citizens Council. [*Applause*] There will be no crosses burned at any bus stops in Montgomery. (*Well. That's right!*) There will be no white persons pulled out of their homes and taken out on some distant road and lynched for not cooperating. [*Applause*] There will be nobody among us who will stand up and defy the Constitution of this nation. [*Applause*] We only assemble here because of our desire to see right exist. [*Applause*]

My friends, I want it to be known that we're going to work with grim and bold determination to gain justice on the buses in this city. [*Applause*] And we are not wrong; we are not wrong in what we are doing. (*Well!*) If we are wrong, the Supreme Court of this nation is wrong. (*Yes, sir!*) [*Applause*] If we are wrong, the Constitution of the United States is wrong. (*Yes!*) [*Applause*] If we are wrong, God Almighty is wrong. (*That's right!*) [*Applause*] If we are wrong, Jesus of Nazareth was merely a utopian dreamer that never came down to Earth. (*Yes!*) [*Applause*] If we are wrong, justice is a lie, (*Yes!*) love has no meaning. [*Applause*] And we are determined here in Montgomery to work and fight until justice runs down like water, (*Yes!*) and righteousness like a mighty stream. [*Applause*][55]

The sustained applause elicited after King's announcement that "there comes a time" clearly is the emotional release that accompanies the satisfaction of *qualitative form*. The pathos of

suffering brought about by the elegy clearly calls out for a more heroic response than what King had so far supplied. This qualitative movement is indicated by the *metaphors* of transition, from an "abyss of humiliation" and "bleakness of nagging despair" to "the glittering sunlight of life's July." In addition, with the statement "there comes a time," King signals that he is moving into a *tragic* frame of heroic struggle toward a utopian end. The pitiful victims of the sorrowful elegy have become the valiant heroes of the tragic struggle.

Yet, like after the introductory words to the speech, King once again refuses to give full voice to the tragic sentiment. Instead, he moves abruptly into the *comic* frame of humility and redemption. For the next few paragraphs, King takes care to declare his allegiance to the objects of reverence shared by the majority of Americans—democracy, free speech, the Constitution, the Supreme Court, and God. Each of these objects function together as *emancipatory* symbols that validate their active resistance to unjust law while giving a space to *express* emotions of joy and solidarity—both distinctively comic in orientation. In addition, he makes it clear that those assembled in protest are not advocating violence but rather seeking reconciliation. As American citizens, they only want to carry forward the ideals of American democracy and Christian virtue. The implication here is that the injustice of segregation is a kind of aberration brought about by a misreading of the Constitution and a misunderstanding between people who should otherwise be working together.

The spirit of comedy is made explicit when King employs *repetitive form* to make the point that if they are wrong, everything good about America and God is wrong—which, although about a serious subject matter, is also funny. To argue with a straight face that judging a bus boycott in Montgomery, Alabama, to be illegal means that Jesus of Nazareth was "merely a utopian dreamer that never came down to Earth" cannot help but elicit a smile from the spirit of goodwill that comes with comedy.

---

[55]Ibid.

Yes, of course comedy is an insufficient tool to prepare one for a long struggle against a recalcitrant authority outfitted with the tools of force. Consequently, the last third of the speech finally sees King giving full voice to the tragic frame. He concludes:

I want to say that in all of our actions, we must stick together. (*That's right!*) [*Applause*] Unity is the great need of the hour, (*Well. That's right!*) and if we are united we can get many of the things that we not only desire but which we justly deserve. (*Yeah!*) And don't let anybody frighten you. (*Yeah!*) We are not afraid of what we are doing, (*Oh, no!*) because we are doing it within the law. (*All right!*) And there is never a time in our American democracy that we must ever think we are wrong when we protest. (*All right!*) We reserve that right. When labor all over this nation came to see that it would be trampled over by capitalistic powers, it was nothing wrong with labor getting together and organizing and protesting for its rights. (*That's right!*) We, the disinherited of this land, we who have been oppressed so long, are tired of going through the long night of captivity. And now we are reaching out for the daybreak of freedom and justice and equality. [*Applause*]

May I say to you, my friends, as I come to a close, and just giving some idea of why we are assembled here, that we must keep—and I want to stress this, in all of our doings, in all of our deliberations here this evening and all of the week and while—whatever we do, we must keep God in the forefront. (*Well. All right!*) Let us be Christian in all of our actions. (*All right!*) But I want to tell you this evening that it is not enough for us to talk about love. Love is one of the pivotal points of the Christian faith, but there is another side called justice. And justice is really love in calculation. (*All right!*) Justice is love correcting that which revolts against love. (*Well!*)

The Almighty God himself is not the God just standing out saying through Hosea, "I

love you, Israel." He's also the God that stands up before the nations and says: "Be still and know that I'm God (*Yeah!*), that if you don't obey me I will break the backbone of your power (*Yeah!*) and slap you out of the orbits of your international and national relationships." (*That's right!*) Standing beside love is always justice, (*Yeah!*) and we are only using the tools of justice. Not only are we using the tools of persuasion, but we've come to see that we've got to use the tools of coercion. Not only is this thing a process of education, but it is also a process of legislation. (*Yeah!*) [*Applause*]

And as we stand and sit here this evening and as we prepare ourselves for what lies ahead, let us go out with a grim and bold determination that we are going to stick together. (*Yeah!*) [*Applause*] We are going to work together. (*Yeah!*) [*Applause*] Right here in Montgomery, when the history books are written in the future, (*Yes!*) somebody will have to say, "There lived a race of people (*Well!*), a *black* people, (*Yes, sir!*) 'fleecy locks and black complexion,' (*Yes!*) but a people who had the moral courage to stand up for their rights. [*Applause*] And thereby they injected a new meaning into the veins of history and of civilization." And we're going to do that. God grant that we will do it before it is too late. (*Oh, yeah!*) As we proceed with our program, let us think of these things. (*Yes!*) [*Applause*][56]

The last four paragraphs of King's speech effectively place his audience within a *tragic* narrative. This shift is marked by the transition from love (which is a comic virtue) to justice (which is a tragic virtue). The members of the audience, now unified and identified ("We, the disinherited of this land, we who have been oppressed so long") have transcended the limits of the elegy ("We . . . are tired of going through the long night of captivity") and now have taken on the duty and role of the tragic hero seeking a utopian goal ("And now we are reaching out for the daybreak of freedom and justice and equality"). No longer is it content merely

---

[56]Ibid.

with the language of comedy which seeks reconciliation through mutual understanding. "Persuasion" has given way to "coercion," and "education" has become secondary to "legislation."

Understanding the drama of tragedy, King thus does not shy away from recognizing the necessity of sacrifice, struggle, and suffering. He chides his audience not to "let anybody frighten you" and to be "not afraid of what we are doing." Rather, knowing the violence that looms—as hinted previously by the references to the White Citizens Council and the Ku Klux Klan—King readies his audience to endure the hardships that accompany tragic journeys. They must prepare for "what lies ahead" and "go out with a grim and bold determination." Yet what validates the tragic struggle is always the promised utopian victory that emerges in historical time. Never easy, victory is not promised in weeks, months, or even their lifetimes. Rather, King looks ahead to some future time, which looks back in reverence to "a race of people" with "fleecy locks and black complexion" who "had the moral courage to stand up for their rights" and inject a "new meaning into the veins of history and of civilization."

Finally, the inspirational power of this closing myth acts to give a unifying qualitative form of the whole speech, as King moves from goal, to problem, to caution, to clarification, and finally to struggle and victory. Each of these stages makes way and calls out for the emotional satisfaction of the next, while the myth of historical triumph gives the whole speech the qualitative unity of a tragedy, despite passing through stages of elegy and comedy on the way. With formal style, the actual, qualitative unity is more than the sum of its parts. It can only be determined on completion of the whole speech. Great rhetoric thus seeks more than to piece together a speech out of assorted parts, each analyzed on its own. It strives to achieve a total, qualitative unity that binds together an audience in a shared experience that gives public speaking its unique power.

CHAPTER 8 EXERCISES

1. Analyzing your rhetorical artifact, what forms of style were employed? Choose at least two aspects from each of the form, symbol, and poetic categories.
2. Choose one kind of form and give an impromptu speech describing some part of your morning. Can the class identify which form you used?
3. Break yourselves into small groups. Compose a child's fable that conveys the basic lesson not to talk to strangers. Come up with an original symbol that helps convey that lesson and also performs at least three functions of a symbol. Present your fables to the class and compare them with the others.
4. Reflect on a similar past experience that everyone has shared (e.g., a first kiss). Now choose a specific poetic category and tell that story in that genre. Compare your stories with others who chose the same genre. How similar were they?
5. Break yourselves into groups. Have each group invent a magical product that will help students. Give it a symbolic name that performs one or more of the functions of a symbol. Then select two of the poetic categories to use to persuade students to buy and use this product. Which was the most persuasive?

INDEX